Gresham Reader on
Cabinet Government

Edited by
Giles Edwards

POLITICO'S

First published in Great Britain 2004 by
Politico's Publishing, an imprint of
Methuen Publishing Limited
215 Vauxhall Bridge Road
London SW1V 1EJ

10 9 8 7 6 5 4 3 2 1

Copyright in this selection and introductions © 2004 Giles Edwards.

The author has asserted his moral rights

A CIP catalogue record for this book is available from the British Library.

ISBN 1 84275 053 4

Typeset by SX Composing DTP, Rayleigh, Essex

Printed and bound in Great Britain by
Mackays of Chatham plc, Chatham, Kent

This book is sold subject to the condition that it shall not by way of trade or otherwise be lent, resold, hired out, or otherwise circulated without the publisher's prior consent in writing in any form of binding or cover other than that in which it is published and without a similar condition being imposed on the subsequent purchaser.

Contents

Gresham College		v
Foreword Professor Peter Hennessy		vii
Introduction		ix
1	The Bagehot Template	1
2	From Party Government to War, 1867–1914	6
3	Great War and Lloyd George, 1914–1922	22
4	Interwar, 1922–1939	37
5	The Impact of War, 1939–1945	61
6	The Short Post-war, 1945–1956	64
7	Suez and After, 1956–1964	105
8	Technocracy, 1964–1970	127
9	Seventies stress, 1970–1979	174
10	Cabinet by Handbag, 1979–1990	214
11	Reaction, 1990–1997	244
12	Command and Control, 1997–	257
Bibliography and Acknowledgements		283
Index		297

Gresham College

For over 400 years Gresham Professors have given free public lectures in the City of London. The College is named after Sir Thomas Gresham, son of Sir Richard Gresham who was Lord Mayor in 1537/38 and who conceived the idea of building an Exchange modelled on the Antwerp Bourse. This was brought to fruition by Sir Thomas, on land provided by the Corporation of London, and was given the royal appellation by Queen Elizabeth I.

Sir Thomas was appointed Royal Agent in Antwerp by Edward VI, a position he held throughout Mary's reign and the first nine years of Elizabeth's. His fine mansion in Bishopsgate was the first home of Gresham College. It was there that the Professors gave their lectures until 1768, their salaries being met from rental income from the shops around the Royal Exchange that Sir Thomas had bequeathed jointly to the City Corporation and the Mercers' Company. This period saw the formation and early development at Gresham College of The Royal Society, and the tenure of chairs by a number of distinguished Professors, including Sir Christopher Wren.

In later years lectures were given in various places in the City until the construction of a new Gresham College, opened in 1842, in Gresham Street. The College has been based at Barnard's Inn Hall since 1991. Barnard's Inn was an Inn of Chancery associated with Gray's Inn, and was described by Dickens in *Great Expectations*. In 1892 it was purchased by the Mercers' Company to house the Mercers' School, which remained there until it closed in 1959. In 1985 the Chair of Commerce, funded by the Mercers' School Memorial Trust, was added to the seven ancient Professorships of Astronomy, Divinity, Geometry, Law, Music, Physic and Rhetoric.

Gresham College is an independent institution, governed by a Council and with the Lord Mayor of London as its President. Sir Thomas left his estate and control of his benefaction to the City Corporation and the Mercers' Company, which operate through the Joint Grand Gresham Committee. In addition to the free public lectures, the College runs seminars and conferences, and provides support to initiatives by the Gresham Professors and others which seek to reinterpret the 'new learning' of Sir Thomas Gresham's time in contemporary terms. The College was delighted to be able to support Professor Peter Hennessy, a former Gresham Professor of Rhetoric, in the research required to prepare this publication.

Foreword

This is a theme that will never go cold. The argument about the relative powers of the prime minister and the Cabinet began with the very first incumbent, Sir Robert Walpole, who denied that as First Lord of the Treasury 1721–42, he was any such thing. As I write much (probably too much) is being made of the fact that Tony Blair allowed the Cabinet to discuss for *a whole hour* the question of variable fees for university students on Thursday 4 December 2003 as part of his attempt to rebut charges of 'presidentialism' by consulting more generally as well as encouraging a dash of collectivity in the Cabinet Room.

It is not, however, just a debate for and between political and constitutional nerds. It goes to the heart of the question of accountability and the checks and balances needed for a system with a largely informal constitution. As Mr Gladstone, himself a formidable wielder of prime ministerial power, put it in 1879, the British Constitution 'presumes more boldly than any other the good sense and good faith of those who work it.'

Nobody is better suited than Giles Edwards to gather together the gems and fragments, the analyses and the polemics, the diary entries and the state papers that have gone into the making of this debate since Walter Bagehot wrote his classic *The English Constitution* in the 1860s. As a student of politics at Warwick University, as a Kennedy Scholar in the Kennedy School of Government at Harvard, as a Master's Student on the MA in Contemporary British History Programme at Queen Mary, University of London and as a political researcher at the BBC, he is wonderfully well-primed to select material to fire the imagination of the sixth-former fresh to this debate as much as to an old sweat like me grown grey by time served in library and archive.

The original idea for this volume came from Professor Rod Rhodes of the Australian National University, Canberra. I took it to Gresham College, that little renaissance jewel in the heart of the City of London, which has a sharp eye for the scholarly market and generously funded Giles Edwards' research in the knowledge that early twenty-first century Britain was in need of a *Gresham Reader on Cabinet Government* to bring purpose, detail and poise to a debate Tony Blair, like Margaret Thatcher before him, had relit by their commanding styles of government. Iain Dale and Sean Magee of Politico's were also enflamed by its heat. Enjoy the kindling material herein.

Peter Hennessy,
Attlee Professor of Contemporary British History,
Queen Mary, University of London,
December 2003

Introduction

Just when we thought the debate between Cabinet and prime minister had been decided decisively in favour of the latter, back came Lord Butler . . . His report into the intelligence failures leading up to the Iraq war provided a fascinating glimpse inside government – actually the second in a year, after the revelations of the Hutton Inquiry hearings the previous summer – and a strong case for a more collective approach to information-sharing and decision-taking. In so doing, it enlivened a battle which has been raging for more than a hundred years, but which in recent decades has sometimes read like an episode from the First World War, with the protagonists sunk deep into trenches which had been dug years earlier, the tedium only occasionally relieved when one side lobbed a grenade across the no-man's land between the two front lines. Professor Anthony King reflected this seeming sterility in 1977, when he complained that 'the two sides contend furiously (and interminably); but it is rather like the old argument about whether the bottle is half full or half empty. The evidence is there to support either contention.' The evidence still is, but thanks to Lord Butler, at least people are talking about it again.

Towards the end of the Thatcher era, Professor George Jones sought to straddle the two sides of this debate with his 'elastic' theory of Cabinet government – that it could stretch to accommodate interventionist prime ministers and snap back into place for a more passive PM. The selections in this book suggest that there is some truth to this theory, but that the post-1945 history of Cabinet versus premiership is more of a two steps forward, one step back progression for the prime minister than a pendulum swinging between two equally powerful poles. Periods of excessive prime ministerialism do tend to be followed by corrections, sometimes sharp, but with every swing towards the prime minister, the pendulum never seems to get quite as far back towards Cabinet. In truth, the period covered by this book has seen a steady seepage of power away from Cabinet to the prime minister.

As Michael Foley argues (page 255), the best modern example is probably John Major's premiership, an irony since Major is often seen as a weak premier. After the personal domination exercised by Margaret Thatcher, many of Major's colleagues and external observers alike looked carefully for signs of a gentler touch from the centre. They were not to be disappointed – excerpts from Major himself (page 245) and Michael Heseltine (page 244), reveal how completely his style differed from that of his predecessor. Yet while prime ministerial interventions became less strident, they continued – Major formalised much of the centralisation which had taken place under Thatcher, and, particularly in presentational terms, found himself bound by what Michael Foley called Thatcher's 'conditioning precedents' (page 253).

The 'conditioning precedents' established during Tony Blair's premiership have been tilted even further towards strong leadership at the centre, their bonds harder to break. Blair has personalised policy far more than any previous prime minister – the epitome of which was his decision, in 2001, to take personal control over the national response to an outbreak of Foot and Mouth disease, eventually resulting in a delay in that year's local (and general) elections. He has established a system which sets departments on a course approved by him, meaning he need only intervene to support pet projects, where the department gets off the approved track, or where some unforeseen crisis appears, and he has the time to do so where necessary. The result is that if a political problem arises today, the press and public alike immediately want to know what the Prime Minister is going to do about it, and it is hard to see how a successor could turn back the clock and ignore these expectations. Given such circumstances, it is not hard to understand why so many observers now talk of Cabinet government in the past tense, but even before Lord Butler came along to help swing the pendulum the other way, I think they were wrong to do so.

For a start, not all constitutional change in the last decade has been in one direction: other powers have been devolved and relinquished. The process began with the Citizen's Charter under Major, and has continued under Blair, with the unprecedented voluntary relinquishment of powers to other bodies (to assemblies in Wales, Northern Ireland and London, the Scottish Parliament and some powers in relation to the House of Lords), as well as the Human Rights and Freedom of Information Acts. As Peter Hennessy makes clear in his piece on war powers (see page 275), Foreign Secretary Jack Straw believes that a precedent has now been set which will require all future governments to consult Parliament before going to war, a dramatic development if borne out. Yet with one exception – the publication by John Major of the government's internal rule book and its subsequent development under Tony Blair into today's *Ministerial Code*, which defines the machinery within which every single decision is taken – these changes all relate to broad but confined areas of public life. And in the case of the *Ministerial Code*, as Amy Baker's study makes clear (page 246), control over its contents and interpretation have been zealously guarded by the Prime Minister.

The question, then, is whether any institutional apparatus remains, or can be developed, to counter the 'prime ministerialism' identified by Richard Crossman in 1963 (page 124) or its latter-day equivalent 'presidentialism', described by Michael Foley (page 253) and Graham Allen (page 266). A clue to one such apparatus can be seen in what is sometimes regarded as the finest recent example of the operation of Cabinet government – the resignation of Margaret

Thatcher. In fact, it was not the rebellion of the Cabinet which mattered *per se*, so much as that the Cabinet included all the Conservative Party's senior figures. They withdrew their support because of the fear amongst the party's MPs that, without a change of leader, they would lose their seats at the next general election. It would be the same in any system this side of an elected head of government. In just this way, the difficulties John Major encountered with his Cabinet were the product less of a powerful *Cabinet* and more of his wobbly position in the House of Commons.

Both cases point to Parliament as an institution which, if pulling its weight, might both improve conduct of the people's business (a democratic argument) and do so efficiently and well (one about good government). Reforms to the House of Lords have already had the (for the government) unintended consequence of producing a body more prepared to be aggressive in challenging the government; and there is every reason to suppose that changes to the Commons would do the same. Moves have already been made in this direction – some departments try to facilitate pre-legislative scrutiny of important legislation and attempts are underway to create a career structure for backbench MPs, turning Select Committee assignments into proper jobs. Specialist staff and press officers have been appointed to improve committees' research capabilities and promote their work to the media and Tony Blair now submits himself to six-monthly grillings by the Liaison Committee. [1]

All of these are positive moves, but Parliament still relies too heavily on the goodwill of the executive in providing documents to it, with too little research capacity to assess what they have been given. At present committees lack the resources to look into every nook and cranny of what governments are up to; there is an odd resistance to spending comparatively tiny extra sums to properly

[1] Members of the Liaison Committee are the Chairs of the other Commons Select Committees.

scrutinise the £400bn national budget. Until that resistance is overcome, committee oversight will be disjointed and *ad hoc*, and large parts of government will remain black holes as far as Parliament, and the public, are concerned. And while extra public money has been found to support opposition parties' research, there is still no proper parliamentary budget office, along the lines of the American Congressional Budget Office, which would allow MPs to challenge the government's cost estimates and financial figures. In the bright new world of the Comprehensive Spending Review, where the Treasury decides not just how much departments spend and on what, but when and how, such an innovation would surely improve governance. Of course, any government will resist these moves, arguing that it makes their job more difficult, and in the short term it undoubtedly would. But even with its sometimes cumbrous procedures, the legislative branch could become a partner in developing good legislation and begin to do a better job than it does now, of acting as a brake on unpopular and inept policies.

What, though, of the Cabinet and Cabinet ministers? Well, they are busy, distracted and ambitious, and all too often cannot be relied upon to get involved in collective decision-taking. These are all reasons for the 'creeping bilateralism' described by Nigel Lawson (page 221). Many of the reasons for the accumulation of power in Number 10 are perfectly understandable and are described in detail in this book, and if the slow decline of Cabinet government didn't matter, we could all pack up and go home. But for more than a hundred years this system has had an invaluable dual role as guarantor of democracy and instrument of good government. With ever more significant policy decisions taken amongst small coteries of Cabinet trusties and non-ministerial colleagues in Number 10, the notion that something valuable is being lost has entered the public consciousness. With it, the search for a means of ensuring both that the Prime Minister consults senior colleagues before taking important decisions, and that controversial policies receive wide and detailed scrutiny before their introduction, has become increasingly frantic. Yet the answer is not in some new apparatus (although I think Parliament could and should play a more vital role in ensuring democratic accountability) but in a return to basics. If Cabinet ministers woke up one morning and decided to exercise their constitutional rights as members of a collective body, they would find that while they needed a little dusting off, those rights were essentially intact. They would discover, as Lord Butler did, that 'excellent quality papers [are] written by officials': they are just not discussed. Again, as Lord Butler argued, they might realise that decisions taken after all interests have been consulted and all options considered will be better decisions, with all the right questions asked and considerable 'collective political judgement' brought to bear. What would that mean in practice? Most likely greater institutional acceptance and fewer unintended consequences. Nor need taking decisions in this way be a bar to making 'tough' calls: where problems are anticipated, they can be overcome. The many arguments in favour of Cabinet government, and about how it operates in today's world of complex Cabinet committees and *ad hoc* ministerial groups, are rehearsed elsewhere in this book. But, while they continue to resonate, the continued study of Cabinet government will remain important.

For the time being, at least, government policy is still nominally decided in Cabinet, and the lives of millions are affected in consequence. Becoming a Privy Counsellor and obtaining the right to attend meetings of Cabinet and its committees remains a sought-after privilege not merely for its honorific value, but because it continues to mean something. What that something is, and how it has changed, forms the subject matter of this book. The contributions to the academic and political debate contained within it are the bright sparks which have illuminated the debate. I hope that by removing the padding and bringing them into a single volume, students of Cabinet government will rediscover the importance of the subject. How far it has come – from Bagehot's 'buckle' fastening the legislative to the executive branches of government, to today's complex structures – will be obvious to anyone reading these pages.

Selections have been drawn from government papers, from political memoirs and biographies, from academic commentary and from media reports for the insight they offer into the operation of Cabinet government in the last 130-odd years. To have been included, an excerpt must have staked out some new ground, offered a new insight or provided an excellent summary. Many were controversial when first published – Richard Crossman's diaries, for example, or Mo Mowlam's admission, just months out of Cabinet herself, that Tony Blair was 'acting more like a president than a prime minister . . . the Cabinet itself is dead.' Others – for example the 1904 Treasury minute establishing the Committee of Imperial Defence and the 1938 memorandum on the shape of a future War Cabinet – were the key operational documents of their era. All continue to be important for the depth of research, the historical perspective or the entirely different paradigm (witness 'core executive studies') they offered to the study of central government.

They will be useful to historians for the light they shed on the operation of Cabinet government in the pre-1939 period, when it was far more central to how government worked. It would be hard to explain how Britain survived four years of the First World War without understanding the changes wrought by Maurice Hankey and David Lloyd George after December 1916, for example. And this book provides plenty of primary material – evidence of what actually happened – as well as plenty of theory about why and how. These passages will be useful, too, to political scientists because these more recent contributions to the discipline – from theorists of the 'core executive' and contemporary historians alike – describe the processes by which the decisions are taken which affect us all.

They are ordered, with few exceptions, in chronological order, with the chapters following the important breaks in British political history. This could produce occasional unfortunate jolts between selections written about similar subjects, and where that would have happened the strict chronological approach has been suspended. Historical assessments are also generally included in the section they were written about.

While the anoraks amongst our number (and I count myself one of them) will always find the study of the processes in central government interesting for its own sake, it provides the context in which all important decisions are taken – from uprating social security benefits to changes to local authorities' planning guidance to public sector investment and matters of war and peace. These are not minor issues, and every voter (and non-voter, for that matter) deserves to have an understanding of how those decisions are taken.

Every author represented in this book – and hundreds of others – has sought to further this understanding. I should like to thank them all. I have hugely enjoyed reading their output, and am grateful to those who have given permission for their work to be included here. I am particularly grateful to Lords Hunt and Butler, who were kind enough to send me copies of their speeches, and to Michael Cockerell, several of whose television documentaries are quoted in this book, and who has been kind enough to share his reminiscences, and insights born of them, on a regular basis.

This book couldn't have been produced without support from three institutions of varying vintage – Gresham College, Politico's Publishing, and Queen Mary, University of London. Gresham funded and supported my research, and its staff have been uniformly kind and helpful. Iain Dale and Sean Magee of Politico's have been supportive from the start – not to mention doing a good hand-holding job through the daunting process of actually producing a book. The book would be less coherent and less useful if it were not for the tender ministrations of Emma Musgrave, also of Politico's. The History Department at Queen Mary provided an academic home for me while conducting my research, for which I'm hugely grateful. QMUL library staff, as well as those at the University of London Library, the British Newspaper Library at Colindale and the National Archives (still the Public Record Office when I started my work), have been wonderful: I've frequently screeched in five minutes before closing time and expected to find a whole reading list worth of books.

Some personal thanks are also in order. First, and foremost, to Professor Peter Hennessy. He first suggested this project to me, and has read and commented on everything I've written since. His support throughout this project, and for the last six years of my academic life, has been unstinting. Constantly on the look-out for what Donald Rumsfeld famously called 'known unknowns' and 'unknown unknowns', Peter's engagement with his subject is notable for his desire to learn more and share it with others, rather than to boast about how much he already knows. It is an inspiring example.

I must also thank David Cowling, Editor of Political Research at the BBC, without whose support I would have been able to complete neither my MA nor this book. Paul Flatters, Sue Inglish, Nathan Yeowell and my other colleagues at the BBC have been unnaturally understanding. Friends around the world – notably Tanya and Hilary – have remained uncomplaining as I've worked on piles of papers in their apartments, and friends and family have gone way beyond the call of duty by reading and proofing sections as they were completed. My mother, in particular, typed parts of it, read all of it and I think enjoyed most of it. My other friends, particularly my housemates, have taken frequent unavailability, late arrivals, and an unhealthy obsession with library opening hours, in good spirits, and I'd like to thank them all, particularly Vinita, for that.

As ever, of course, any errors and omissions are mine, and mine alone.

Giles Edwards
Richmond, July 2004

1
The Bagehot Template

Walter Bagehot (1826–77) was the editor of The Economist *and an astute observer of the political scene. In 1865 he wrote* The English Constitution, *a description of how British politics operated before the 1867 Reform Act. That legislation, which extended the franchise to the urban working class and transformed politics forever, rendered many of Bagehot's conclusions immediately redundant. Yet his book became a classic because its analysis extended beyond the daily political grind, and introduced the concept of the 'efficient' and 'dignified' parts of the constitution, with the Cabinet as the 'efficient secret' at its heart. Its influence has been such that few political observers since have placed the Cabinet anywhere but at the heart of their own analyses.*[1]

The efficient secret of the English Constitution may be described as the close union, the nearly complete fusion, of the executive and legislative powers. No doubt by the traditional theory, as it exists in all the books, the goodness of our constitution consists in the entire separation of the legislative and executive authorities, but in truth its merit consists in their singular approximation. The connecting link is the *Cabinet*. By that new word we mean a committee of the legislative body selected to be the executive body. The legislature has many committees, but this is its greatest. It chooses for this, its main

---

[1] Walter Bagehot, *The English Constitution* (ed. Miles Taylor), Oxford University Press, Oxford, 2001, pp. 11–14.

committee, the men in whom it has most confidence. It does not, it is true, choose them directly; but it is nearly omnipotent in choosing them indirectly. A century ago the Crown had a real choice of ministers, though it had no longer a choice in policy. During the long reign of Sir Robert Walpole he was obliged not only to manage Parliament but to manage the palace. He was obliged to take care that some court intrigue did not expel him from his place. The nation then selected the English policy, but the Crown chose the English ministers. They were not only in name, as now, but in fact, the Queen's servants. Remnants, important remnants, of this great prerogative still remain. The discriminating favour of William IV made Lord Melbourne head of the Whig Party when he was only one of several rivals. At the death of Lord Palmerston it is very likely that the Queen may have the opportunity of fairly choosing between two, if not three statesmen. But, as a rule, the nominal prime minister for most purposes – the leader of the House of Commons – almost without exception is so. There is nearly always some one man plainly selected by the voice of the predominant party in the predominant house of the legislature to head that party, and consequently to rule the nation. We have in England an elective first magistrate as truly as the Americans have an elective first magistrate. The Queen is only at the head of the dignified part of the Constitution. The prime minister is at the head of the efficient part. The Crown is, according to the saying, the 'fountain of honour'; but the Treasury is the spring of business. Nevertheless, our first magistrate differs from the American. He is not elected directly by the people; he is elected by the representatives of the people. He is an example of a 'double election'. The legislature chosen, in name, to make laws, in fact finds its principal business in making and in keeping an executive.

The leading minister so selected has to choose his associates, but he only chooses among a charmed circle. The position of most men in Parliament forbids their being invited to the Cabinet; the position of a few men ensures their being invited. Between the compulsory list whom he must take, and the impossible list whom he cannot take, a prime minister's independent choice in the formation of a Cabinet is not very large; it extends rather to the division of the Cabinet offices than to the choice of Cabinet ministers. Parliament and the nation have pretty well settled who shall have the first places; but they have not discriminated with the same accuracy which man shall have which place. The highest patronage of a prime minister is, of course, a considerable power, though it is exercised under close and imperative restrictions; though it is far less than it seems to be when stated in theory, or looked at from a distance.

The Cabinet, in a word, is a board of control chosen by the legislature, out of persons whom it trusts and knows, to rule the nation. The particular mode in which the English ministers are selected; the fiction that they are, in any political sense, the Queen's servants; the rule which limits the choice of the Cabinet to the members of the legislature – are accidents unessential to its definition – historical incidents separable from its nature. Its characteristic is that it should be chosen by the legislature out of persons agreeable to and trusted by the legislature. Naturally these are principally its own members – but they need not be exclusively so. A Cabinet which included persons not members of the legislative assembly might still perform all useful duties. Indeed, the peers, which constitute a large element in modern Cabinets, are members, nowadays, only of a subordinate assembly. The House of Lords still exercises several useful functions; but the ruling influence – the deciding faculty – has passed to what, using the language of old times, we still call the lower house – to an assembly which, though inferior as a dignified institution, is superior as an efficient institution. A principal advantage of the House of Lords in the present age indeed consists in its thus acting as a *reservoir* of Cabinet ministers. Unless the composition of the House of Commons were improved, or unless the rules requiring Cabinet ministers to be members of the legislature were relaxed, it would undoubtedly be difficult to find, without the Lords, a sufficient supply of chief ministers. But the detail of the composition of a Cabinet, and the precise method of its choice, are not to the purpose now. The first and cardinal consideration is the definition of a Cabinet. We must not bewilder ourselves with the inseparable accidents until we know the necessary essence. A Cabinet is a combining committee – a *hyphen* which joins, a *buckle* which fastens, the legislative part of the State to the executive part of the State. In its origin it belongs to the one, in its functions it belongs to the other.

The most curious point about the Cabinet is that so very little is known about it. The meetings are not only secret in theory, but secret in reality. By the present practice, no official minute in all ordinary cases is kept of them. Even a private note is discouraged and disliked. The House of Commons, even in its most inquisitive and turbulent moments, would scarcely permit a note of a Cabinet meeting to be read. No minister who respected the fundamental usages of political practice would attempt to read such a note. The committee which unites the law-making power to the law-executive power – which, by virtue of that combination, is, while it lasts and holds together, the most powerful body in the State – is a committee wholly secret. No description of it, at once graphic and authentic, has ever been given. It is said to be sometimes like a rather disorderly board of directors, where many speak and few listen – though no one knows.

But a Cabinet, though it is a committee of the legislative assembly, is a committee with a power which no assembly would – unless for historical accidents, and after happy experience – have been persuaded to entrust to any committee. It is a committee which can dissolve the assembly which appointed it; it is a committee with a suspensive veto – a committee with a power of appeal. Though appointed by one Parliament, it can appeal if it chooses to the next. Theoretically, indeed, the power to dissolve Parliament is entrusted to the sovereign only, and there are vestiges of doubt whether in *all* cases a sovereign is bound to dissolve Parliament when the Cabinet asks him to do so. But neglecting such small and dubious exceptions, the Cabinet which was chosen by one House of Commons has an appeal to the next House of Commons. The chief committee of the legislature has the power of dissolving the predominant part of that legislature – that which at a crisis is the supreme legislature. The English system, therefore, is not an absorption of the executive power by the legislative power; it is a fusion of the two. Either the Cabinet legislates and acts, or else it can dissolve. It is a creature, but it has the power of destroying its creators. It is an executive which can annihilate the legislature, as well as an executive which is the nominee of the legislature. It *was* made, but it *can* unmake; it was derivative in its origin, but it is destructive in its action.

2
From Party Government to War, 1867–1914

Bagehot's description of the late-nineteenth century cabinet as the centre of the political system, and the decision-making body for government, was widely shared. Crucially, in their writings and their practice, the era's great political actors subscribed to his analysis. Greatest of all, as Chancellor and later as the century's most commanding Prime Minister, was William Ewart Gladstone (1809–1898). This was his own firm statement of the role of Cabinet, written in 1894.[1]

In the public mind and in ordinary practice the Cabinet is viewed as the seat of ultimate responsibility.

Gladstone began to broaden and regularise the application of the principles of Cabinet government, and the changes can be seen described in a series of letters. This one is to the Foreign Secretary, Lord Granville (1815–1891), on 1 July 1883, after a speech made by the President of the Board of Trade, Joseph Chamberlain (1836–1914). Gladstone emphasises the doctrine of collective responsibility: because Cabinet ministers decide policy collectively, they must defend it as one once it has been decided, and must not diverge from it in their public

---

[1] Quoted in PRO, CAB 21/1625, *Notes for Government Spokesman*, for a House of Lords debate initiated by Lord Cecil, on the power of the Cabinet, 17.5.1950.

*statements. The doctrine is the key building block of Cabinet government.*²

Now I should be as far as possible from asserting that under all circumstances speech must be confined within the exact limits of which action is tied down. But I think the dignity and authority, not to say the honour and integrity, of government require that the liberty of speaking beyond these limits should be exercised sparingly, reluctantly, and with much modesty and reserve. Whereas Chamberlain's Birmingham speech exceeded it largely, gratuitously and with a total absence of recognition of the fact that he was not an individual but a member of a body.

*This letter from Gladstone to General Ponsonby (1825–1895), Private Secretary to Queen Victoria, on 12 May 1881, emphasises the 'cuts both ways' nature of ministerial collective responsibility.*³

Undoubtedly members of the Cabinet are bound to vote in every case – apart from accidental absences.

I think it likely that the two Ministers you name may have deemed themselves too sharply committed, by declarations touching Lord Beaconsfield as contra-distinguished from his policy, to make it suitable for them to vote.

There is no doubt that the case was a peculiar one, without any precedent covering the whole breadth of it.

It was also one in which circumstances made it proper for me to arrive at a decision without waiting for the re-assembling of my colleagues: and the rule I have stated as to the obligation of Cabinet

---

² John Morley, *The Life of William Ewart Gladstone,* Vol. 3, Macmillan, London, 1903, p. 113.
³ Philip Guedella, *The Queen and Mr Gladstone, 1880-1898,* Hodder & Stoughton Ltd., London, 1933, pp. 156-57.

ministers has for its correlation the supposition that they have been parties to the discussion of the subject in the Cabinet.

In an earlier letter to Lord Granville, at that time Foreign Secretary, Gladstone had already effectively removed the right of a group of ministers to call a Cabinet meeting without the Prime Minister's authorisation. In December 1870, when he had been Prime Minister for just two years, Gladstone wrote:[4]

The Cabinet appears not to have been called in the usual manner through me.

Here are Gladstone's thoughts on the Prime Minister and his relationship with the Cabinet.[5]

The head of the British Government is not a Grand Vizier. He has no powers, properly so called, over his colleagues: on the rare occasions, when a Cabinet determines its course by the votes of its members, his vote counts only as one of theirs. But they are appointed and dismissed by the Sovereign on his advice. In a perfectly organised administration, such for example as was that of Sir Robert Peel in 1841–6[6], nothing of great importance is matured, or would even be projected, in any department without his personal cognisance; and any weighty business would commonly go to him before being submitted to the Cabinet. He reports to the Sovereign its proceedings, and he also has many audiences of the august occupant of the Throne.

[4] J. P. Mackintosh, *The British Cabinet*, Stevens & Sons Ltd., London, 1962, p. 299.
[5] W. E. Gladstone, *Gleanings of Past Years, 1875–8*, Volume I, John Murray, London, 1879, pp. 242–43.
[6] Gladstone served under Peel, and greatly admired his administration, but the workload in mid-century was much lighter than it became later, rendering impossible 'personal cognisance' of every significant matter.

He is bound, in these reports and audiences, not to counterwork the Cabinet; not to divide it; not to undermine the position of any of his colleagues in the royal favour. If he departs in any degree from strict adherence to these rules, and uses his great opportunities to increase his own influence, or pursue aims not shared by his colleagues, then, unless he is prepared to advise their dismissal, he not only departs from rule, but commits an act of treachery and baseness. As the Cabinet stands between the Sovereign and the Parliament, and is bound to be loyal to both, so he stands between his colleagues and the Sovereign, and is bound to be loyal to both.

This is one of the more famous civil service minutes of the nineteenth century, and reveals the very real problems of the system of having no formal minutes of Cabinet meetings. It was written in 1882, from Lord Hartington's Private Secretary, addressed to Gladstone's Private Secretary.[7]

Harcourt and Chamberlain have both been here this morning and at my Chief about yesterday's Cabinet proceedings. They cannot agree what occurred. There must have been some decision, as Bright's resignation shows.[8] My Chief has told me to ask you what the devil was decided, for he be damned if he knows. Will you ask Mr G. in more conventional and less pungent terms?

On 8 April 1878, Lord Salisbury (1830–1903) set out in Parliament what has remained the definitive statement of Cabinet collective responsibility. It came in reply to complaints from Lord Derby, recently

---

[7] Quoted in John F. Naylor, *A Man and an Institution: Sir Maurice Hankey, the Cabinet Secretariat and the custody of Cabinet secrecy*, Cambridge University Press, Cambridge, 1984.
[8] John Bright, (1811–1889) was Chancellor of the Duchy of Lancaster, and had in fact resigned over plans for Home Rule for Ireland.

resigned from the government and whose place as Foreign Secretary Salisbury had taken, about policies he could not accept.[9]

Now, my Lords, am I not defending a great constitutional principle when I say that, for all that passes in Cabinet each member of it who does not resign is absolutely and irretrievably responsible, and has no right afterwards to say that he agreed in one case to a compromise, while in another he was persuaded by one of his colleagues ... It is only on the principle that absolute responsibility is undertaken by every member of a Cabinet who, after a decision is arrived at, remains a member of it, that the joint responsibility of ministers to Parliament can be upheld, and one of the most essential conditions of parliamentary responsibility established.

In this remarkable extract from her Journal, on 6 February 1886, Queen Victoria (1819–1901) describes a conversation with the new Foreign Secretary, Lord Rosebery (1847–1929), himself a later Prime Minister. As interesting, a later letter to Lord Salisbury indicated that she offered this advice to Rosebery having been offered it herself by Salisbury.[10]

I urged Lord Rosebery not to bring too many matters before the Cabinet, as nothing was decided there, and it would be far better to discuss everything with me and Mr Gladstone.

Debate about the personal prerogatives of the monarch was pretty vigorous during the reign of Victoria, at least in part due to episodes like this. Bartle Frere was the British High Commissioner for South Africa, who, in sending an ultimatum which caused the Zulu War, disobeyed

[9] Lady Gwendolen Cecil, *Life of Robert, Marquis of Salisbury*, Vol. 2, Hodder and Stoughton, London, 1921, pp. 219–20.
[10] George Earle Buckle (ed.), *The Letters of Queen Victoria*, Third series, Vol. 1, John Murray, London, 1930, p. 48; the letter to Lord Salisbury is on p. 211.

orders from London. This is described by future Prime Minister Arthur Balfour in a memorandum from 8 May 1880.[11]

Bartle Frere should have been recalled as soon as news of his ultimatum reached England. We should then have escaped in appearance, as well as in reality, the responsibility of the Zulu War. So thought the majority of the Cabinet, so thought Dizzy himself. But the Queen was strong opposed to it; Hicks Beach was strongly opposed to it; and the Prime Minister was unable to resist Sovereign and the Colonial Secretary together.[12]

The late Victorian era also saw the demise of the notion that Cabinet ministers had any existence independent of their appointment by the prime minister. After the death of Queen Victoria (the last monarch to make successful interventions over appointments) there was no doubt that Cabinet ministers were appointed by the prime minister, and that the ministry fell when he did. In 1884 Sir William Harcourt (1827–1904), Home Secretary and a later Chancellor, one of Gladstone's great rivals, acknowledged this in a letter to the Prime Minister.[13]

I confess I have never doubted that Cabinet offices were held *durante bene placito*[14] of the Prime Minister . . . in the ordinary working of the Cabinet I have always supposed that the Prime Minister had the same authority to modify it as he has to construct it . . . In my opinion it is no more open to the head of a department in the

---

[11] Arthur James Balfour, *Chapters of Autobiography*, Cassell & Company Ltd., London, 1930, pp. 113–14.
[12] Sir Michael Hicks Beach (1837–1914), Colonial Secretary; Dizzy was the Prime Minister, Lord Beaconsfield, formerly Benjamin Disraeli (1807–1881).
[13] A. G. Gardiner, *The Life of Sir William Harcourt: Volume 1, 1827–1886*, Constable and Company Ltd., London, 1923, p. 508.
[14] 'at the pleasure'.

Cabinet to say to the potter that he will be an *urceus* or an *amphora* than it is to a Commander of a Division to say to the Commander in Chief that he will not be superseded in the command by another officer. The interests at stake are far too serious to admit of the doctrine of fixity of tenure.

In his 1890 biography of the great eighteenth-century Prime Minister Robert Walpole (1676–1745), John Morley (1838–1923), a member of Gladstone's Cabinet and later his biographer, coined perhaps the most famous phrase ever used to describe the Prime Minister's relationship with his Cabinet.[15]

The Prime Minister is the keystone of the Cabinet arch. Although in Cabinet all its members stand on an equal footing, speak with equal voice, and, on the rare occasions when a division is taken, are counted on the fraternal principle of one man, one vote, yet the head of the Cabinet is *primus inter pares*,[16] and occupies a position which, so long as it lasts, is one of exceptional and peculiar authority.

In his memoirs almost forty years later, Herbert Asquith, another later prime minister himself (1852–1928), revealed that this may actually have come from Gladstone himself.[17]

Lord Morley says in a letter to me (March 3, 1919): 'By the way, the chapter in my book upon the Cabinet was in truth the work of W. E. G.'

---

[15] John Morley, *Walpole*, Macmillan and Co., London, 1890, p. 157.
[16] 'First among equals'.
[17] Earl of Oxford and Asquith, *Fifty Years of Parliament*, Vol. 2, Cassell and Company Ltd., London, 1926, p. 183.

Harcourt wrote himself a memorandum (dated 12 July 1889) on Morley's book in these terms.[18]

On a question of policy there can be no doubt that the most successful administrations are those where there is a strong prime minister and a subordinate Cabinet. Where the individual members of the Cabinet are too strong there are perpetual elements of discord and disunion ... Though in theory *primus inter pares* the prime minister should really be *inter stellas luna minores*.[19] This was evidently the case with Walpole, Pitt and Peel.

Still, the prime minister's unambiguous right to make appointments did not contribute to a less febrile atmosphere when the Cabinet was being formed. Lord Salisbury left this priceless quote describing these occasions.[20]

The Carlton Club[21] resembles nothing so much at this moment as the Zoological Garden at feeding time.

Salisbury also strongly believed that in order to have full and frank exchanges, the secrecy of those exchanges must be sacrosanct. This is how his niece and biographer described his views.[22]

Originating in a spontaneous gathering of friends, legally unrecognised, it [Cabinet] had inherited a tradition of freedom and

---

[18] A. G. Gardiner, *The Life of Sir William Harcourt: Volume 2*, Constable and Company Ltd., London, 1923, p. 612.
[19] 'A moon among lesser stars.'
[20] Herman Finer, *The Theory and Practice of Modern Government*, Fourth ed., Methuen & Company Ltd., London, 1961, p. 582.
[21] London club which has long been a social centre for the Conservative Party.
[22] Lady Gwendolen Cecil, *Life of Robert Marquis of Salisbury: Volume II, 1868–1880*, Hodder and Stoughton Ltd., London, 1921, pp. 223–24.

informality which was in his eyes indispensable to its efficiency. A Cabinet discussion was not the occasion for the deliverance of considered judgements but an opportunity for the pursuit of practical conclusions. It could only be made completely effective for this purpose if the flow of suggestions which accompanied it attained the freedom and fullness which belong to private conversations – members must feel themselves untrammelled by any consideration of consistency with the past or self-justification in the future. The convention which forbade any note being taken of what was said, – futile as a safeguard for secrecy, – was invaluable as a guarantee for this irresponsible licence in discussion. Lord Salisbury would have extended it in principle to the record preserved in each man's memory. The first rule of Cabinet conduct, he used to declare, was that no member should ever 'Hansardise' another, – ever compare his present contribution to the common fund of counsel with a privately expressed opinion. Any record kept of the discussions must gravely restrict this invaluable liberty; – if public reference to them were ever to be tolerated, it must disappear.

Although regular interventions on appointments had died with Queen Victoria, monarchs still attempted to influence public policy decisions through the prime minister. They were rarely successful, and in 1902, after King Edward VII had urged him not to establish an inquiry into the Boer War, Lord Salisbury (then Prime Minister) firmly established the prerogatives of the office.[23]

[The King] has no power to impose such a veto against a decision of the Cabinet. His colleagues would have the right to refuse to be overruled by the Prime Minister; and in a matter which they regard

---

[23] J. P. Mackintosh, *The British Cabinet*, Stevens & Sons Ltd., London, 1962, p. 229.

as a question of honourable adherence to a pledge they would doubtless do so.

Not only did this dispel any lingering illusions the King may have had about the monarch's role in political decision-taking, it also described a powerful and central role for the Cabinet, which the King recognised in a letter to Lord Knollys (1837–1924), Private Secretary to the Prince of Wales, through whom he had originally tried to influence Salisbury.[24]

[Lord Salisbury] ought to have let me know sooner the decisions of the Cabinet. The latter is apparently so powerful a body neither I or *(sic)* the Prime Minister can gainsay them.

Collective and ministerial responsibility was occasionally used for more mundane purposes, even before the decline of Cabinet government usually associated with the late twentieth century, as Sidney Low, writing in 1904, described.[25]

The government can always meet an attack, which ought otherwise be successful, on the administration of a particular department, by making the question one of confidence. A good illustration is supplied by the debate of January 27th 1902, on the National Telephone Company. The agreement was condemned by many of the supporters of the administration, and a hostile amendment was moved by the Lord Mayor of London, a strong Conservative. There was no real question of government policy involved; it was simply the judgement and good sense of a minister, as the head of a branch of the public service, that was challenged. It was not easy to defend

---

[24] J. P. Mackintosh, *The British Cabinet*, Stevens & Sons Ltd., London, 1962, p. 229.
[25] Sidney Low, *The Governance of England*, T. Fisher Unwin, London, 1904, p. 146.

the agreement on its merits; but the ministerialists were warned not to condemn it, as such condemnation would be considered by the government equivalent to a vote of censure.

One key challenge in government was the lack of co-operation between the armed service departments, each of which had its own Cabinet minister representing its interests, and little incentive to change. They had previously derailed one attempt to facilitate their better co-operation – the 1890 Hartington Commission – which considered reforms to their intelligence departments and eventually decided against making such a recommendation.[26]

The amalgamation of the existing departments would, in our opinion, give rise to increased friction; while if, as we believe, the administration of the Admiralty and War Office should remain under separate heads, the practical difficulties in the working of a single Intelligence Department are evident, and to place either under the direction of an officer of the other service would impair its efficient working. While, therefore, we are strongly of opinion that the fullest intercommunication of all information of mutual value should be maintained by the two Intelligence Departments, we are opposed to their amalgamation.

In the early years of the century, recognition grew that greater inter-service cooperation would be required. The chosen vehicle was the Committee of Imperial Defence (CID), widely seen as the forerunner to the Cabinet Office (which initially inherited its staff). Yet prior to the Hankey/Lloyd-George reforms during the First World War, its strategic

[26] C. 5979, *Preliminary and Further Reports of the Royal Commissioners appointed to enquire into the Civil and Professional Administration of the Naval and Military Departments and the relation of those departments to each other and to the Treasury*, HMSO, London, 1890, p. viii.

capabilities, in line with contemporary assessments of the proper role of Cabinet Government, were tightly constrained. The Treasury minute which established the CID in 1904 set out its functions.[27]

... collect and co-ordinate for the use of the Committee information bearing on the wide problem of Imperial Defence ... [and] to make possible a continuity of method in the treatment of the questions which may from time to time come before the Committee.

The Dutch academic Hans Daalder, examining in 1963 the CID's role in the development of the machinery of government, concluded as follows:[28]

Later claims notwithstanding ... the CID, cannot be said to have been effectively in charge of strategic planning before 1914. Even Hankey [Secretary to the CID and later the first Cabinet Secretary, responsible for establishing the Cabinet Office], who can hardly be accused of lack of parental appreciation for the CID, has admitted that 'there was not that close and minute joint scrutiny of plans which a more perfect system should ensure.' The CID did not control or even succeed in clearing business between the two service departments in major fields of war preparation. It engaged in interesting discussions that did not definitely commit anyone. It collected important documentation. It prepared extensive instructions for action to be taken at the outbreak of war. But neither long-term strategy nor the effects of war on civilian life was adequately studied or foreseen. Stated differently, the CID formed a useful piece of machinery. But it did not prevail against the

---

[27] Quoted in Cd. 8490, Dardanelles Commission, *First Report*, HMSO, London, 1917, p. 4.
[28] Hans Daalder, *Cabinet Reform in Britain, 1914–1963*, Stanford University Press, Stanford, 1963, p. 153.

concentrated power of the individual Service departments. Nor did it really transcend the limitations that a century of almost unbroken peace had fixed in the minds of British politicians and public alike.

Shortly after the establishment of the Committee of Imperial Defence, Lord Esher (1852–1930), a former Conservative MP, wrote to Arthur Balfour (1848–1930), the Prime Minister, recommending some changes to ensure its continued survival. This is from his letter, dated 5 October 1905, written after a conversation with the King, Balfour, Haldane (1856–1928), the Secretary of State for War.[29] and Lord Knollys.[30]

In view of a possible change of government next year, is there not a great risk of the partial or total collapse of the Defence Committee?

The existing safeguards for its continuance under a new administration, are first, the permanent Secretariat, and, second, the one permanent member, Lord Roberts.

The danger consists, however, in the vague definition of the duties of the Committee, and the numerical weakness of the permanent element.

The Committee does not, and cannot (under a representative form of government), possess executive functions. But as a permanent deliberation committee, with powers of enquiry and recommendation, it could be made to fulfil many duties hitherto delegated to 'Commissions' appointed ad hoc, and it could also be made to relieve public departments of certain responsibilities which in view of our growing Imperial needs they are not qualified to bear.

Recent events have proved that large questions of reorganisation, dealing with Imperial Defence, cannot adequately and efficiently be

---

[29] (1856–1928) Liberal MP and future Secretary for War and Lord Chancellor.
[30] Maurice J. Brett (ed.), *Journals and letters of Reginald Viscount Esher*, Vol. 2, Ivor Nicholson & Watson Ltd, London, 1934, pp. 114–15.

dealt with by the War Office in conjunction with the India Office, the Colonial Office and the Admiralty, all of which are vitally concerned with them.

Nor are these questions, in their constructive stages, matters which can be adequately treated by the Cabinet; the departments named are absorbed by laborious and complex administrative detail. They have neither time nor machinery adequate to deal with questions requiring careful enquiry, much common deliberation and mutual forbearance.

The Cabinet, composed of men absorbed in administrative and parliamentary duties, growing heavier year by year, cannot undertake to enquire into, nor to construct elaborate schemes involving much technical consideration. The special function of the Cabinet is to arrive at decisions upon facts or theories carefully presented in concrete form; it is not contended that any violent wrench should be given to the existing constitution, or that the supremacy of the Cabinet should be questioned. The Defence Committee, as conceived by the Prime Minister, is an Evolution and not a Revolution.

The question is whether, in the interests of the stability of the fabric, Mr Balfour, before quitting office, should, by numerically strengthening the permanent element in that Committee, give fresh assurance of its continuity. The proposal is, that two permanent sub-committees should be formed under the presidency of Mr Balfour, specially constituted to deal with:

a Certain scheduled recommendations made by the Elgin Commission.
b Certain strategical questions raised last summer by Sir John Fisher.[31]

---

[31] Sir John Fisher was First Sea Lord, 1904–10, and in 1905 was responsible for organising the redistribution of the Fleet.

A change of government, taking place while these sub-committees are engaged upon work of the kind suggested would not threaten (for reasons which appear obvious) their continuance, and consequently the existence of the committee itself.

The issue of ministerial conflicts of interest originally arose under Gladstone. But as the scope of government increased, prime ministers increasingly recognised the potential pitfalls, and moved to avoid them. This is Sir Henry Campbell-Bannerman (1836–1908), Prime Minister from 1905–08, answering a question in 1906 about directorships recently held by government ministers.[32]

The condition which was laid down in the formation of the government was that all directorships held by ministers must be resigned except in the case of honorary directorships, directorships in connection with philanthropic undertakings, and directorships of private companies. Every member of the government has either complied with this understanding or is in the process of complying with it. I do not think it is necessary to say more except to add that my right hon. friend the Secretary of State for India, whose name is mentioned in the question, has never held a directorship, and the same remark applies to my hon. friend the Civil Lord of the Admiralty.

Despite this caution, in 1913 the Marconi scandal erupted. Two ministers were accused of owning Marconi shares while having access to inside information. While they escaped censure, Asquith used the occasion (on 19 June 1913) to renew and expand Henry Campbell-Bannerman's rules on ministerial propriety.[33]

[32] HC Debs, 4 Series, Volume 154, 20 March 1906, Col. 234.
[33] J. A. Spender and Cyril Asquith, *Life of Herbert Henry Asquith, Lord Oxford and Asquith,* Vol. 1, Hutchinson & Co, London, 1932, p. 364.

The first, of course, and the most obvious, is that (1) ministers ought not to enter into any transaction whereby their private pecuniary interests might, even conceivably, come into conflict with their public duty. There is no dispute about that. Again (2) no minister is justified, under any circumstances, in using official information, information that has come to him as a minister, for his own private profit or for that of his friends. Further (3) no minister ought to allow or to put himself in a position to be tempted to use his official influence in support of any scheme, or in furtherance of any contract, in regard to which he has an undisclosed private interest. That again is beyond dispute. Again (4) no minister ought to accept from persons who are in negotiation with or seeking to enter into contractual or proprietary or pecuniary relations with the State, any kind of favour. That, I think, is also beyond dispute. I will add a further proposition, which I am not sure has been completely formulated, though it has no doubt been adumbrated in the course of these debates, and that is that (5) ministers should scrupulously avoid speculative investments in securities as to which, from their position and their special means of early or confidential information, they have, or may have, an advantage over other people in anticipating market changes.

3

Great War and Lloyd George, 1914–1922

Herbert Asquith was Liberal Prime Minister from 1908 to 1916. A notably successful peacetime premier, his reputation suffered irretrievable damage during the war, as many members of the government felt that his leisurely conduct of government was not suited to the new reality of 'total war'. Asquith continued to argue, for example, that taking Cabinet minutes was unconstitutional. He was forced to make a number of concessions before his eventual resignation, and in his memoirs, sought to defend his actions as both improving the efficiency of governance and upholding the principles of Cabinet collective responsibility.[1]

The root difficulty in the early conduct of the War on our part – a difficulty experienced in nearly the same degree in France – was how to combine rapid and effective executive action in the various theatres with the maintenance of Cabinet responsibility and control. This was the case quite as much after as before the formation of the Coalition in May, 1915. Various expedients in the way of delegation were tried, and on September 22 I proposed to the Cabinet the creation of two committees – one to deal with the actual conduct of the War and its problems: the other to concern itself with the financial outlook. I recorded at the time that 'after a good deal of

---

[1] Earl of Oxford and Asquith, *Memories and Reflections 1852–1927*, Vol. 2, Cassell & Co. Ltd., London, 1928, pp. 23–24.

discussion' the proposal was 'approved in principle'. When the details came to be worked out, there was for a time a fusillade of cross-criticism, but by the end of October I was able to make the following announcement on the subject of the War Committee to my colleagues:

> The proposal, as I understand it, is that there should be a small Committee of the Cabinet, not fewer than three or more than five in number to deal executively with the conduct of the War.
>
> It is understood that the Committee will from time to time call to their aid, for the purposes both of discussion and decision, other members of the Cabinet, either because their departments are concerned in the particular matter which is being dealt with or for other special reasons.
>
> The Cabinet to remain as it is, in numbers and composition.
>
> The *plenum* of the Cabinet to be kept constantly informed of the decisions and actions of the Committee, and in all questions which involve a change or new departure in policy to be consulted before decisive action is taken.

In addition to these proposals and the formation of the coalition government in May 1915, Asquith had already made one significant change to the machinery of government. In November 1914, recognising that the old Committee of Imperial Defence machinery was not suitable for the war, he created the War Council. This is from the later report of the Dardanelles Commission on the key changes which took place.[2]

The main change which was effected was, however, in connection with the powers of the Council as compared to those of the

---

[2] Cd. 8490, *Dardanelles Commission*, First Report, HMSO, London, 1917, pp. 6–7.

Committee of Imperial Defence. Whilst the latter body was in existence, the responsibility for all important decisions remained, theoretically in all, and practically in most cases, with the united Cabinet. The War Council remained, like the Committee of Imperial Defence, a Committee of the Cabinet with some experts added. Theoretically, the powers of the united Cabinet remained the same as before. Practically, they underwent a radical change. It was the Council, and not the united Cabinet, which finally decided the most important matters, and gave effect to its decisions without necessarily waiting for any expression of assent or dissent from the Cabinet. The Cabinet appear to have been generally informed of any important decisions which may have been taken by the Council, but not until after the necessary executive steps had been taken to give whole or partial effect to those decisions.

Still, the management of the war sometimes did not appear to be taken as a serious enterprise by those in control. One particular criticism focused on the lack of a meeting of the War Council between 19 March and 14 May 1915. This was how Asquith's biographers described his later response to the charge.[3]

... after 19th March there had been no new departure of any kind of policy, and that the operations which took place were 'the actual and necessary consequences of what had gone before, coupled with the decision of the Admiral not to continue the naval attack.' They were, however, he added, the subject of daily, even hourly communication between himself and his principal colleagues, and of long and careful discussions in the thirteen Cabinets which had taken place in these weeks.

---

[3] J. A. Spender and Cyril Asquith, *Life of Herbert Henry Asquith, Lord of Oxford and Asquith*, Vol. 2, Hutchinson & Co, London, 1932, pp. 160–61.

The Treasury had long been the crucial Department of State, and the political significance of the Chancellorship was set out in this letter from Austen Chamberlain (1863–1937), a former and future Chancellor who was himself to become Secretary of State for India in the Asquith Government, to Andrew Bonar Law (1858–1923) on 17 May 1915, as Asquith was building his coalition National Government.[4]

I attach great importance to your being Ch. of the Ex. That office gives its holder great authority and power. There is none other except the prime ministership which gives such influence, or such a starting point for influence in the whole field of policy. It is second in the Govt. when in the right hands.

Internal government problems got worse after Asquith was forced to create a coalition. This is how Winston Churchill (1874–1965), First Lord of the Admiralty, described business slowing even further as the new government met for the first time on 26 May 1915.[5]

Whereas practically all the important matters connected with the war had been dealt with in the late government by four or five ministers, at least a dozen powerful, capable, distinguished personalities who were in a position to assert themselves had now to be consulted.

The progress of business therefore became cumbrous and laborious in the last degree, and though all these evils were corrected by earnest patriotism and loyalty, the general result was bound to be disappointing. Those who had knowledge had pasts to defend; those free from war commitments were also free from war experience. At

---

[4] Robert Blake, *The Unknown Prime Minister: The Life and Times of Andrew Bonar Law, 1858–1923*, Eyre & Spottiswoode, London, 1955, p. 249.
[5] Winston Churchill, *The World Crisis, Volume 2: 1915*, Thorton Butterworth Ltd., London, 1923, p. 385.

least five or six different opinions prevailed on every great topic, and every operative decision was obtained only by prolonged, discursive and exhausting discussion. Far more often we laboured through long delays to unsatisfactory compromises. Meanwhile the destroying war strode remorselessly on its course.

Historians judged it similarly. Arthur Berriedale Keith, in his classic work The British Cabinet System, *explained the problem twelve years later.*[6]

Such a galaxy of talent failed to produce efficiency in decisions, and, so far was their collective judgement from impressing the Cabinet as a whole, that questions were raised again in the whole body.

Asquith's harshest contemporary critic was the War Minister, David Lloyd George (1863–1945). Lloyd George became increasingly disenchanted with the slow pace of decision-taking in the coalition government. In his memoirs, he recalled how it looked to him.[7]

A paralysis of will seemed to have seized the government. Whatever the subject, it was impossible to get and move on. I am not sure that this palsy did not account for the unanimity of the Cabinet on the question of rejecting overtures for peace. These would have meant action. The pacifist element were easily persuaded to do nothing. The government was getting into that nervous condition where they could neither wage war nor negotiate peace.

---

[6] Arthur Berriedale Keith, *The British Cabinet System, 1830–1938*, Stevens & Sons Ltd., London, 1939, p. 158.

[7] David Lloyd George, *War Memoirs,* Vol. 1 (New edition), Odhams Press Ltd., London, 1938, p. 580.

In a House of Lords debate in June 1918 the Leader of the Lords, Lord Curzon (1859–1925), provided perhaps the most damning indictment of the operation of the Asquith Cabinet.[8]

Meetings of the Cabinet were most irregular; sometimes only once, seldom more than twice, a week. There was no agenda, there was no order of business. Any minister requiring to bring up a matter either of departmental or of public importance had to seek the permission of the Prime Minister to do so. No one else, broadly speaking, was warned in advance. It was difficult for any minister to secure an interstice in the general discussion in which he could place his own case. No record whatever was kept of our proceedings, except the private and personal letter written by the Prime Minister to the Sovereign, the contents of which, of course, are never seen by anybody else. The Cabinet often had the very haziest notion as to what its decisions were; and I appeal not only to my own experience but to the experience of every Cabinet minister who sits in this House, and to the records contained in the memoirs of half-a-dozen prime ministers in the past, that cases frequently arose when the matter was left so much in doubt that a minister went away and acted upon what he thought was a decision which subsequently turned out to be no decision at all, or was repudiated by his colleagues. No one will deny that a system, however embedded in the traditions of the past, and consecrated by constitutional custom, which was attended by these defects was a system which was destined, immediately it came into contact with the hard realities of war, to crumble into dust at once.

[8] HL Debs, 5 series, Volume 30, 19 June 1918, Col. 265.

Asquith resigned in December 1916, but in his memoirs, published a decade later, he provided the most expansive interpretation to date of the potential powers of a prime minister vis á vis his Cabinet.[9]

The Latin phrases which have been resorted to – *'primus inter pares'*, *'velut inter ignes Luna minores'* – do not carry the matter any further. The office of prime minister is what its holder chooses and is able to make of it.

When David Lloyd George became Prime Minister in 1916, he brought some dramatic changes. Out went the old committee structures, with their need to consult the full Cabinet on any change of policy. In their place stood a new, executive War Cabinet of five members served by the secretariat of the old Committee of Imperial Defence. The changes were to have a dramatic long-term effect on the operation of Cabinet government, but Lloyd George was more immediately concerned with the conduct of the war.[10]

I had decided to make one fundamental change in the constitution of the Cabinet. I had long come to the conclusion that a body of 20 Members was a futile instrument for the conduct of any business which required immediate action. I ultimately resolved to set up a Cabinet of five to whom the whole control of the War should be entrusted. I felt that they must remain in almost constant session to review events from day to day. Ministers who were in charge of departments could rarely be available for purposes of consultation, and their minds would naturally be taken up with the innumerable details of their respective Offices. The War Cabinet must therefore

---

[9] Earl of Oxford and Asquith, *Fifty Years of Parliament*, Vol. 2, Cassell & Co. Ltd., London, 1926, p. 185.

[10] David Lloyd George, *War Memoirs*, Vol. 3, Ivor Nicholson & Watson, London, 1934, pp. 1064, 1080–81.

consist of men who were free from all departmental cares, and who could devote the whole of their time and thought to the momentous questions which were involved in the successful direction of a world war. When matters arose which affected any particular department, the head of that department could be summoned to attend the Cabinet, bringing with him appropriate experts. It was made quite clear that the Cabinet would have the same direct access to those experts as their departmental chiefs; that questions could be addressed to them directly; and that they were to speak their minds freely without awaiting the permission or opinion of their political chiefs.

. . . Another departure from Cabinet traditions which I had decided to initiate was the setting up of a Cabinet Secretariat. Hitherto no written record was ever made of even the most important decisions of the Cabinet, let alone the discussions which preceded them. I have no recollection of Sir Henry Campbell-Bannerman or Mr Asquith ever making a note of the conclusions arrived at, except in very exceptional cases where the decision taken was embodied in the form of an answer to be given to a question about to be put in the House of Commons. The result was that now and again there was a good deal of doubt as to what the Cabinet had actually determined on some particular issue. I came to the conclusion that it was desirable to have a secretary present who would make a short précis of the discussions on all important issues and take a full record of all decisions. Where these decisions affected one of the departments, a copy of the minute was immediately sent to the Minister concerned. I thought it was of primary importance that a written intimation of the character and terms of the decision of the Cabinet should be sent formally to the department, not merely as a reminder to the minister, but in order that the officials who advised him and carried out his orders should be fully informed. I also thought it not only desirable but imperative, having regard to the number of decisions taken in the past which had not been carried out, to charge the Secretary with the duty of keeping in touch with further developments and of reporting to me from time to time what action had been taken in the various departments concerned on these Cabinet orders. I subsequently found that these enquiries addressed from the Cabinet Office and the reports which had to be made in response, were very helpful in keeping the departments alert and well up to the mark. Where the Secretary reported failure or delay in carrying out decisions, I sent for the minister, and where unexpected difficulties had arisen, steps were taken to remove them.

In March 1946 Lord (Maurice) Hankey, the former Cabinet Secretary who had gone on to serve in the Cabinet from 1939–42, gave a series of broadcasts on the Cabinet system. This is how he described the functions of the original 1916 War Cabinet Secretariat, as laid down by Lloyd George.[11]

(1) To record the proceedings of the War Cabinet.
(2) To transmit the decisions of the War Cabinet to those departments which are concerned in giving effect to them or otherwise interested.
(3) To prepare Agenda Papers; to arrange for the attendance of ministers and other persons concerned; and to procure and circulate the documents required for discussion.
(4) To attend to the correspondence connected with the work of the War Cabinet.

---

[11] PRO, LCO 2/3215, Principles of the Cabinet system and the work of the Cabinet Secretariat: Broadcast by Lord Hankey, Draft of Broadcast by Lord Hankey.

Hankey's original draft Rules of Procedure *was a crucial document. It was the first official guidance about the operation of Cabinet government, and amounted to a considerable increase in power for the Cabinet Secretariat. Many of its key components remain in the document – now the* Ministerial Code *– to this day.*[12]

(1) Questions may be referred for decision by the War Cabinet by the prime minister, or by members of the War Cabinet, or by any member of the government or by any government department. The normal procedure for raising any question should be a communication to the secretary, accompanied, when practicable, by a short memorandum containing a summary of the points on which a decision is required.

(2) Before reaching their final conclusions on any subject the War Cabinet will, as a general rule, consult the ministers at the head of the department concerned, who will lay before them all the evidence, written or oral, relevant and necessary to a decision.

(3) After each meeting the secretary will circulate the copies of the draft minutes to members for their remarks. He will also circulate to ministers summoned for particular subjects, drafts of the minutes on those subjects for their remarks. When their remarks have been received, the secretary will submit a final draft of the minutes for the approval of the prime minister. After the prime minister has initialled the minutes of the War Cabinet, the conclusions formulated therein will become operative decisions to be carried out by the responsible departments. The prime minister can delegate his powers in this respect in case of absence or the claims of other urgent business.

(4) As soon as the prime minister's initials have been received, the decisions of the War Cabinet will be communicated by the

---

[12] PRO, CAB 21/102, *The War Cabinet: Rules of Procedure*, 24 January 1917.

secretary to the political and civil heads of the departments concerned, who will be responsible for giving effect to them.

In a separate memorandum, Hankey set out the responsibilities of the Cabinet Secretariat in two broad areas – 'machinery' and 'ideas'.[13]

Under 'machinery' are included the keeping of accurate and adequate records of the proceedings and decisions of the War Cabinet; the preparation of Agenda Papers, and the collection and distribution of all information required for the War Cabinet's deliberations; the dissemination of the decisions of the War Cabinet to those concerned in carrying them out, and the elaboration of the machinery to ensure that such decisions are actually carried out and not lost sight of; and the collection from the departments of all information required to keep the members of the War Cabinet abreast of all necessary information . . .

Presumably, under the new system there is no desire in the least to fetter the formulation of ideas by the departments. But the War Cabinet, composed of selected ministers without portfolios, is in a position to view every question from a wider point of view, and to formulate ideas far beyond the probable scope of any minister engaged in the heavy task of administering a great government department.

I conceive that, to help them on this side, the ministers on the War Cabinet will require expert staff to assist them. This is not with the idea of diminishing the responsibility of the departments, which would be fatal to sound government. The expert staff is required rather to collect from the departments, or elsewhere, the data which the War Cabinet require for the development of the ideas and the

---

[13] PRO, CAB 21/102, *Functions of the War Cabinet*, Note on the Composition of the Secretariat of the War Cabinet, undated, 1917.

formulation of the wider schemes which have been referred to. I presume that the schemes will be discussed with the departments concerned before they are put into force, so that the departments will not feel that schemes have been forced on them without examination by the executive who have to carry them out.

The 'Haldane Committee', named after its chairman, Lord Haldane, was established during the war to consider how the wartime innovations and new governmental responsibilities could best be meshed with the needs of parliamentary oversight and good governance during peacetime. It provided the first clear statement of the Cabinet's responsibilities, and several of its recommendations, in particular the need for proper research support, were later followed up.[14]

The main functions of the Cabinet may, we think, be described as:
  (a) the final determination of the policy to be submitted to Parliament;
  (b) the supreme control of the national executive in accordance with the policy prescribed by Parliament; and
  (c) the continuous co-ordination and delimitation of the activities of the several departments of state.

For the due performance of these functions the following conditions seem to be essential, or, at least, desirable:
  (i) the Cabinet should be small in number – preferably ten or, at most, twelve;
  (ii) it should meet frequently;
  (iii) it should be supplied in the most convenient form with all the information and material necessary to enable it to arrive at expeditious decisions;

[14] Cd. 9203, *Report of the Machinery of Government Committee*, Ministry of Reconstruction, 1918, p. 5.

(iv) it should make a point of consulting personally all the ministers whose work is likely to be affected by its decisions; and
(v) it should have a systematic method of securing that its decisions are effectually carried out by the departments concerned.

Amongst Lloyd George's other changes, he brought a number of bright young men to Number 10 to work for him personally. Because there was no room in the building itself, they worked in sheds in the garden, and became known as the 'Garden Suburb'. Lloyd George kept the Garden Suburb and many of his innovations as the country returned to peace, and was criticised for it. But while his seeming omnipotence temporarily prevented his critics moving against him, the judgement of contemporary historians was harsh. This is Arthur Berriedale Keith.[15]

No doubt Mr Lloyd George never succeeded in realising the essential change brought about by the advent of peace, and the necessity of restoring the old practices of Cabinet government. He delayed as long as he dared the restoration of the normal Cabinet, and he actually seems to have thought it possible that Mr Austen Chamberlain would accept office as Chancellor of the Exchequer without a seat in the Cabinet. When this idea was rejected with firmness, all that he would concede was a place in the Cabinet, but the restoration of the full Cabinet was further delayed, without, it seems clear, any public advantage.

* * *

It is plain that in the war period, its [the Cabinet Office's] activities bordered on the mischievous, though the Prime Minister's own secretariat was a prime offender.

[15] Arthur Berriedale Keith, *The British Cabinet System, 1830–1938*, Stevens & Sons Ltd., London, 1939, pp. 81, 134.

Variously feared for their influence and praised for their effectiveness, it was not until 1980 that a proper study of the Garden Suburb was published, by historian John Turner. With access to the official papers, he was able to provide a more balanced assessment.[16]

The Garden Suburb undertook the work of actively seeking information, before and after the War Cabinet made a decision, and presenting it in a useful form to the Prime Minister. The secretaries could use their access to departmental papers and permanent officials to digest essential information and comment critically on arguments put forward by the departments. Specialised knowledge and personal acquaintance with officials were particularly valuable. Some difficulties could even be resolved by the Secretariat on its own, leaving only a formal decision to be taken by the War Cabinet. After a decision, the Garden Suburb could find out whether departmental action was having the desired effect. Five men could not monitor every decision, nor evaluate every area of policy; but they could at least identify some possible failures in time for preventive action . . .

As contemporaries had anticipated, members of the Garden Suburb did much to interpret Lloyd George to the world and the world to Lloyd George: 'cultivating the Prime Minister's mind' in Massingham's hostile phrase, and cultivating public opinion at the same time. They helped to create a body of thought which influenced the Prime Minister's public statement and, to a lesser extent, his acts of policy. They had no monopoly in the cultivation of Lloyd George's mind, nor were they unaffected by his own active intelligence, but they were frequently in his company and therefore able to put their positions to him more often than others who

---

[16] John Turner, *Lloyd George's Secretariat*, Cambridge University Press, Cambridge, 1980, pp. 5, 139.

competed for his attention. Their interpretation of events, their own private and published writings, and their recommendation for the public presentation of the government's case all contributed to the intellectual foundations of Lloyd George's political position.

4
Interwar, 1922–1939

With the war over, many of Lloyd George's critics (and some of his friends) felt that the time had come for a return to the normal way of doing things, in Cabinet government terms as in others. They, and many historians, viewed Lloyd George's later rule with disdain. In a resignation speech to his constituency Liberal Club on 13 March 1922, E. S. Montagu, the former Secretary of State for India, hit out at the effect of the Prime Minister's style of government.[1]

An accusation of a breach of the doctrine of Cabinet responsibility from the Prime Minister, of all men in the world, is a laughable accusation. It is grotesque. What are the circumstances? The head of our government, at the present moment, is a Prime Minister of great, if eccentric, genius, whose contributions to the well-being of his country, and of the world, have been so well known but who has demanded the price which it is within the power of every genius to demand – and that price has been the total, complete, absolute disappearance of the doctrine of Cabinet responsibility ever since he formed his government.

Nor was he the only one. This is the draft of a letter from Lord Curzon, at the time Foreign Secretary, to Lloyd George, bemoaning the Prime Minister's heavy involvement in foreign affairs. The government fell

---

[1] Edwin Montagu, 'Mr. Montagu's Reply', *The Times*, 13 March 1922.

*before it could be sent, but Curzon was far from the last Foreign Secretary to make this complaint.*²

There has grown up a system under which there are in reality two Foreign Offices: the one for which I am for the time being responsible, and the other at Number 10 – with the essential difference between them that, whereas I report not only to you but to all my colleagues everything that I say or do, every telegram that I receive or send, every communication of importance that reaches me, it is often only by accident that I hear what is being done by the other Foreign Office; and even when I am informed officially of what has passed there, it has nevertheless been done, in many cases, without the Foreign Office, for which I am responsible, knowing that the communication was going to be made or the interview take place.

This condition of affairs has reached such a pitch that not only is it a subject of common knowledge and daily comment in my office, but it is known to every journalist in London, and it has been the subject of open complaints and censure in well-nigh every newspaper in the United Kingdom, the Foreign Office and myself in particular having been held up to contempt for having abdicated our functions, or allowed them to be stolen away. There cannot be a doubt that opinion has not merely condemned this procedure as unconstitutional and improper, but has clamoured without a dissentient voice for its cessation. In this way there has grown up a situation which has for long rendered my own position one of extreme delicacy and difficulty, and to which, in the common interest, an end should be sought.

During this period – I have now been Secretary of State for three

---

² Earl of Ronaldshay, *The Life of Lord Curzon*, Vol. 3, Ernest Benn Ltd, London, 1928, pp. 316–17.

years – I have borne this situation with such equanimity as I could. I have on several occasions mentioned it or written about it to you. I have repeatedly mentioned it to your Private Secretaries. I have discussed it at length with my principal colleagues. Throughout I have gladly recognised the exceptional and commanding influence which you exercise over the Foreign Affairs both of this country and of the world, by virtue of your personality and of the power which your unexampled experience in conferences and councils during and since the war has very naturally placed in your hands; and I have constantly deferred from making more serious representations in the interests of loyalty to yourself and unity in the government.

But the case has not been confined even to a long series of such minor incidents as those to which I have referred at the beginning of this letter. I could, if required, draw up a list of important cases in which agents have been employed, instructions given, policies initiated at Number 10 Downing Street – all in the Department of Foreign Affairs – of which the Foreign Office has either known nothing or has been informed only when the action had already been taken.

I have for long felt that such a situation should not be permitted to continue, and that, if it were not checked, you ought to have a Foreign Secretary who will more easily than I conform to this novel conception of Foreign Office duties. Indeed, I should find no pleasure in continuing now, were I not to receive a definite assurance from you that the constitutional relations between the two departments should be re-established and the Foreign Office shall resume its proper function in the state.

Pray believe me that this resolve on my part indicates no desire to question the prerogative or the paramount influence of the Prime Minister in general or of yourself in particular. These are undisputed and indisputable, and, with due co-ordination, can be wielded as effectively in the domain of Foreign Affairs as in every other department of government.

I have discussed this matter at length with Chamberlain and at earlier dates with Balfour; and I shall be ready to come with the former and see you upon it at any time which you may desire. I could also, if it were found necessary, draw up the fuller statement, for which I have the materials.

Perhaps Lloyd George's stark assessment of the composition of most Cabinets provided some explanation for his behaviour.[3]

In most governments there are four or five outstanding figures who by exceptional talent, experience, and personality constitute the inner council which gives direction to the policy of a ministry. An administration that is not fortunate enough to possess such a group may pull through without mishap in tranquil seasons, but in an emergency it is hopelessly lost. The rest do not count in a crisis. The hummocks that look like eminences in fine weather are quickly submerged in a great flood, when the highest peaks alone are visible above the surface of the waters.

His cynicism went further than that, though. Perhaps it is no surprise after the intriguing which had marked his political career. Looking at some of the great clashes between senior ministers down the years, might it also be a supremely accurate view?[4]

There can be no friendship between the top five men in a Cabinet.

---

[3] David Lloyd George, *War Memoirs*, Vol. 3, Ivor Nicholson & Watson, London, 1934, p. 1042.
[4] Thomas Jones, *A Diary with Letters, 1931–1950*, Oxford University Press, London, 1954, p. 52.

As the criticism of Lloyd George built, former Prime Minister Herbert Asquith, speaking in a House of Commons debate in June 1922, expressed his concerns about the constitutional implications of the new Cabinet Secretariat, at least during peacetime.[5]

I am perfectly certain, if I may venture to say so – for I have not had experience of the new system – that Mr Gladstone and Lord Beaconsfield[6] would have shuddered in their graves at the thought of an outsider being present and taking notes of what was going on. They would have considered it a breach of the fundamental practice of the Constitution.

This was the response from Austen Chamberlain, Chancellor of the Exchequer at the time.[7]

The right hon. gentleman asks, 'Has this Cabinet Secretariat bettered legislation?' It is not its business to better legislation. 'Has it bettered finance?' It is not its business to better finance. The business of legislation is the business of ministers; the business of finance is the business of the Chancellor of the Exchequer and the Treasury and ministers at large. 'Has it bettered foreign affairs?' It is not its business to deal with foreign affairs. That is the business of the Secretary of State and the Foreign Office. Those questions are based on a misconception of what the duties of the Cabinet Secretariat are. Its duties are to receive from ministers or departments notification of questions on which Cabinet decisions are required; to see that the papers which the Cabinet has to have before it, before it takes those decisions, are properly presented; to record so much of the discussions as from time to time they may be directed to record; to

---

[5] HC Debs, 5 Series, Volume 155, 13 June 1922, Col. 225.
[6] Benjamin Disraeli had become Lord Beaconsfield in 1876.
[7] HC Debs, 5 Series, Volume 155, 13 June 1922, Col. 225.

take note of the decisions, and to communicate them to those who have to execute them. But they are not themselves authorised to take the initiative in any matter of legislation, or in any matter of executive action.

Lord Balfour, who by that time had served as both Prime Minister and Foreign Secretary (under Lloyd George), contributed to the debate when he wrote, in 1926, the introduction to a new edition of Bagehot's English Constitution. *In it, he argued that Bagehot's analysis – with Cabinet at the very centre of government – remained true for the practice in the early twentieth century.*[8]

To my thinking at least, the gradual growth and final establishment of the Cabinet system has been of greater importance than anything in our constitutional history since the Revolution settlement, greater, for instance, than the series of Reform Bills which began in 1832.

H. A. L. Fisher (1864–1940), President of the Board of Education 1916–22, is unusual amongst ex-ministers in not sharing the view that a large Cabinet is necessarily deleterious to the good conduct of business.[9]

My experience is that a Cabinet of some twenty-three members is not too large, for the bulk of the discussion is naturally carried on by the principal ministers sitting round the prime minister at the centre of the long table, the juniors seldom intervening unless their special departments are involved. Much, however, must depend on the

---

[8] Earl of Balfour, Introduction to Walter Bagehot's *English Constitution*, Oxford University Press, London, 1926, p. xii.
[9] H. A. L. Fisher, *An Unfinished Autobiography*, Oxford University Press, London, 1940, p. 139.

chairmanship of the prime minister. A strong chairman has nothing to fear from a large Cabinet and much to gain, for the growing volume of business necessitates many Cabinet committees, and even in a large Cabinet there is more work than its members are able properly to discharge.

Austen Chamberlain had been Leader of the Conservative Party, but when the coalition collapsed and the Conservatives returned to office he was replaced by Andrew Bonar Law. Bonar Law took a far less rosy view of Lloyd George's innovations, and was committed to abolishing the Cabinet Secretariat. Hankey, the Cabinet Secretary, fought a furious (and ultimately successful) rearguard action to save the Cabinet Office. This is the minute he eventually agreed with Sir Warren Fisher, Permanent Secretary to the Treasury, that went to Bonar Law on 7 November 1922. Hankey had also sent a separate minute opposing the absorption of the Cabinet Office by the Treasury (on 6 November).[10]

1. In the course of the Prime Minister's election address and of his speech at Glasgow on 20th Ultimo he said in regard to the Cabinet Secretariat that the government 'intend to bring that body in its present form to an end, and I am certain that the necessary work can be centralised and the invaluable services of the present Secretary retained in connection with the Treasury which in the past has always been the central department of government': also, 'I am convinced that the work can be done quite as efficiently, and far more economically, by having the Cabinet Secretariat, who is also the Secretariat of the Committee of Imperial Defence – in having him and whatever help he needs

---

[10] PRO, CAB 63/33, *War Cabinet and Cabinet Office: Lord Hankey: Papers*, Hankey and Fisher to Bonar Law, 7 November 1922.

treated as part of the Treasury, which is the central department of government.'

2. The Treasury, unlike finance ministries in other countries, is not merely the finance department but also, under the Prime Minister (First Lord) and the Cabinet, the central and co-ordinating organ of government. As such it is the natural body to provide for the secretarial needs of the Cabinet.

3. Effect could be given to the Prime Minister's statements either by merging the staff required to do the secretarial work of the Cabinet in the headquarters staff of the Treasury or by reverting to the system in operation until March 1921, under which the Cabinet Secretariat and the Committee of Imperial Defence were shown as a unit on the vote for the 'Treasury and Subordinate Departments'. I think the Prime Minister's announcement is not inconsistent with the latter arrangement under which the cost of this service would be shown on the face of the vote as a distinct item.

4. I should like to suggest that, on a vacancy occurring in the post of Clerk to the Privy Council, Sir Maurice Hankey should succeed to it and thus be the officer immediately attached both to the working Privy Council and to the Ceremonial Privy Council. (The title would appear, in addition to those of Secretary to the Cabinet and Secretary to the Committee of Imperial Defence, on the vote for the Treasury and Subordinate Departments, and also in its present place, but without salary, on the Privy Council vote.) This course would have certain constitutional as well as practical and financial advantages.

Yet the future of the Cabinet Office was still unclear when the first Labour government came to office in 1924. Labour Ministers were to prove unlikely saviours, but their experience of working on committees with records of decisions taken helped give the Cabinet Office life after

Lloyd George. Martin Burch and Ian Holliday paid Ramsay MacDonald and his Cabinet their due.[11]

In demonstrating that a bureaucratic machine might function smoothly, the first Labour government set standards for subsequent governments to meet. The Cabinet Secretariat, operating as guardian of the institutional memory, ensured that these standards deemed workable were communicated to successor Cabinets.

Despite this ability to use the new systems, the first Labour government was not always the most harmonious, with some of its members chafing against the influence of Prime Minister Ramsay MacDonald. This is from the diaries of Beatrice Webb (1858–1943), one of the party's founders, the movement's leaders and wife of Sidney Webb (1859–1947), President of the Board of Trade.[12]

7 April 1924
Altogether, personal relations within the Cabinet are not happy. Cabinet meetings are quite harmonious – but at these meetings only routine daily business is transacted – very few big questions of policy are discussed. The PM carries on his foreign policy without discussion. Meanwhile each of his ministers goes his own way in his own department without consulting his chief. I could not have imagined a body which has less *corporate* responsibility than MacDonald's Cabinet. Are all Cabinets congeries of little autocrats with a super-autocrat presiding over them?

---

[11] Martin Burch and Ian Holliday, *The British Cabinet System*, Prentice Hall, Hemel Hempstead, 1996, p. 18.
[12] Margaret Cole (ed.), *Beatrice Webb's Diaries, 1924–1932*, Longmans, Green & Co., London, 1956, p. 20.

Earl Grey (1862–1933), Foreign Secretary between 1905 and 1916, here describes the qualities he felt were necessary in a good Cabinet minister.[13]

One of these is to put his mind into the common stock; to work sincerely in matters of difference of opinion and difficulty for a Cabinet decision. This does not mean that what is regarded by a minister as vital to the public interest should be compromised. A minister should resign rather than agree to that. It means that a minister should not press his personal views unduly about what is not essential, that he should contend for substance not for form, that he should consider without *amour-propre* how his own opinion can be reconciled with that of others. Subject to the one qualification of not sacrificing what he regards as vital to the public interest, he should not contend for victor, but work for agreement in the Cabinet.

The other qualification is that of accepting full personal responsibility for Cabinet decisions, when once agreed to. Perhaps a third qualification might be mentioned, that of never threatening resignation or talking about it, except in the last resort on a matter of vital importance, and then only when resignation is really intended.

In 1928 Maurice Hankey, still Secretary to the Committee of Imperial Defence, wrote a memorandum to the Committee outlining options for updating the 'War Book' about control in a time of war. In this important document, Hankey divided the options between that – Cabinet assisted by a special committee – which might work in a minor crisis, and that which might be required in a full-blown conflict. This is what he wrote about the latter.[14]

[13] Viscount Grey, *Twenty-five years, 1892–1916*, Vol. 1, Hodder & Stoughton, London, 1925, pp. 67–68.
[14] PRO, CAB 104/124, Committee of Imperial Defence, *Supreme Control in War*, 24 May 1928.

In the case of actual war, however – at any rate, other than a minor war – it is probable that some very authoritative organisation would be required, with which the Chiefs of Staff can be permanently associated, and which might be termed a *War Committee* . . . The experience of the War shows that a War Committee should be clothed with full powers of decision, subject to the right of the prime minister (or chairman) to reserve any point for the full Cabinet; at least some of its members should be sufficiently free from administrative duties to devote their whole time to the central problem of the war, and to take the chair at Sub-Committees; the Chiefs of Staff Committee should be assembled in order to advise on all joint problems of a military character, and the chiefs of staff themselves should be present, at least whenever military questions are discussed; their assent should be asked for to all decisions in military matters. All decisions of a War Committee should be communicated as soon as possible to the full Cabinet, those of a more secret character, on which the success of operations or the lives of men may depend, being communicated verbally. The experience of the war showed that for the smooth working of Cabinet government it was essential that the general results of the War Committee's deliberations should be known to the Cabinet. Otherwise suspicion and friction are apt to be engendered.

The War Committee should, it is thought, suffice for the control of anything except a maximum unlimited war in which all available resources within the Empire are being mobilised. When that stage had been reached in the Great War, the War Committee's system almost broke down under the strain, and in the autumn of 1915 its work fell into arrears. Mr. Lloyd George's *War Cabinet* . . . restored the situation, overtook arrears of business, and managed to keep abreast of the work; but only by meeting on an average more than once a day, and by delegating much of the business to committees over which its members presided. The proceedings were facilitated by the fact that the members of the War Cabinet were (with the exception of Mr Bonar Law) all free from departmental duties.

Although the War Cabinet proved by far the most efficient method for the exercise of the supreme control of our war effort in the Great War, it does not follow that this plan should be followed in all wars. For example, to take an extreme case, it would be absurd to unsettle the ordinary constitutional machinery of government by setting up a War Cabinet in order to conduct a war with Ibn Saud or the Imam! Each case must be considered on its merits by the prime minister of the day. It must be remembered that the appointment of a War Cabinet involves a very considerable dislocation of the ordinary machinery of government. Moreover, the exclusion of ministers who in normal times are members of the Cabinet from the vital affairs of the nation could never be popular among the excluded ministers, and would only be tolerated in case of a national emergency of the very gravest kind.

When the second Labour government broke down over economic policy in 1931, King George V persuaded Ramsay MacDonald (1866–1937) to stay on as Prime Minister in charge of a National Government. It was a controversial intervention in politics, and the party leaders all met to seal the deal. This was the memorandum Viscount Samuel (1870–1963), the Acting Liberal Leader, wrote himself after the meeting.[15]

1. A National Government to be formed to deal with the present financial emergency.
2. It will not be a coalition in the ordinary sense of the term, but a co-operation of individuals.
3. When the emergency is dealt with, the government's work will have finished and parties will return to their ordinary positions.

[15] John Bowle, *Viscount Samuel: A Biography*, Victor Gollancz Ltd., London, 1957, p. 273.

4. The economies shall be equitable and shall generally follow the lines of the suggestions attached, designed to enable a loan to be raised in New York and Paris.
5. The election which may follow the end of the government will not be fought by the government but by the parties.
6. If there is any legislation which it is necessary to pass for special departmental or other reasons, and is generally accepted by the different parties, it may be undertaken.
7. The Cabinet shall be reduced to a minimum.

In 1932 the Cabinet was divided over the issue of free trade. It eventually backed some protectionist measures, and threatened to split, with several key members ready to resign. At the Cabinet meeting on 22 January, Viscount Hailsham (1872–1950), the Secretary of State for War, suggested that Cabinet ministers should be allowed to publicly disagree with the policy.[16] The Prime Minister, Ramsay MacDonald agreed, and collective responsibility was suspended as part of what became known as the 'Agreement to Differ'. This is the announcement which was made to the press on 22 January.[17]

The Cabinet, however, is deeply impressed with the paramount importance of maintaining national unity in the presence of the grave problems now confronting this country and the whole world.

It has accordingly determined that some modification of usual ministerial practice is required, and has decided that ministers who find themselves unable to support the conclusions arrived at by the majority of their colleagues on the subject of import duties and

---

[16] David Marquand, *Ramsay MacDonald*, Jonathan Cape, London, 1977, p. 713.
[17] Philip Snowden, *An Autobiography, Volume 2: 1919–1934*, Ivor Nicholson & Watson Ltd., London, 1934, p. 1012.

cognate matters are to be at liberty to express their views by speech and vote.

The Cabinet being essentially united on all other matters of policy believes that by this special provision it is best interpreting the will of the nation and the needs of the time.

The 'Agreement to Differ' was criticised as an attack on collective responsibility. This is how Viscount Hailsham defended the Agreement in the House of Lords.[18]

I think, to be quite frank with your Lordships, it would be rather quibbling to suggest that we are merely following the precedents to which I have alluded. Equally I think it is not quite fair to speak of what we are doing as an abandonment of the doctrine of Cabinet responsibility. I find myself in complete agreement with my noble friend Lord Peel when he says that he believes in the doctrine of collective Cabinet responsibility and that he would be very sorry to see it abandoned. So would I.

I am not myself in favour of the course which we are taking on the ground that it is to be a permanent new departure. I justify it to myself and, I hope, your Lordships' House as an exception to a very sound constitutional principle which can only be justified by exceptional circumstances. I do not agree with my noble friend Lord Banbury that because it has been once allowed therefore it must become the habitual practice. It can only be justified by exceptional circumstances such as I hope are not likely to recur.

Viscount Sankey (1866–1948), the Lord Chancellor, had spoken earlier in the debate, and took a more constitutionally radical position. [19]

---

[18] HL Debs, 5 series, Volume 83, 10 February 1932, Cols. 551–52.
[19] HL Debs, 5 Series, Volume 83, 10 February 1932, Col. 545.

Your Lordships must therefore see that the doctrine of collective responsibility is not a creed, nor is it even an Eleventh Commandment. It is a good working rule for normal times, but there is no obligation upon a prime minister always to adhere to the rule in its entirety, nor does it bind succeeding generations when conditions have changed or when circumstances are abnormal.

In this 1935 letter, Sir John Simon (1873–1954), the future Chancellor of the Exchequer and Lord Chancellor, made clear that the power to call a dissolution now belonged to the prime minister alone. While other members of Cabinet might be consulted, they had no formal role in the decision.[20]

The decision whether there shall be an immediate general election and, if so, on what date the country shall go to the polls, rests with the Prime Minister, and until the Prime Minister has decided, and has announced his decision, all anticipations are without authority.

Immediately prior to the Second World War, Sir Ivor Jennings and Arthur Berriedale Keith produced their famous works on Cabinet government. Jennings' better stood the test of time, but was nevertheless of its time. He described the position of the Cabinet and its relationship with the prime minister in the mid-1930s, and foreshadowed some later developments which were eventually to unbalance that relationship.[21]

The administration becomes a whole – in so far as it is a whole – only because of the supreme political control of the Cabinet, having at its command the supreme legislative authority of Parliament, and

---

[20] Sir John Simon, 'Letter to Sir Alfred Mowat, President of the Spen Valley Liberal Association', *The Times*, 18 October 1935.
[21] Sir W. Ivor Jennings, *Cabinet Government*, Cambridge University Press, Cambridge, 1936, pp. 70–71, p. 114, p. 150, p. 178, p. 189, p. 239.

providing correlation through the constitutional practices that regulate its operation.

* * *

The Treasury must necessarily be the most important of the departments. It must necessarily be a prime element in co-ordinating. For every governmental activity involves finance; and unless an effective check is imposed, and co-ordination provided for, the financial consequences of departmental action cannot be foreseen.

* * *

The prime minister's actual authority has tended to increase. He is not merely *primus inter pares*. He is not even, as Harcourt said, *inter stellas luna minores*. He is, rather, a sun around which planets revolve. Though he may rise to office because of the King's choice or the election of his parliamentary colleagues, he owes his majority to the choice of the electorate. Generally, a party obtains office because of a general election. A general election is, primarily, an election of a prime minister. The wavering voters who decide elections support neither a party nor a policy, they support a leader.

* * *

The Cabinet is a general controlling body. It usually meets once a week only and for two hours. Many of its members are departmental ministers, with important departmental duties to perform. It neither desires nor is able to deal with all the numerous details of government. It expects a minister to take all decisions which are not of real political importance. Every minister must therefore exercise his own discretion as to what matters arising in his department ought to receive Cabinet sanction. The minister who refers too much is weak; he who refers too little is dangerous.

* * *

The question of the right of the prime minister to refuse to summon a Cabinet is perhaps of some theoretical interest. As a matter of practice, it never arises. If a matter is of great urgency, it is inconceivable that the prime minister will not recognise it as such. If a dispute has arisen between the prime minister and a minister, that alone is a question of urgency upon which the prime minister himself will desire an immediate decision.

* * *

The experience of the war teaches several lessons. First, the ordinary Cabinet system provides insufficient control where day-to-day decisions of outstanding importance have to be taken. The Cabinet system assumes that the main lines of departmental policy can be laid down well in advance, so that the departments can take consequential decisions without constant reference to the Cabinet. Where the pace of national activity has to be speeded up, as in war and in time of financial crisis, the Cabinet system has to be modified.

Keith's book was even more of its time, but is valuable for the light it sheds on contemporary perceptions of Neville Chamberlain's practice of Cabinet government, in particular. Keith shared Jennings' view that the office of prime minister had outgrown the Cabinet, and that this was the result of elections based on personality and not policy.[22]

It is clear, therefore, that the polite description of the prime minister as *primus inter pares*, which satisfied Lord Morley, or the higher claim of Sir William Harcourt that he should rank as *inter stellas luna minores* is inadequate to describe the real position of the prime

---

[22] Arthur Berriedale Keith, *The British Cabinet System, 1830–1938*, Stevens & Sons Ltd., London, 1939, pp. 83, 130–31, 163, 271, 560, 128.

minister if by temperament he is willing to assert to the full position which he can assert if he so desires. The power of the prime minister grows, not diminishes, and this is inevitable when the sources whence it is derived are borne in mind. The root of the matter lies in the fact that since the Reform Act of 1832, the prime minister has become the choice of the electorate, and a general election is fought largely on personalities rather than principle.

* * *

It is clear that in the earlier days of the Cabinet a simple procedure sufficed. The premier was informed by his colleagues of any points which they desired to raise, and any minister who so desired could order the circulation to the Cabinet of a memorandum setting forth his views. Naturally, any member who received such a memorandum could circulate a counter-memorandum, as did Lord Balfour and Mr Ritchie when Mr Balfour circulated his meditations on possible modification of the free trade system in 1903. The meeting was summoned in the name of the Prime Minister by his secretary, normally once a week. The Prime Minister controlled the proceedings; the Foreign Secretary made his observations on any important incidents and answered, politely, as Mr Lloyd George admits, questions, arising thence or out of the Foreign Office papers which had been circulated. Then the premier allowed the several ministers to put their questions before the Cabinet, guided the discussion to some final or provisional conclusion, recorded the result and then called on another minister to open his subject and so on. There was neither Secretariat or record other than the letter from the premier to the King, a copy of which was kept by the premier's private secretary.

* * *

One experiment was made under the War Cabinet system, that of giving ministries to men not professional politicians. It may fairly be said that its success often was dubious, and in the best cases not distinguished. Government is a business with rules of its own, and it is best conducted by men who have made it their lifework to familiarise themselves with these rules. The advent of normal government saw the hasty retreat to their normal sphere of the neophytes, without leaving any personal contribution of lasting value to the welfare of their people, though recognition is due to their eager labour and desire to help their country.

* * *

The advent, however, of the Labour Party, and its rapid rise to the position of the second party in the state, as shown by the elections of 1922 and 1923, have considerably affected the position by creating the possibility of the emergence of a three-party system. Very important effects might thus be produced on the operation of Cabinet government. The dictatorial power of the prime minister would obviously be undermined if he did not command a majority in the Commons. It would become necessary for him to seek collaboration with the other parties to endeavour to pass such measures as commanded general support, or, at least, the support of another party, and he could no longer expect to be able to hold over his supporters the threat of a dissolution, for under this state of things he could not claim the right authoritatively to advise the Crown to dissolve. In the same way it would be necessary for the government of the day to leave issues so far as possible open. The government whips could not be put on unless the matter were clearly vital.

* * *

As a result of his initiative, he [Neville Chamberlain] presented the Cabinet with virtually no option but to accept his views and to homologate them. He had interviewed the Fuehrer, and could insist that war was inevitable, unless the action he advocated was taken. If the Cabinet had refused to yield, he could have resigned, giving as his reason that the course rejected was the sole alternative to war, or have advised a dissolution, when the country would have been asked to vote for peace or war. In either case the country would have been paralysed by a Cabinet crisis at a critical moment, while it was only too notorious that Herr Hitler struck at Austria at the moment when France was undergoing one of her normal Cabinet difficulties and a ministry with power to act was wanting . . . Cabinet responsibility involves in principle the determination of policy of a novel kind by the Cabinet without undue pressure. When the prime minister determines it, and presents his colleagues with the choice of acceptance or his resignation, the deliberative power of the Cabinet disappears in favour of one-man rule, and democracy is *pro tanto* weakened.

Anthony Eden (1897–1977) resigned as Foreign Secretary in 1938 in protest at both Neville Chamberlain's management of foreign policy (he had been conducting many key negotiations himself) and its course. Lord Halifax was appointed in his place. In this debate in 1938, many MPs complained about having a Foreign Secretary in the House of Lords, rather than the Commons. Winston Churchill rejected these criticisms, arguing that the Prime Minister's role was so much greater that having access to the Foreign Secretary hardly mattered.[23]

Let me look at this question of whether it is in some sense derogatory to the House of Commons to have a Foreign Secretary in the House of Lords. We must not have anything which is derogatory to the House of Commons. Certainly not, but when you have a Prime Minister, what is the good of worrying about the Foreign Secretary? What is the point of crying out for the moon, when you have the sun,

[23] HC Debs, 5 Series, Volume 332, 28 February 1938, Cols. 869–70.

and you have that bright orb of day from whose effulgent beams the lesser luminaries derive their radiance.

This is how Ian Colvin described the Cabinet control over foreign policy during Chamberlain's premiership. No surprise, perhaps, that Eden had resigned.[24]

What emerges from the Cabinet papers is that the real decisions were taken before the Cabinet meetings. A few ministers only had access to the Intelligence reports. The Prime Minister sought their agreement to his policy first in an inner Cabinet. Both the decision to go to Berchtesgaden and the ultimatum to President Beneš were related to the Cabinet only after action had been taken. The public proposal for a firm warning to Hitler was explained to the Cabinet as having already been rejected by 'all those in possession of the facts'. It was presented as no longer an open question. The Cabinet was allowed to debate, but asked to endorse and approve actions taken. The real Cabinet may be said at this time to have consisted of the Prime Minister acting as his own Foreign Secretary, the Foreign Secretary proper, and two previous Foreign Secretaries.

Christopher Hill examined Cabinet's involvement in foreign policy by looking at six examples in the period from 1938 to 1941. He concluded that the two key factors which determine the level of collectivity in decision-making are the clarity of the options facing the Cabinet, and the extent to which the problem disturbed the settled views of foreign policy held by ministers.[25]

---

[24] Ian Colvin, *The Chamberlain Cabinet*, Victor Gollancz Ltd, London, 1971, pp. 166–67.
[25] Christopher Hill, *Cabinet decisions on foreign policy: The British experience October 1938–June 1941*, Cambridge University Press, Cambridge, 1991, p. xx.

Essentially, this book is built on the key assumption of foreign policy analysis, that there will always be a two-way flow between process and policy; each affects the other. The theme of Cabinet government demonstrates how foreign policy decisions are subject to internal political argument, just as the pattern of influence within the Cabinet is partly shaped by the demands made by external events. At this highest level of responsibility, foreign policy-making is made up of a set of moving relationships, played out within the limits laid down by institutions, precedents, personalities and the structure of the issue of the moment. Dynamic equilibrium is the condition generally sought by the Cabinet and its members, in the sense that they seek to preserve major values in various arenas simultaneously, but the complexity of the interplay involved means that it cannot always be sustained. The compelling hold which politics can exert derives from our knowledge that human beings can both rise above and fall beneath the structures which normally contain them. When this happens at the level of the Cabinet and foreign policy, whole societies feel the effects.

With a strong Prime Minister, ministerial autonomy, and the need to behave as a Cabinet, rather than purely departmental, minister, were important issues. For Leo Amery (1873–1955), a Cabinet Minister in the 1920s and Secretary of State for India and Burma in 1940, a year after he made these remarks, independence and the willingness to stand up and be counted were crucial qualities.[26]

I have no time for governments in which members of the Cabinet go around calling each other by their Christian names. They have no independence. I would rather they did not speak to each other

---

[26] Quoted in Edward Heath, *The Course of My Life: The Autobiography of Edward Heath*, Hodder & Stoughton, London, 1998, pp. 64–65.

outside the Cabinet room if it meant they would stand up for what they believe in once they are inside it.

The Munich crisis of September 1938 created the realisation that much war planning was out of date, and senior civil servants took steps to rectify that, with a series of minutes to the Prime Minister about 'Supreme Control in War'. This is the opening minute from Edward Bridges, then Cabinet Secretary, to Sir Horace Wilson, then Chief Industrial Adviser, describing the two options: a 'War Cabinet' or a 'War Committee'. There was some considerable symmetry between this minute and Hankey's earlier memorandum.[27] Chamberlain later accepted Bridges' recommendation, and implemented it when war broke out.[28]

In deciding which system to adopt, there are, I think, two fundamental considerations to bear in mind.

The first is that in a big war there must be a body which meets every day, or twice a day if need be, and which can give immediate and authoritative decisions. From these two conclusions flow: (a) that the body must be small in numbers, so as to shorten discussion: (b) that it ought to be mainly composed of ministers who are not engaged in day-to-day administration of departments vitally concerned in our war effort.

The second point is to reconcile the direction of the war by a body of six ministers, or super-ministers, with the doctrine of Cabinet responsibility. The War Cabinet system solves the problem quite simply by cutting the Gordian Knot. If this system is adopted, members of the government outside the War Cabinet in effect cease

---

[27] See page 38.
[28] PRO, CAB 104/124, *Supreme Control in War*, Bridges to Wilson, 5 November 1938; Chamberlain's approval is in *Minute by the Prime Minister*, 7 December 1938.

to be Cabinet ministers, since they can have no *collective* responsibility for the government's war policy. The position can, of course, be eased a little by setting up a Home Affairs Committee.

The War Cabinet solution is drastic. The War Committee system – on the other hand – is an attempt to slur over the difficulty by elevating a Committee of the Cabinet into a body which has considerably wider powers than a Sub-Committee usually possesses. Thus it is contemplated that the War Committee would have power to act in certain respects without reference to the Cabinet.

The root difficulty inherent in a solution on the lines of a War Committee arises from division of responsibility. To take an example from the last War, the Evacuation of the Dardanelles was referred by Mr Asquith's War Committee to the full Cabinet. This led to a most unfortunate delay, and a delay of this kind is precisely what must be avoided at all costs in war. Discussion of important subjects by two bodies also means an added strain on members of the War Committee. Further, the line of demarcation of responsibility between the War Committee and the Cabinet is difficult to define and may well result in friction.

Again, international affairs and military operations are both conducted at a far greater speed than a few years ago. It is difficult to avoid the conclusion that in any future war a War Cabinet will have to be adopted as the organ of supreme control.

5
The Impact of War, 1939–1945

The outbreak of the Second World War was to herald another upheaval in how government was run. When Winston Churchill (1874–1965) was brought back into the government as First Lord of the Admiralty in 1939, he returned to an office he had last held during the First World War (1911–1915). Then, he had been a harsh critic of the incompetent decision-making procedures and general conduct of the war, and this time around his criticism was no less damning. This is what he wrote later about the operation of a key Defence Committee in April 1940.[1]

There was a copious flow of polite conversation, at the end of which a tactful report was drawn up by the secretary in attendance and checked by the three Service Departments to make sure there were no discrepancies. Thus we had arrived at those broad, happy uplands where everything is settled for the greatest good of the greatest number by the common sense of most after the consultation of all.

When he became Prime Minister in May, 1940, Churchill appointed himself Minister of Defence and chaired the Committee.[2] *In his memoirs Lord Ismay (1887–1965), Churchill's staff officer and*

---

[1] Winston Churchill, *The Second World War, Volume 1: The Gathering Storm,* Cassell & Col. Ltd., London, 1948, p. 464.
[2] Lord Ismay, *The Memoirs of General The Lord Ismay*, Heinemann, London, 1960, p. 159.

personal representative to the Chiefs of Staff Committee, described how far the changes Churchill made to the Defence Committee improved the consideration of business.

It might seem on the face of it that these two innovations made little change in existing arrangements; but the practical effects were revolutionary. Henceforward the Prime Minister himself, with all the powers and authority which attach to that office, exercised a personal direction, ubiquitous and continuous supervision, not only over the formulation of military policy at every stage, but also over the general conduct of military operations. There was a remarkable intensification of national effort in every field. All the considerations affecting any problem – political and economic, as well as military – could now be brought into focus more readily, and thanks to Mr Churchill's personal exercise of the wide powers given to him by the War Cabinet and to his astounding drive, firm decisions could be reached and translated into action far more quickly than had hitherto been the case. For the first time in their history, the Chiefs of Staff were in direct and continuous contact with the head of the government, and were able to act as a combined Battle Headquarters – 'a superchief of a War Staff in Commission' – as had always been contemplated.

During the War, an efficient but informed decision-taking apparatus was crucial, and a vigorous debate took place about the best means of achieving it. This is Winston Churchill's explanation for why he did not establish a purely non-departmental War Cabinet.[3]

---

[3] Winston Churchill, *The Second World War, Volume 1: The Gathering Storm*, Cassell & Col. Ltd., London, 1948, pp. 327–28.

Put shortly, 'Five Men with nothing to do but to run the war' was deemed the ideal. There are however many practical objections to such a course. A group of detached statesmen, however high their nominal authority, are at a serious disadvantage in dealing with the ministers at the head of the great departments vitally concerned. This is especially true of the Service Departments. The War Cabinet personages can have no direct responsibility for day-to-day events. They may take major decisions, they may advise in general terms beforehand or criticise afterwards, but they are no match for instance for a First Lord of the Admiralty or a Secretary of State for War or Air who, knowing every detail of the subject and supported by his professional colleagues, bears the burden of action. United, there is little they cannot settle, but usually there are several opinions among them. Words and arguments are interminable, and meanwhile the torrent of war takes its headlong course. The War Cabinet ministers themselves would naturally be diffident of challenging the responsible minister, armed with all his facts and figures. They feel a compunction in adding to the strain upon those actually in executive control. They tend therefore to become more and more theoretical supervisors and commentators, reading an immense amount of material every day, but doubtful how to use their knowledge without doing more harm than good. Often they can do little more than arbitrate or find a compromise in inter-departmental disputes. It is therefore necessary that the ministers in charge of the Foreign Office and the fighting departments should be integral members of the supreme body. Usually some at least of the 'Big Five' are chosen for their political influence, rather than for their knowledge of, and aptitude for, warlike operations. The numbers therefore begin to grow far beyond the limited circle originally conceived. Of course, where the prime minister himself becomes minister of defence, a strong compression is obtained. Personally, when I was placed in charge I did not like having unharnessed ministers around me. Everyone should do a good day's work and be accountable for some definite task, and then they do not make trouble for trouble's sake or to cut a figure.

Churchill's War Cabinet machinery did not prevent the Prime Minister from talking, on occasion at considerable length. These sections from the memoirs of Sir Anthony Eden, Defence and then Foreign Secretary under Churchill during the war, illustrate the two qualities.[4]

A Cabinet as conducted by Mr Churchill could be a splendid and unique experience. It might be a monologue, it was never a dictatorship. The disadvantage, to those with specific duties to perform or departments to run, was the time consumed. All the same, none of us should have grudged these Cabinets, enlivened by the sweep and dive of the Prime Minister's discourse.

* * *

The War Cabinet which Churchill assembled came to function with the sense of authority and power which this crucial period demanded... It must seem fantastic to modern eyes that throughout this time the whole government of the country and direction of the war in its every aspect should have been the responsibility of the War Cabinet and the Defence Committee. The former was composed of six or seven members, three of whom, Mr Churchill, Mr Attlee and myself, doubled on the Defence Committee, with Mr Lyttelton added to us on his return from Cairo.

The machinery for the military and political conduct of the war had been discerningly built and it worked, withstanding all strains, including the exhausting eccentricity of hours dear to the Prime

---

[4] Earl of Avon, *The Reckoning: The Eden Memoirs*, Cassell & Company Ltd., London, 1965, pp. 497, 552.

Minister. Churchill knew how to get the best out of it and though he never spared himself he never wasted himself either. Don't be put upon, he once said to me, and he lived up to his advice. The Chiefs of Staff as professionals of proven ability, had to endure and to know when to accept any of the variety of theories and suggestions constantly put to them. Equally they were free to propound their own ideas and did so, even if the timing could be a matter of nice judgement.

This tendency to verbosity made it difficult to know what had been decided. On one occasion, future Prime Minister and then-civil servant Harold Wilson (1916–1995) was asked to help resolve the resultant mess.[5]

In 1940, on a famous occasion, I recorded the Cabinet minutes, at the age of 24. Sir Edward Bridges, Secretary of the Cabinet, came into my room – a gross breach of protocol: he should have sent for me – and said 'I want you to write the Cabinet minutes. I can't make head or tail of the discussion.' I stuttered that I had not been there and did not know what they had said. He said if I had been, I would not have been any better informed than he was. I tried vainly to excuse myself, and he thrust his notes across the table and asked me to read them. I was still no better informed. In the event he ordered me to produce the minutes in one hour, saying 'This is your subject. You know what they ought to have decided, presumably. Write the minutes on those lines, and no one will ever question it.' He was right. They didn't. That could not have happened under Attlee, whose summing-up was superb, crisp, clear – and let no one try to go against it.

---

[5] Sir Harold Wilson, *The Governance of Britain*, Weidenfeld & Nicolson, London, 1976, p. 53.

Churchill's verbosity also produced the occasional sharp retort, as this from Attlee proves.[6]

A monologue is not a decision.

Yet Churchill was able to continue working under the most extreme pressure. Here he describes his priorities immediately after the 1942 reshuffle: more concerned with a successful outcome than with personal fatigue.[7]

I did not suffer from any desire to be relieved of my responsibilities. All I wanted was compliance with my wishes after reasonable discussion.

Oliver Lyttelton (1893–1972), later Lord Chandos, added in his memoirs to the picture of Churchill as a consensual premier, even during the war.[8]

... it is generally supposed that he loomed so large that the other members of the War Cabinet were merely his lieutenants, and that he overrode them whenever he wished. This is not the truth, because for one thing Mr Churchill's respect for constitutional propriety extended as much to the collective responsibility of his Cabinet as to the ultimate power and dominance of the House of Commons.

I can think of a number of highly important matters upon which Mr Churchill did not get his own way or had his first wishes greatly

---

[6] Anthony Jay (ed.), *The Oxford Dictionary of Political Quotations*, Oxford University Press, Oxford, 1996, p. 19.
[7] Winston Churchill, *The Second World War, Volume IV: The Hinge of Fate*, Cassell & Co. Ltd., London, 1951, p. 78.
[8] Oliver Lyttelton, *The Memoirs of Lord Chandos*, The Bodley Head, London, 1962, pp. 290–91.

modified. He fought hard on these occasions, but when a changed or modified policy was agreed, he rarely looked over his shoulder or bore resentment.

After a further reshuffle, in 1942, Churchill explained to the House of Commons how the new Cabinet would work, in particular the crucial role in domestic policy of the Lord President's Committee.[9]

Let me explain how the duties are divided. The members of the War Cabinet are collectively and individually responsible for the whole policy of the country, and they are the ones who are alone held accountable for the conduct of the war. However, they have also particular spheres of superintendence. The Leader of the Labour Party, as head of the second largest party in the National Government, acts as Deputy Prime Minister in all things, and in addition will discharge the duties of the Dominions Secretary, thus meeting, without an addition to our numbers, the request pressed upon us from so many quarters that our relations with the Dominions, apart from those between His Majesty's various prime ministers on which the Dominions are most insistent, shall be in the hands of a member of the War Cabinet.

The Lord President of the Council presides over what is, in certain aspects, almost a parallel Cabinet concerned with home affairs. Of this body a number of ministers of Cabinet rank are regular members, and others are invited as may be convenient. An immense mass of business is discharged at their frequent meetings, and it is only in the case of a serious difference or in very large questions that the War Cabinet as such is concerned.

---

[9] HC Debs, 5 series, Volume 378, 24 February 1942, Col. 38.

As the Second World War drew to a close, the political truce which had held throughout the war broke. In the 1945 general election Labour won a stunning victory, all the more surprising because few had expected it. The War had brought dramatic changes to the operation of government, and hugely increased state control, and co-ordination, of the economy. As Britain experienced acute post-war difficulties, these controls could hardly be immediately relaxed. So it was that, just as the Hankey/Lloyd George reforms during the First World War had endured in peacetime, many of the changes (if less dramatic) made by Churchill would outlast his wartime administration. And as for how he ran the War Cabinet, his example was still being studied fifty years later.

6
The Short Post-war, 1945–1956

In 1945 Clement Attlee (1883–1967) became the first Labour Prime Minister with a proper majority of his own. Having been Deputy Prime Minister during the war, he had a keen sense of the qualities he sought in colleagues and how he wanted to run his Cabinet. In this interview with Francis Williams (1903–1970), his former Press Secretary, after he had left office, the famously terse Attlee explained some of his thinking.[1]

You've got to have a certain number of solid people whom no one would think particularly brilliant, but who between conflicting opinions can act as middle-men, give you the ordinary man's point of view. I'll tell you who was an ordinary man and a very useful man. You remember little George Tomlinson. He was Minister of Education after Ellen Wilkinson. A Lancashire man. I can remember a thing coming up which looked like a good scheme, all worked out by the civil service. But I wasn't quite sure of how it would go down with ordinary people, so I said: 'Minister of Education, what do you think of this?' 'Well,' says George, 'it sounds all right but I've been trying to persuade my wife of it for the last three weeks and I can't persuade her.' A common-sense point of view like that's extremely valuable.

* * *

[1] From Francis Williams, 'The Making of a Cabinet: Lord Attlee interviewed by Francis Williams', in Anthony King (ed.), *The British Prime Minister: A Reader*, Macmillan, London, 1969, pp. 70–71, 71, 72–73.

You don't take a vote. No. Never. You might take it on something like whether you meet at 6.30 or 7.30, I suppose, but not on anything major. In the same way you never take a vote at a Commonwealth Meeting of Prime Ministers. The presiding prime minister collects the voices.

* * *

Williams: What other qualities are needed for a prime minister?

Attlee: ... Another thing: a fairly egocentric Cabinet minister can get along, but an egocentric prime minister can't. He must remember he's only the first among equals. He necessarily has, if he's any use at all, a good deal of experience and authority. Some people may think he has a certain amount of wisdom. His voice will carry the greatest weight. But you can't ride rough-shod over a Cabinet unless you're something very extraordinary. What you do generally is give guidance.

Here Attlee's biographer, Kenneth Harris, describes his style in Cabinet.[2]

Attlee's conduct of Cabinet meetings, like all his administrative work, was crisp, and authoritative and to the point. His Cabinet meetings were on average shorter than those held by any prime minister since the First World War; and his object, visible from the opening of business, was to get the meeting over as soon as possible. He sat with Bevin on one side of him, Morrison on the other ... On major issues, when all the senior members were present, he would ask for Morrison's opinion first, and work around the table to end with Bevin's. Attlee's Cabinets were relatively easy to minute and act on, largely because of the concise and concrete terms in which he had delivered his summing-up.

[2] Kenneth Harris, *Attlee*, Weidenfeld & Nicolson, London, 1995, p. 403.

The committee system, as it was developed during the war and evolved during the post-war period, came to play an increasingly vital role in the operation of Cabinet government. But the membership and indeed existence of Cabinet committees was a closely-guarded secret until John Major's premiership (except for four, Economic Affairs, Foreign and Defence, Home Affairs and Future Legislation, whose existence was acknowledged by Margaret Thatcher). In this 1945 note, Cabinet Secretary Sir Edward Bridges set out why.[3]

It has been the general practice of the government to refuse to disclose in public the functions or the composition of Cabinet committees, though there were exceptions in peacetime and since the outbreak of war it has been found expedient on occasion to disclose some of the features of the War Cabinet committee system. It might similarly be desirable to reveal the general nature of the arrangements made for a system of standing Cabinet committees in peacetime. It is most important, however, that disclosures should not go too far. The underlying reason for the practice of non-disclosure is that decisions are those of the government as a whole, and that the internal arrangements which may be made by ministers for discussion among themselves are essentially a domestic matter and no concern of Parliament or the public. Free and frank discussion between ministers is hampered if the processes by which it is carried on are laid bare. Decisions of the government normally fall to be announced and defended by the minister concerned as his own decision, and it is only rarely desirable to state that a decision has been taken by the Cabinet or by a particular Cabinet committee, since such announcements may have the embarrassing result of causing some decisions of government to be regarded as less

---

[3] PRO PREM 4/6/9, *Cabinet Committees – various*, Bridges to Martin, 23 May, 1945.

authoritative than others. It is even more important to maintain the anonymity of membership of Cabinet committees, since individual members might come to be regarded by Parliament and the public as specially responsible for the policy adopted in the sphere covered by the committees' activities. This would weaken the authority of the departmental minister principally concerned and the collective responsibility of the Cabinet as a whole.

In his book Triple Challenge, *Francis Williams emphasised the centrality of the 'Big Four' during the Attlee governments.*[4]

The control of Labour policy and thus of the direction Britain shall take in domestic, imperial and international affairs during this decisive period in her history lies primarily in the hands of four men, Clement Attlee, Ernest Bevin, Stafford Cripps, Herbert Morrison . . .

inevitably their special status and authority give their views great weight in all Cabinet discussions. Moreover although they do not act as an inner Cabinet they form the principal membership of a number of important Cabinet committees – of which the Economic Policy Committee is only one example – and work together in very many matters as a team.

It is therefore no exaggeration to describe them as holding, under the Prime Minister, all the significant strings of power in their hands. Attlee, Bevin, Cripps and Morrison are in fact responsible for the broad direction and planning of the whole of British policy at home and abroad.

[4] Francis Williams, *The Triple Challenge: The Future of Socialist Britain*, William Heinemann Ltd., London, 1948, pp. 41, 47–48.

Attlee regarded appointing his Cabinet as one of the most important, and difficult, tasks he had as Prime Minister. Here he recounts why it was difficult, and how he overcame one Labour Party rule that might have made his task even more difficult.[5]

The choosing of ministers is, I think, the most difficult of all the tasks which fall to the lot of a prime minister, while their dismissal is the most distasteful. Yet it is essential, if a party is to live, to bring on the younger members. On a number of occasions I had to tell ministers that the time had come when they must give place to younger men and, in one or two instances, to tell them that I thought that they were not quite up to their jobs. I should like to record that, with the exception of one person who was clearly unfit, all my colleagues took my decision with complete loyalty and never displayed the least resentment. Nevertheless, it is a most distasteful thing to have to say to an old friend and colleague that it is time for him to make room for a younger man and I am eternally grateful to my colleagues for their magnanimity ...

It is not without interest to recall that after the 1931 election débâcle, with the very strong feeling that had naturally arisen against MacDonald, proposals were made to restrict the powers of any future Labour prime minister. He was to have colleagues selected by the party to act with him in choosing members of the government. The passage of time and further experience has led to these proposals being tacitly dropped. In my view, the responsibility of choosing the members of the government must rest solely with the prime minister, though in practice he will consult with his colleagues. If he cannot be trusted to exercise this power in the best interests of the nation and the party without fear, favour or affection, he is not fit to

[5] Clement Attlee, *As it Happened*, William Heinemann Ltd., London, 1954, pp. 155, 156.

be prime minister. I am quite sure that the method of the Australian Labor Party, whereby a number of members are elected by the Caucus and all that is left to the prime minister is to fit the pieces into a jigsaw puzzle as best he may, is quite wrong.

After a busy first year in office, senior ministers' minds began to turn to the costs of a broad interpretation of collective responsibility. The Chancellor, Sir Stafford Cripps, felt that ministers wasted much of their valuable time at meetings where they were not really needed. This was speedily relayed to Attlee through the Whitehall civil service grapevine. A fastidious time-saver himself, the Prime Minister wrote to his Cabinet colleagues to ask for a streamlining of the process.[6]

1. . . . The burden of work imposed on many ministers last Session was made more heavy by the amount of time which they had to spend in attending meetings of Cabinet committees. It is perhaps inevitable that in the first months after a new government has taken office an exceptionally large number of problems should be put forward for collective decision by ministers. In the coming Session, however, means must be found of reducing the demands which committee work has hitherto made on the time of busy ministers. The Cabinet committee system has a valuable part to play in the central machinery of government, both in relieving the pressure on the Cabinet itself and in helping to give practical effect to the principle of collective responsibility at times when the Cabinet does not include all ministers in charge of departments. Its value will, however, be impaired if ministers are asked to spend an excessive

---

[6] PRO, CAB 21/1701, Organisation of Cabinet Committees, C.P. (46) 357 Cabinet Committees, Note by the Prime Minister, 26 September 1946; the note about Sir Stafford Cripps's original observation is PRO, CAB 21/1701, Organisation of Cabinet Committees, Sir Edward Bridges to Sir Norman Brook, 7 July 1946.

amount of time at committee meetings. This can be avoided if ministers will (a) refrain from referring to committees questions which do not engage the collective responsibility of ministers and can readily be dealt with by other means; and (b) assist in securing that business which must be discussed in committee is handled speedily. To this end I ask my colleagues to keep in mind, in the coming months, the suggestions set out in the following paragraphs of this note.

2. First I look for a marked reduction in the number of problems put forward for discussion by ministerial committees.

In many fields the broad lines of government policy have now been settled; and ministers should find it possible to decide themselves, without discussion among their colleagues, many questions which in the last Session had to be referred to committees.

Where colleagues have to be consulted, but only two or three are directly concerned, agreement can often be reached by correspondence or by personal meetings. Where it is thought likely that a serious conflict of view will develop, it may be convenient to ask a senior minister – possibly the chairman of the Cabinet committee to which the problem would otherwise be referred – to convene a meeting of the ministers directly affected and seek to arrive at a settlement between them.

Reference to one of the standing committees of the Cabinet will still be necessary when important questions of policy are involved, and it is also a convenient method of handling less important matters which are of interest to a number of departments normally represented on that committee. Committees should not, however, be used for the purpose of transacting less important business which directly concerns only two or three of the members of the committee.

3. Chairmen of committees should be vigilant to prevent papers coming forward for discussion in committee which could be settled

otherwise. Apart from the methods mentioned in the preceding paragraph, discussions in committee can often be avoided by intimating, when a paper is circulated, that its recommendations will be taken to be approved unless comments are sent to the secretary of the committee by a specified date.

Chairmen should encourage the secretaries of their committees to submit to them suggestions for reducing, by these and similar means, the amount of business to be transacted at full meetings of the committee.

4. A committee cannot transact its business with efficiency and despatch if papers are discussed before ministers have had time to consider and obtain advice upon them. It is the rule that a paper for consideration by the Cabinet, other than one commenting on a paper already circulated, must be circulated two clear days before the meeting at which it is to be considered; and exceptions to this rule are made only for matters of extreme urgency, with the sanction of the prime minister. This rule applies also to Cabinet committees, and their business would be facilitated if chairmen insisted that it should be complied with, save in the most exceptional circumstances.

5. Attendance at committees should be restricted to the permanent members and other ministers who have a major interest in the questions under discussion. Ministers should not be required to sit through lengthy discussions in case points affecting their departments should be raised. Nor should they insist on attending meetings for the purpose of making departmental points which have no important bearing on the main issues under discussion. Such points can always be brought to the committee's notice by a letter to the chairman or a message to the secretary.

Chairmen and secretaries of committees should keep this in mind in deciding which ministers, other than the permanent members of the committee, should be invited to meetings.

6. Ministers are responsible for seeing that memoranda circulated to the Cabinet and its ministerial committees are kept as short as possible and contain, wherever appropriate, a concise summary of the proposals put forward for decision.

Chairmen of committees are responsible for re-establishing the normal practice whereby ministers assume that the papers which they have circulated have been read and refrain from opening discussion of each item by oral repetition of the arguments already set forth in the papers.

The chairman of a committee is responsible for the orderly conduct of its business. He should see that discussion is kept to the point and irrelevance or repetition is checked. It is also his duty, in advance of the meeting, to make himself thoroughly familiar with the papers circulated and to think out tentative lines along which the issues for discussion might be resolved and, where appropriate, to take preliminary soundings among his colleagues with a view to avoiding unnecessary discussion.

7. The chairman of a committee is also responsible for ensuring that the secretary, under his direction, follows up questions which are not settled at meetings and takes steps either to get them disposed of or to have preliminary points discussed outside the committee so that the issues remaining for decision may be clearly defined when the matter is again put on the committee's agenda.

C.R.A., 10 Downing Street, SW1, 26th September, 1946

Attlee's plea was not entirely successful. This is an extract from the diary of the future Labour Leader Hugh Gaitskell, (1906–1963), from 14 October 1947, whilst he was Minister of Fuel and Power. It also demonstrates that some Cabinet ministers are less concerned about form, and more interested in seeing government conducted with maximum efficiency.[7]

Sometimes Cabinet meetings horrify me because of the amount of rubbish talked by some ministers who come there after reading briefs which they do not understand. I do not know how this can be avoided, except perhaps by getting more things settled at the official level, and when they cannot be settled there having the issues presented plainly to ministers.

Also, I believe the Cabinet is too large. A smaller Cabinet, mostly of non-departmental ministers, would really be able to listen and understand more easily and hear the others arguing the matter out.

Others shared Gaitskell's view. This letter, about the nationalisation of the Bank of England, is from John Maynard Keynes (1883–1946) to Lord Halifax, the British Ambassador to Washington, written in January 1946.[8]

One final conclusion. My impression is that the *fait accompli* is now being accepted, at any rate in official circles and in the Bank of England, as something which must be loyally and sincerely carried out. I think you can reassure the Americans on this, if the public reception to the programme here leads them to doubt it. Political trouble there will certainly be, for the Cabinet is a poor, weak thing.

---

[7] Philip M. Williams (ed.), *The Diary of Hugh Gaitskell, 1945–1956*, Jonathan Cape, London, 1983, p. 36.
[8] R. F. Harrod, *The Life of John Maynard Keynes*, Macmillan & Co. Ltd., London, 1951, p. 619.

Foreign Secretary Ernest Bevin (1881–1951), a former Bristol carter and founder of the Transport and General Workers' Union, was one of the key figures in both the wartime coalition and post-war Labour administration. At a Cabinet committee meeting in October 1946, considering whether Britain should develop an independent nuclear capability, he arrived late. Sensing that the meeting was about to decide not, he put a strong pro case – an illustration of the power of an individual, and of an argument, on even so important an issue as this.[9]

That won't do at all . . . we've got to have this . . . I don't mind for myself, but I don't want any other foreign secretary of this country to be talked to or at by a secretary of state in the United States as I have just had in my discussions with Mr Byrnes. We have got to have this thing over here whatever it costs . . . We've got to have the bloody Union Jack on top of it.

By August 1950 Aneurin Bevan (1897–1960), another major figure in the Labour administration because of his establishment of the National Health Service, had become an increasingly dissenting voice in the Cabinet. In August, he asked for his objection to a Cabinet decision about defence spending to be formally recorded. This is the reply penned by Sir Norman Brook, the Cabinet Secretary, after consulting the Prime Minister. Brook explained to Bevan that since the decision had been taken collectively, he could not opt out, since this would imply the suspension of the doctrine of collective Cabinet responsibility.[10]

---

[9] Quoted by Sir Michael Perrin, in a BBC *Timewatch* interview, from a Cabinet committee meeting on 25 October 1946, in Peter Hennessy, 'The Attlee Governments', 1945–51, in Peter Hennessy and Anthony Seldon, *Ruling Performance: British Governments from Attlee to Thatcher*, Basil Blackwell, Oxford, 1987, p. 38.

[10] PRO, CAB 21/4324, Cabinet Government: Principle of Collective Responsibility, Sir Norman Brook to Aneurin Bevan, 19 August 1950.

So far as concerns my practice in recording Cabinet discussions, it is not 'normal for members of the Cabinet to have their dissent recorded'. For the constitutional point of view, there is an important difference between dissenting from or opposing a colleague's proposal and registering dissent from the conclusion finally reached. The first is 'normal' and is reflected in Cabinet minutes in the record of the discussion. The second would, however, in my view raise acutely the question of collective responsibility. When a minister who dislikes a particular proposal has deployed all his arguments against it and has failed to convince his colleagues, I believe that the doctrine of collective responsibility requires him to acquiesce in the decision taken. He cannot, in Cabinet, 'reserve his position'; for under our system of Cabinet government it is the ultimate forum. He must either subordinate his view to that of his colleagues or part company with them.

You suggest that he can register dissent in Cabinet so long as he does not proclaim it publicly. I cannot find, in anything which prime ministers or constitutional authorities have said in the past, any support for this very negative view of collective responsibility. All the books confirm the often-quoted remark of Lord Salisbury that 'for all that passes in Cabinet each member of it who does not resign is absolutely and irretrievably responsible'. This doctrine, if it is correct, would clearly invalidate any practice of recording that a particular minister continued to dissent from a Cabinet decision after it had been reached.

In the not-so-old days, before there were formal Cabinet minutes, there was no means by which a minister could seek to diminish in this way his share of collective responsibility. There would have been no caveats in the letters recording Cabinet decisions which the prime minister sent in those days to the King, for Gladstone and other premiers always insisted that the Cabinet must present a united front to the Crown. I cannot think that a purely mechanical development, such as the recording of minutes, can have introduced such an important modification of the ordinary conventions about collective responsibility.

At the end of Labour's time in office, several former Cabinet ministers took the opportunity to put pen to paper with their reflections on their time in office. Harold Laski (1893–1950), the former Chairman of the Labour Party, gave a series of lectures at Manchester University. He provided further fodder to the emerging debate about extended prime ministerial power, but as importantly set out to tackle as impractical proposals from former Conservative Minister Leo Amery about 'time out' for Cabinet ministers for what might today be called 'blue sky thinking'. [11]

The immense growth in the authority of the Cabinet in the first half of the twentieth century is, in many ways, the most striking aspect of constitutional change in this period. It has, of course, been greatly assisted by the impact of two world wars, in each of which the centralisation of power in its hands, was an inevitable concomitant of organisation for victory, and this centralisation was, in its turn, strengthened by the fact that in each of the conflicts, the Prime Minister became, in the first case just after two years, and in the second just after nine months, almost a dictator by consent upon whose leadership the general character of the war effort came to depend.

* * *

It is clear, on any showing, that the whole *modus operandi* of the Cabinet depends upon the habits of the prime minister, but, even

---

[11] Harold Laski, *Reflections on the Constitution*, Manchester University Press, Manchester, 1951, pp. 106, 132, 168–69.

more, that little short of revolt, whether in or outside the Cabinet, can really shake his position as the master of its fortunes. It was a combination of intrigue and revolt which overthrew Mr Asquith in 1916; it was revolt which overthrew Mr Lloyd George in 1922; and it was revolt which overthrew Mr Neville Chamberlain in 1940. Elections apart, a prime minister can virtually stay in office for as long as he chooses, provided he does not estrange a group of powerful colleagues, and is able to hold the general loyalty of the mass of his followers.

* * *

The prime minister always apart, Mr. Amery's idea of a Cabinet as a collection of ministers thinking firmly and imaginatively about the future, with a day or two off each week in which they consider the flow of current affairs, or, maybe the cross-currents in the stream that prevent the boat from going forward, is exactly that divorce of theory from practice that is as fatal not only to getting things done as they should be done, but getting them so done that what is achieved is itself a preparation for the next achievement. I am not arguing that a minister who reflects upon the future must bury himself in his departmental papers; but I do not think that the best way to prevent that burial is mainly to make of him a brooding omnipresence in the sky who darts, two or three times a week, down to earth, and then flies back to whatever special area of the stars the prime minister may have allocated to him as his special residence.

I am arguing the quite explicit thesis that a good Cabinet minister is a man who is always in the closest touch with his department, but never bogged down in its details; that he should know pretty quickly whom he can trust there and who he should watch with his best weather eye. But just as all discoveries, both in the natural and in the social sciences, are made at the boundaries of a subject, and not at its centre, so a good Cabinet minister will be constantly watching the work of his department as though he were making a pilot survey, as it were, of its future activities, and be making it in relation to what he knows is happening in other departments.

Herbert Morrison (1888–1965), had been Deputy Prime Minister, Leader of the House of Commons and Lord President, and then Foreign Secretary, in the 1945–51 Labour government. His book Government and Parliament *was interesting for the light it shed on the inner workings of government. Much was later superseded by Attlee's own observations, but his comments on chairing a Cabinet committee are interesting because they are so similar to those from several prime ministers about chairing Cabinet itself.*[12]

The work of co-ordination or the chairmanship of a Cabinet committee requires certain qualities. If such a minister seeks to be a dictator or to act in the spirit of giving orders to departmental ministers, or is impatient or irritable in listening to relevant arguments, he will not win that goodwill of his colleagues which is vital to the success of his work. His business is to be an understanding friend who is seeking to assist his colleagues in finding a way through the maze of conflicting considerations, for there is nearly always more than one side to a question. Whilst he needs to take trouble to understand the matters under consideration to the fullest practicable extent and whilst it is good that he should have a mind of his own he must remember that his business is to be a helpful conciliator and not an additional irritant. The confidence of the departmental ministers in him is very important.

---

[12] Herbert Morrison, *Government and Parliament: A Survey from the Inside*, third edition, Oxford University Press, London, 1964, pp. 38, 69.

Attlee was small, average-looking and famously terse. Yet he dominated his government, and is considered by many to be one of the most notably successful prime ministers of the twentieth century. According to John Mackintosh, writing in 1962, this is proof positive that the powers of the office were already substantial – certainly far greater than those of a premier's Cabinet colleagues.[13]

The record of the Labour governments after 1945 shows that prime ministers do not have to be exceptional individuals in order to dominate their ministries.

When he returned to Downing Street in October 1951, Winston Churchill was keen to re-introduce the system of 'supervising ministers' which he had used during the war. In an effort to both reduce the size of the Cabinet and improve inter-departmental coordination in overlapping policy areas, Lords Leathers (Fuel and Power, Transport and Civil Aviation) and Woolton (Agriculture and Food) were appointed by Churchill to 'supervise' groups of departments. This experiment with 'overlords' was controversial both in Parliament, where the opposition were concerned about accountability, and in the civil service. In this memorandum to Churchill written shortly after the election, Cabinet Secretary Sir Norman Brook argued that Cabinet committees, which Churchill had sharply criticised whilst in opposition, remained the best means of improving efficiency.[14]

The conception of a super-minister, responsible for supervising the work of other ministers of Cabinet rank, is fraught with serious

---

[13] J. P. Mackintosh, *The British Cabinet*, Stevens & Sons Ltd., London, 1962, p. 430.
[14] PRO, CAB 21/2654, Papers prepared on the assumption that a Conservative government was formed after the general election, October 1951, Note from Brook to Churchill, undated.

difficulties, both constitutional and practical. Thus –

(a) It is difficult to reconcile with the doctrine of ministerial responsibility. Each departmental minister is personally accountable to Parliament for the policy and administration of his department; and this responsibility would be blurred if, on all matters of major importance, he was subject to the directions of another minister.
(b) It is inconsistent with the principle that policies and plans should be formulated by those who have the executive responsibility for carrying them out.
(c) It rests upon the assumption that policy can be divorced from administration. In fact the two are inextricably intertwined: policy cannot safely be formulated *in vacuo*: it should be founded on experience in administration, and should be capable of modification in the light of practical experience.
(d) It is contrary to our traditions of Cabinet government that one minister of Cabinet rank should be subordinated to another. This new relationship would be likely to give rise to frictions.
(e) Among officials, difficulties would certainly arise if staff attached to the super-minister attempted to dictate to the departmental staffs who have greater knowledge and experience of the subjects which they handle.
(f) Advocates of a system of supervising ministers claim that it would enable a few senior ministers to concern themselves with broad issues of policy, undistracted by the details of administration. Even if this were desirable (see (b) and (c) above), it seems doubtful whether it would be achieved in practice. For once it was announced that the responsibility for final decision rested with the super-minister, Members of Parliament would insist on referring to him all matters which *they* considered important and would be reluctant to accept a

final answer from the departmental minister. This lead would be followed by local authorities, industry and individual members of the public concerned with the subjects falling within the jurisdiction of the super-minister. He would thus be drawn into the details of administration – and might well find himself, in the end, doubling the work of the departmental minister (and, incidentally, providing himself with a staff for that purpose). Meanwhile the position of the departmental minister would have been undermined.

2. These difficulties have been avoided by the system of standing Cabinet committees, which was developed under the war-time coalition government and has since come to be accepted as a normal piece of government machinery. The chairman of a standing Cabinet committee (usually a senior minister without heavy departmental duties, like the prime minister or the lord president, or a departmental minister with 'central' functions, like the chancellor of the exchequer) can play a co-ordinating role in the formulation of policy without undermining the responsibility of the departmental ministers to Parliament. For –

(a) The chairmen of standing committees control groups of subjects, not groups of departments. This avoids any implication that they have an authority superior to that of departmental ministers.
(b) Their authority derives, not from any superior powers, but from their personality and position as chairmen of committees.
(c) The decisions of standing committees are not taken by the chairmen, but are collective decisions in which all the ministers concerned share responsibility. Having shared in the formulation of the policy, the departmental ministers can be left to defend it in Parliament.

3. The powers and duties of the minister of defence were so defined

as to avoid the difficulties noted in paragraph 1 above. He is not a supervising minister in that sense. He is responsible to Parliament for inter-Service questions, e.g. strategy, for which no one of the Service ministers could be accountable. Thus, while the minister of defence is responsible for the distribution between the three Services of the total resources available for defence, in men, money and materials, each of the Service ministers remains responsible directly to Parliament for the manner in which his share of those resources is used.

Not only the civil service was critical. Sir John Anderson (1882–1958), a Cabinet Minister during the Second World War, a Whitehall Permanent Secretary before it, and one of those closest to Winston Churchill, argued as early as 1946 that the overlords, or 'supervising ministers' would not work in peacetime, and that the Cabinet committee structure, with proper support mechanisms, would be a far better bet. He had made similar arguments in a report of the Committee on the Machinery of Government (which Anderson had chaired) presented to Churchill shortly after the end of the war in Europe, in 1945. Ironically, when Churchill appointed the overlords in 1951, he wished Anderson to be one.[15]

There is undoubtedly a case that might be argued in favour of the supervising ministers, as they may be called, but experience has convinced me – and, I believe, others of my late colleagues – that any such arrangement would speedily break down in practice. It would, in fact, be found to be inconsistent both with the parliamentary responsibilities of departmental ministers and with departmental control. Authority over departments must be undivided and

---

[15] Sir John Anderson, *The Machinery of Government: The Romanes Lecture, delivered in the Sheldonian Theatre, 14 May 1946*, Oxford University Press, Oxford, 1946, pp. 13, 31–32.

unquestionable. A supervising minister would mean, in practice, a supervising staff, with endless possibilities of friction and clash ...

While I emphasise the departmental responsibilities of ministers as a necessary and vital principle, I at the same time stress the importance, as a practical matter, of adequate machinery for making a reality of collective responsibility. The need for this has been proved in two wars and will increase now that the government is so much more concerned with economic affairs, with the need for making sure that the policies of different departments are consistent with each other and form a coherent whole. As a means to this end, I would rely on the institution, in conjunction with a Cabinet of moderate size, of a permanent but flexible system of Cabinet committees, on the strengthening of the machinery of the Cabinet Secretariat, and on the association with that secretariat of technical sections organized for joint planning and intelligence and for economic, statistical, and scientific studies ...

Herbert Morrison, the Labour Deputy Leader, put the opposition case in the debate on the Queen's Speech on 13 November 1951.[16]

There are some other very curious appointments in His Majesty's government. Certainly it is a very lordly Cabinet. There are six lords in this Cabinet compared with three in the last one – a somewhat different picture from that which was given by the Prime Minister. The number of lords has gone up by 100 per cent. One of my backbench friends said to me the other day, 'This is "the Lords-help-us" Government'. It may indicate the shortage of Tory ability in the House of Commons, but still the Prime Minister might have done the best with what he had available.

Among the six, there are three mystery lords. Let us start with

[16] HC Debs, 5 Series, Volume 493, 13 November 1951, Cols. 833–34.

Lord Woolton. His duty, as I understand it – I can be corrected if I am wrong – is to be responsible for the over-all or higher policy of the Ministries of Agriculture and of Food. He is to co-ordinate and be responsible for the higher policy and direction, which of course is a limitation on the functions of the departmental ministers.

Lord Leathers has similar duties in relation to the Ministry of Fuel and Power, the Ministry of Transport and the Ministry of Civil Aviation, which I understand is now to be merged with the Ministry of Transport.

Lord Cherwell has other duties which are not so clear. I gather that science is among them. Presumably that means that the Lord President of the Council has lost the functions he had many years ago of general responsibility for civil science. I know that Lord Cherwell is a scientist of some ability. [HON. MEMBERS: 'Oh.'] It is so. I am trying to be nice; give me a chance and do not discourage me. I understand he is a scientist. That is not disputed. But I am very doubtful, from my experience in handling our scientific research departments and so on – [*interruption.*] – I have had considerable experience of it – and did some good work there, too.

In this world of science, in which there is plenty of disagreement, plenty of conflict of opinion and plenty of legitimate argument about scientific opinion, I am very doubtful about the wisdom of putting a scientist there to supervise, especially a somewhat controversial character such as Lord Cherwell. No doubt he will assist the Prime Minister by briefing him about other ministers, and he will be handy for that purpose. No doubt they are looking forward to that situation, and I wish them luck.

But I come to this serious constitutional point about Lord Leathers and Lord Woolton and any other Ministers in a similar position. It has been publicly announced that they are specifically responsible for certain things, either coordination or the over-all policy of the Departments with which they are connected. The Prime

Minister says there is nothing new about this; it was done during the war. With great respect, I do not agree with him, and I think my right hon. friend the Leader of the Opposition, who had a hand in that, will bear me out.

There were Cabinet committees and there were chairmen of Cabinet committees, as there were in the late Labour government. That is domestic to a government, and Sir John Anderson always took the view that it is desirable that they should be secret and not announced. I respectfully agree with that. But this is a domestic matter within the government. There is no need for there to be answerability for chairmen of Cabinet committees, in other than exceptional cases where the chairman of a Cabinet committee is announced, as mine was in relation to the Information Services.

These have been announced. These ministers have specific responsibilities which will move the responsibilities away from departmental ministers. Let us make no mistake about that. Therefore, I want to know who is to answer for those two noble Lords in the House of Commons. This is an important matter. If it is said that the departmental ministers will answer, that is an impossible situation, because the departmental ministers have no longer responsibility for this sphere of activity.

Where more than one minister is responsible, there is the Prime Minister in reserve. Should policy questions on transport, civil aviation, fuel and power, food, and agriculture and fisheries all be put to the Prime Minister? I hope we can be told, because obviously someone must answer for these two Ministers with specifically stated public functions who sit in another place.[17] I do not think this kind of expedient will work particularly well. We shall see. The Conservatives have said that they wish to strengthen the powers of

---

[17] By parliamentary convention, MPs refer to the House of Lords as 'another place'.

the House of Lords. Well, they have done so already at the expense of the House of Commons.

Parliamentarians continued to challenge the government about the overlords, eventually producing from Lord Woolton this declaration – in a debate on food production – that the arrangement was a purely administrative one. The overlords, he argued, had little effective power.[18]

I must explain what I conceive to be the clear issue of responsibility, and it is this. Ministers of the Crown are responsible to Parliament for the departments to which they are charged. The Minister of Agriculture is responsible to Parliament for what he does. In this House, when your Lordships raise issues, then either his Parliamentary Secretary or I reply for him. The Minister of Food is responsible to the House of Commons. Of course, there is no Parliamentary Secretary here, and I reply for him just as I reply for the Minister of Health in this House. My own parliamentary responsibilities as Lord President of the Council are quite clearly defined. I am responsible for the work of the Privy Council and I am responsible for civil science in this country. In my view, the work of the coordinators is not a responsibility to Parliament; it is a responsibility to the Cabinet. It is true that in Mr Churchill's present government we have not, as we had in his previous government and as I gather noble Lords opposite had in the last government, a Committee for Food and Agriculture. Instead, ministers are good enough to confer with me, bringing their departmental staff with them. The noble Earl need not be frightened that this coordinator is adding very considerably to the cost of conducting the affairs of the country, because I have not any staff for this purpose. There has been

[18] HL Debs, 5 Series, Volume 176, 30 April 1952, Cols. 475–76.

no increase, as a result of this office, in the very small staff which the Lord President of the Council has.

Woolton's words caused chaos. The following day the Leader of the House of Lords, Lord Salisbury tried to clear up the confusion.[19]

My Lords, what my noble friend had in mind was that the co-ordination of the work of departments is a function within the government, an allocation of duties by the Prime Minister for the purposes of administrative convenience. It does not affect the direct responsibility to Parliament of departmental ministers, which, as before, remains with these ministers once the government have taken their decisions; nor, equally, does it affect the long-established ministerial responsibility to Crown and Parliament.

Eventually, Churchill was forced clarify the position. He defended the appointments, but his statement that the overlords had 'no power to give orders or directions to a departmental minister' sounded the death knell for the experiment, which was abandoned the following year.[20]

Every departmental minister is responsible to Parliament for the policy and administration of his department. This is a fundamental principle in our system of parliamentary democracy. But it is an equally respectable and necessary principle that ministers as a body are collectively responsible for government policy as a whole. This means that a minister's personal responsibility for his departmental policy must be exercised in harmony with the views of his ministerial colleagues.

The work of the so-called 'co-ordinating Ministers' is an aspect

---

[19] HL Debs, 5 Series, Volume 176, 1 May 1952, Col. 523.
[20] HC Debs, 5 Series, Volume 500, 6 May 1952, Cols. 188–91.

of collective responsibility. In former days all reconciliation of departmental policies was done in the Cabinet, of which all departmental ministers were members, or by the Prime Minister himself. But for many years past prime ministers have from time to time entrusted to a senior colleague the duty of keeping a general oversight, on the Cabinet's behalf, over subjects of special importance not falling wholly within the jurisdiction of a single Department of State.

These tasks have usually been assigned to holders of the old offices involving no heavy departmental duties, notably the offices of Lord President and Lord Privy Seal. An early example of this was the arrangement by which in 1929 Mr Ramsay Macdonald assigned to Mr J. H. Thomas, as Lord Privy Seal, a special responsibility for co-ordinating measures for dealing with unemployment.

With the growing complexity of government business, and the increasing extent to which policies have to be administered jointly by two or more departments, prime ministers have found it increasingly convenient to ask senior ministers to act in a co-ordinating role. And in recent times this arrangement has been more regularly adopted because, under modern conditions which have called into existence so many new departments of state, the Cabinet no longer normally includes all ministers in charge of departments.

This has led to the development of the system of standing Cabinet committees, which assist the Cabinet in discharging its collective business and include departmental ministers who are not themselves members of the Cabinet. The chairmanship of these standing committees has normally been assumed by senior ministers without departmental duties; and it is mainly in their capacity as chairmen of these committees that these ministers have exercised their co-ordinating functions, subject to Cabinet review. This is a natural evolution in the processes of conducting the collective business of government, and there is nothing new about it.

During the war the Lord President of the Council, in particular, discharged extensive co-ordinating responsibilities on this basis; and it is well known that similar arrangements were in force during the period of the last government. The responsibilities assigned under the present government to Lord Woolton and Lord Leathers carry this development a stage further in one respect, and in one respect only, namely, that the specific area of co-ordination assigned to each of them was publicly announced on his appointment.

Indeed, so far as concerns my noble friend, Lord Leathers, it was made explicit in his title. Coal, gas, electricity, oil and transport represent a homogeneous group of subjects which call for co-ordination. Moreover, it includes the basic services which have passed under public ownership under Socialist schemes of nationalisation; and there is clear scope for co-ordination – I am sorry to use that hard-worn word so often – of the government's relations with the public corporations administering those services. Lord Leathers' co-ordinating functions do not differ, in the constitutional sense, from those of my noble friend, Lord Woolton.

The co-ordinating Ministers have no statutory powers. They have, in particular, no power to give orders or directions to a departmental minister. A departmental minister who is invited by a co-ordinating Minister to adjust a departmental policy to accord with the wider interests of the government as a whole always has access to the Cabinet; and, if he then finds that he cannot win the support of his ministerial colleagues, he should accept their decision. No departmental minister can, of course, be expected to remain in a government and carry out policies with which he disagrees.

Thus, the existence and activities of these co-ordinating Ministers do not impair or diminish the responsibility to Parliament of the departmental ministers whose policies they co-ordinate. Those ministers are fully accountable to Parliament for any act of policy or administration within their departmental jurisdiction. It does not follow that the co-ordinating Ministers are 'non-responsible'. Having no statutory powers as co-ordinating Ministers, they perform in that capacity no formal acts. But they share in the collective responsibility of the government as a whole, and, as Ministers of the Crown, they are accountable to Parliament.

Some felt that the experiment with overlords did not take the concept of non-departmental supervising ministers far enough. Former Cabinet Minister Leo Amery, in his book Thoughts on the Constitution, *suggested that Cabinet would operate much better if only non-departmental ministers were members. He based his arguments, in part, on some of the recommendations from the Haldane Committee.*[21]

I would have a Cabinet of about half a dozen, all entirely free from departmental duties. This Cabinet would deal with current administrative questions, as did the War Cabinets of the last two wars, by bringing into its discussions the departmental ministers directly affected. But it should also have regular meetings definitely set aside for the discussion of future policy. The work of the former type of meetings would be expedited by standing and *ad hoc* committees, such as those outlined by Sir John Anderson, over which members of the Cabinet would preside with the advantage both of their higher authority and of their freedom from other routine work.

Lord Percy (1887–1958), a former President of the Board of Education, joined the debate in his 1958 memoirs, at least in part replying to Leo Amery's argument.[22]

---

[21] Leo Amery, *Thoughts on the Constitution*, Oxford University Press, London, 1953, pp. 90–91.
[22] Eustace Percy, *Some Memories*, Eyre & Spottiswoode, London, 1958, pp. 124–25.

The Bonar Law and Baldwin Cabinets were a more or less conscious return to the traditional system, after Lloyd George's experiments in various kinds and degrees of overlordship. My own view has always been that no Cabinet can be trusted which does not consist mainly of ministers responsible for departmental administration. Cabinet ministers must not only have 'time to think'; they must also have food for responsible thought; nor can decisions on policy be effectively conveyed to departments through the medium of impersonal Cabinet minutes. But departmental responsibility could, in theory, be reconciled with a quite small Cabinet if departments were grouped under a Cabinet minister, each with his own sub-Cabinet, as it were, of departmental ministers, over whom he exercised a real superintendence. There are, however, two practical difficulties about this idea. The lesser of the two is the one that sprang at once to the mind of Baldwin, the party manager, when one tried the idea on him: that, at any rate during the transition when the scheme was being put into operation, it would not offer a sufficient number of 'plums' for aspiring members of Parliament who would not be content with what would seem relegation to a mere Second Eleven – and a discontented Second Eleven would be strong enough to ruin the *morale* of a government. The greater difficulty is that, if such grouping were to be a reality, it would have to be geographical, including a comprehensive re-planning of departmental buildings. Superintendence would be a fiction, and would become a mere nuisance, if superintending ministers had to follow their scattered flocks over all the area from Whitehall to Blackfriars and Mayfair. It was on this rock, I think, that Churchill's rather half-hearted experiment in overlordship in his last administration floundered; and I doubt whether the Ministry of Defence will become an administrative reality until the geographical problem has been better solved.

The tortured parliamentary explanations of the overlords' roles were not, according to Hans Daalder, what Churchill had intended them to be, and his epitaph on the experiment was more generous than those of many contemporary commentators.[23]

It was evidently Churchill's intention that Woolton, Leathers, Alexander, Cherwell, and others would indeed have the actual direction over their specific spheres of action, on the strength of his *plenitudo potestatis* and in full responsibility to himself. This intention was defeated, on the one hand, because Churchill could not regain the almost dictatorial position he had held during the war, let alone delegate full powers to his personal friends. The scheme was defeated, on the other hand, because the departments held on to their customary right to fight out differences of opinion, if necessary, before the supreme tribunal of the Cabinet itself. Peacetime differed from wartime, and during the six years of Attlee's leadership the departments had regained much of their traditional status.

On 23 June 1953 Churchill suffered a serious stroke, and was largely incapacitated for several weeks. Remarkably, he and his closest advisers managed to keep it a secret. During that period, the advisers essentially governed on his behalf, although as this extract from the memoirs of John Colville (1915–87), Joint Principal Private Secretary to the Prime Minister, makes clear, trying very hard to preserve constitutional propriety.[24]

---

[23] Hans Daalder, *Cabinet Reform in Britain, 1914–1963*, Stanford University Press, Stanford, 1963, p. 119.
[24] John Colville, *The Fringes of Power: Downing Street Diaries 1939–55*, Hodder & Stoughton, London, 1955, pp. 668–70.

The staff at No.10, Christopher Soames[25] and myself in particular, were in a quandary. Two days after his stroke, when I drove down to Chartwell alone with the Prime Minister (Lady Churchill having gone on ahead to prepare the household), he gave me strict orders not to let it be known that he was temporarily incapacitated and to ensure that the administration continued to function as if he were in full control. We realised that however well we knew his policy and the way his thoughts were likely to move, we had to be careful not to allow our own judgement to be given prime ministerial effect. To have done so, as we could without too great difficulty, would have been a constitutional outrage. It was an extraordinary, indeed perhaps an unprecedented, situation...

A second factor of great help to us was the wisdom and coolness of the Secretary of the Cabinet, Sir Norman Brook, whom I consulted as soon as the crisis occurred. My colleagues and I had to handle requests for decisions from ministers and government departments entirely ignorant of the Prime Minister's incapacity. Discussion of how best to handle such enquiries, whether by postponement, by consultation with the minister or under secretary responsible or, in some cases, by direct reply on the Prime Minister's behalf were the subject of daily discussions with the Secretary of the Cabinet. It was the more difficult for us because Anthony Eden, the second in command, had his operation on the very day Churchill had his stroke, and because although R. A. Butler took charge of the Cabinet with tact and competence, we knew that Churchill was unwilling to delegate his powers to anybody.

This situation lasted the best part of a month. It was eased for Pitblado[26] and me by a third factor, the sense of responsibility

---

[25] Soames (1920–87) was the Prime Minister's son-in-law and MP for Bedford.
[26] David Pitblado (1912–97) was Joint Principal Private Secretary to the Prime Minister.

and the down-to-earth intelligence of Churchill's son-in-law, Christopher Soames, Member of Parliament for Bedford. He had over the previous five years won the affection and trust of his formidable and, in the first instance, somewhat doubtful father-in-law... but he was not in principle supposed to see Cabinet papers or secret documents. That indeed had accounted for Sir Norman Brook's worries described in my entry for June 20th, 1952. However, in the unusual circumstances prevailing, it seemed to me that, whatever the rules might be, Christopher should be given access to many papers he was not supposed to see, including Cabinet papers. In the event the shrewdness of his comments, combined with his ability to differentiate between what mattered and what did not, was of invaluable help in difficult days.

Before the end of July the Prime Minister was sufficiently restored to take an intelligent interest in affairs of state and express his own decisive views. Christopher and I then returned to the fringes of power, having for a time been drawn perilously close to the centre. For the next two years the distance between the fringes and the centre was far shorter than it had once been.

During his second Conservative government, Churchill was seen as one of the most collegial of post-war prime ministers. He often stated his belief in both the form and substance of Cabinet government.[27]

I am a great believer in bringing things before the Cabinet. If a minister has got anything on his mind and he has the sense to get it argued by the Cabinet he will have the machine behind him.

---

[27] Lord Moran, *Winston Churchill: The Struggle for Survival, 1940/1965*, Constable, London, 1966, p. 404, diary entry for 28 April 1953.

Churchill oversaw the decision to build the hydrogen bomb, the second great nuclear weapons decision of the post-war years. He was criticised at the time for a lack of consultation, but according to Peter Hennessy, an historical perspective suggests this was unfair.[28]

The summer of 1954 was a protracted season of Cabinet recrimination over Churchill's lack of consultation even in one policy area – nuclear weapons – where, rightly, he has been seen as a more fully collegial premier than his predecessor, Attlee, or any of his successors, Macmillan excepted. This was unfair. Unlike Attlee who, as we have seen, did not lift the original atomic bomb decision up from his Cabinet committee, GEN 163, to the full Cabinet, Churchill told the second of his hydrogen bomb Cabinet committees, GEN 464 (the original decision had been taken in the Defence Committee) on 13 April 1954, that he would 'like to invite the Cabinet at an early date to decide in principle that hydrogen bombs should be made in the United Kingdom'.

This intention was in stark contrast to his atomic practices during the Second World War, when Churchill declined to consult even the service ministers, let alone the War Cabinet, about the development of the atomic bomb. Yet when the question did reach the full Cabinet on 7 July 1954, Crookshank, the Leader of the House of Commons, recoiling from the surprise announcement from Churchill, as Macmillan recorded in his diary, 'that the decision had been taken to make the hydrogen bomb in England', and the preliminaries were in hand, at once made a most vigorous protest at such a momentous decision being communicated to the Cabinet in so cavalier a way, and started to walk out of the room. We all did the same and the Cabinet broke up – if not in disorder – in a somewhat ragged

---

[28] Peter Hennessy, *The Prime Minister: The office and its holders since 1945*, Penguin, London, 2000, pp. 198–99.

fashion. Walter Monckton [Minister of Labour and National Service] and Woolton seemed especially shocked; not, I think, at the decision (which is probably right) but at the odd way in which things are being done.'

The H-bomb question returned to Cabinet the following day before being finally resolved on 26 July 1954, leaving Churchill bruised by what he called 'the constitutional aspect' of the thermo-nuclear decision and the 'considerable feeling in the Cabinet about the H-bomb decision not having been formally imparted to our colleagues earlier'.

This is from one of Churchill's letters to the Queen. It is notable that, despite the consultation, the outcome does not seem to be in question.[29]

It is my duty to inform your Majesty that the Cabinet are considering whether it would be right and advantageous for this country to produce the hydrogen bomb, and have meanwhile agreed to the continuation of the preparatory work which has been going on for the last few months. Your Majesty will, I understand, be receiving the account of the proceedings in the Cabinet at which this matter was recently discussed. A final decision is to be taken before the end of the month.

There is very little doubt in my mind what that will be.

---

[29] PRO, PREM 11/747, The Queen: 1954, *Churchill to HMQ*, 16 July 1954.

In 1954 Sir Thomas Dugdale resigned over the 'Crichel Down' Affair in what appeared to be the clearest post-war example of ministerial responsibility. John Griffith, an academic who shared that view at the time of the resignation, later looked back at the files when they were opened and rejected his earlier judgement.[30]

It seems clear that at the time of the first debate on 15 June 1954 there was no question of Dugdale's resignation. He drew attention to Clark's finding that there had been no bribery, corruption or personal dishonesty and added: 'The inquiry has thus achieved my main purpose which was to deal with any rumours or suggestions of this kind' and suggested that his civil servants were not as black as Clark had painted them. Nothing changed between then and 20 July except the rising howl of a pack of hounds behind him and failure of his Cabinet colleagues to give him any cover. And if Lord Boyle was right, he was unwilling to accept the abandonment of his department's policy over what should be done with Crichel Down.

After Labour's election defeat in 1955, Attlee for the first time named a 'Shadow Cabinet'. Since then, the system has been important in the development of opposition policy and credibility. This is the assessment by historian R. M. Punnett.[31]

In face of this, it is probably fair to say that the main practical significance of the post-1945 shadow government system lies not so much in the extent to which it prepares potential ministers for office,

---

[30] John Griffith, *Crichel Down:* 'The Most Famous Farm in British Constitutional History', *Contemporary Record*, Vol. 1, Number 1, Spring 1987, p. 40.

[31] R. M. Punnett, 'Her Majesty's Shadow Government: Its Evolution and Modern Role', in Valentine Herman and James Alt (eds.), *Cabinet Studies: A Reader*, Macmillan, London, 1975, p. 155.

but rather in the two very real contributions, noted earlier in the chapter, that it makes to the opposition's attempts to achieve office in the first place: that is the way in which the clear division of responsibilities among a front bench team adds to the efficiency of the opposition as a critic and scrutineer of the government's activities, and also the way in which the public presence of shadow ministers enhances the opposition party's image as an alternative government, waiting in the wings, primed for office with a team of potential ministers. In short, the shadow government system can contribute quite considerably to the chances of electoral victory, but can contribute less to the success of a period in office once it is achieved.

For the decade following the Second World War, Cabinet government, properly operated, had served three different administrations well. In 1955, in his extensive examination of how committee structures operated in local government, Sir Kenneth Wheare (a distinguished political scientist and eventually member of the Franks Committee on Administrative Tribunals and Inquiries, and Chancellor of Liverpool University) concluded with a fairly typical mid-century appraisal of the benefits of this balance between unitary and collective executive in central government. Yet within a year, Cabinet government was to be tested more severely than it had been at any point since the war's end.[32]

Writers on political theory have sometimes discussed the question whether it is better to entrust the process of administration to single individuals or to groups of individuals, whether the unitary executive is preferable to the plural executive. In Britain we have examples of both systems. In the central government, the

---

[32] Sir Kenneth C. Wheare, *Government by Committee: An Essay on the British Constitution*, Oxford University Press, London, 1955, p. 163.

responsibility for the administration of the departments is entrusted to single individuals – the ministers – each one of whom is responsible to Parliament and to the electorate for the proper conduct of the affairs of his department. It is true that we do not stop at this. We provide also that these single individuals shall be members of a team – the Cabinet and ministry – so that they do not act in complete isolation from each other. Their individual responsibility is supplemented by a collective responsibility. It may well be that this particular mixture of the unitary and the plural systems of administration in Britain – and in other countries where the Cabinet system is adopted – provides as good a solution as you can get to the problem of how to organise central administration. It appears to combine the advantages of the two systems.

7
Suez and After, 1956–1964

Anthony Eden (1897–1977) had been Foreign Secretary under Winston Churchill since the Second World War and, for an equally long time, had been the great man's heir apparent. So when Eden finally succeeded Churchill in April 1955 he had some firm ideas about both the policies he wished to pursue, and how he wished to run his administration. After holding a swift general election, which increased the Conservative majority to sixty, Eden seemed to be master of both areas. Yet it was to be an eruption in the area of his supposed expertise – foreign policy – and his subsequent handling of it, which proved fatal for his administration. The issue was the nationalisation of the Suez Canal by Egyptian leader Gamal Abdel Nasser. Eden saw this, and the subsequent rejection of his diplomatic efforts to resolve the situation peacefully, as a personal insult and a latter-day example of dictatorial tyranny to be resisted. His collusion with the French government in an Israeli attack on Egypt, after which British and French troops would be sent to the canal zone, ostensibly to separate the warring parties, proved a disastrous miscalculation and 'Suez' is regarded today as the point at which British illusions about a world role were shattered. It is also an intensely controversial moment in the history of Cabinet government, as Eden is generally regarded as having operated a personal foreign policy, and kept key details from his colleagues – lying to them, in effect. In this significant revisionist piece, John Barnes argues that far from remaining in the dark, his Cabinet colleagues were in fact fully apprised of the details of the situation.[1]

Although Eden sought to save his Cabinet some of the stress of business by following Baldwin's habit of frequent private consultation with his principal colleagues, and took a high view of the part a prime minister has to play in government, there is little evidence that he by-passed the Cabinet on anything that really mattered. The extent to which it was involved in the Suez decisions has been much questioned, but the official record shows that, from the initial decision on 27 July that every effort should be made to restore effective international control over the canal – if necessary by the threat and, in the last resort, the use of force – to the final decision on 6 November to accept a cease-fire, the Cabinet was involved in all the key decisions. It was, for example, the Cabinet that took the decision on 11 September to try out the scheme for a Suez Canal Users' Association rather than follow Nasser's rejection of the Eighteen Power proposals with an immediate reference to the UN Security Council, and, while it is true that the Prime Minister and Foreign Secretary were responsible for the precise timing of the eventual appeal to the Security Council on 23 September, there can be no question but that they were acting in pursuance of an earlier Cabinet decision. The only important exceptions concern the possibility of collaboration with Israel; and it is clear that even here, although they may not have known the full story of Eden's decision to go along with Franco-Israeli collusion, the rest of the Cabinet were told enough to know that their discussions of a possible Israeli break-out against the Egyptians were far from hypothetical and that the British government had an insight into Israeli intentions which had come directly from the Israelis themselves. Nor was this

---

[1] John Barnes, 'From Eden to Macmillan, 1955–1959', in Peter Hennessy and Anthony Seldon, *Ruling Performance: British Governments from Attlee to Thatcher*, Basil Blackwell, Oxford, 1987, pp. 113–14.

knowledge confined to ministers. In a significant phrase on 2 November Sir Richard Powell told his fellow permanent secretaries on the Defence (Transitional Arrangements) Committee that the French should be asked in their publicity to avoid any material 'which might be construed as confirming the accusation' of collusion.

What was kept from ministers was the precise nature of the arrangement with the Israelis. When the Cabinet discussed the situation on 24 October, ministers were told that the military operations which had been planned could not be held in readiness for many days longer; that, if such an operation were launched, Israel would undoubtedly mount a full-scale attack on Egypt; and that Britain would 'never have a better pretext for intervention against [Nasser] than we had now as a result of his seizure of the Suez Canal'. At the decisive meeting on the following day, in the light of further talks with the French, ministers were told that the Israelis were advancing their attack, that the French wanted to intervene to limit hostilities, and that they would take military action alone or with the Israelis if Britain declined to do so. Eden then sketched the scenario which was actually set in train on 30 October, and added that they 'must face the risk that we should be accused of collusion with Israel'. His argument was that the accusation was inevitable, since the Israelis would launch a parallel attack in any case, and it was better for Britain that it should be seen to be holding a balance between Israel and Egypt rather than appear to be accepting Israeli co-operation in any attack on Egypt alone. This statement was both disingenuous and over-optimistic, and there were evidently some Cabinet ministers clear-sighted enough to voice their doubts at the time. But no one resigned, and it can scarcely be claimed that ministers had not been given sufficient clues to what was really happening. The decision to intervene, therefore, was quite clearly a decision taken by the full Cabinet, and after very full debate. The actual decision to land troops in the face of UN pressure for a cease-fire was also the subject of a full, and at times agonizing, debate in Cabinet on 4 November, and it is difficult to see how the charges that have sometimes been voiced against Eden – in effect, that he took his Cabinet for a ride – can be sustained.

This extract from a confidential annex to the Cabinet minutes of 23 October lends weight to the view that the rest of the Cabinet had been kept fully in the picture, but not all historians agree that it is a 'smoking minute'.[2]

The Prime Minister recalled that, when the Cabinet had last discussed the Suez situation on 18th October, there had been reason to believe that the issue might be brought rapidly to a head as a result of military action by Israel against Egypt. From secret conversations which had been held in Paris with representatives of the Israeli Government, it now appeared that the Israelis would not alone launch a full-scale attack against Egypt. The United Kingdom and French Governments were thus confronted with the choice between an early military operation or a relatively prolonged negotiation.

'Rab' Butler (1902–82), one of the most experienced ministers of the post-war era, was Lord Privy Seal at the time. This is how he remembered Eden's behaviour.[3]

Eden, who had been so brilliant a negotiator in his prime, became a 'one-man band' at this time. He and his Foreign Secretary, Selwyn Lloyd, had interviewed the French leaders Messrs. Mollet and Pineau near Paris on October 16th, 1956, without even informing Gladwyn

---

[2] PRO, CAB 128/30, CM (56) 72, Confidential Annex, 23 October, 1956.
[3] Lord Butler, *The Art of Memory: Friends in Perspective*, Hodder & Stoughton, London, 1982, p. 100.

Jebb, the British ambassador in Paris, with whom they were staying. Throughout the crisis the Prime Minister hardly consulted his civil servants. Yet I would not call him, as some journalists have done, a dictator, since he continually reported to Parliament, which was in almost constant session, and very stormy sessions they were too. Moreover, although he kept his own counsel, Cabinet meetings, designed to elicit expression and obtain support, were frequent. I would say, however, that Eden at Suez came much nearer to being a dictator than Churchill did at the height of the war. Churchill was *the* great Commoner, greater even than the Elder or the Younger Pitt, for he insisted on his policies being explained in and ratified by Parliament, even if it was necessary to hold 'secret' sessions, with no press present, for security reasons.

This contemporary discussion, with its rather famous exchange about being at war, is a fair representation of how Eden's behaviour was seen by many at the time.[4]

It was at a two-hour Cabinet meeting in the morning that Sir Anthony informed his colleagues of what he planned to do. Until then only the inner Cabinet (Mr Lloyd, Mr Butler, Mr Macmillan, Lord Salisbury and Mr Head) had been in the picture. Now when the Prime Minister read out to the assembled Cabinet the terms of the ultimatum which was shortly to be handed over to the Egyptian and Israeli Ambassadors, some of his colleagues were taken aback. They had not realized that war was barely sixteen hours away. They felt that it was impossible for them at such short notice to discharge their constitutional responsibilities.

When one of the ministers complained about the short notice at

---

[4] Randolph S. Churchill, *The Rise and Fall of Sir Anthony Eden*, Macgibbon & Kee, London, 1959, pp. 277–78.

which they had to make their decision, the Prime Minister rather grandly said: 'A lot of my present colleagues never served in a War Cabinet.' Upon which another Cabinet Minister said: 'Well, Prime Minister, we didn't know we were at war.' There was a ghastly hush. But it was too late to do anything about it. To resign when British troops, ships and aircraft were already committed to the battle was not a thing that any patriotic man could do. And those who disliked what had been done had only four hours or so before the ultimatum became public in which to dissociate themselves, if they so wished, from what was being done in their name.

John Mackintosh, in his 1962 work on Cabinet government, argued that Eden's behaviour during Suez was little different from Chamberlain's at Munich: an example of extreme 'prime ministerialism'.[5]

This Suez crisis is often cited as the most extreme example of how a premier, backed by a few ministers in the departments concerned, can act and commit his government relying on the Cabinet to agree or to be carried along. But it is not different in any important respect from the way in which Neville Chamberlain and his close associates planned and executed British policy in the late summer of 1938, the Cabinet being told about the visit to Hitler only after this had been arranged.

Four years after Suez, Attlee wrote to the Daily Telegraph, *explaining why he believed a prime minister should not become over-involved in foreign policy.*[6]

---

[5] J. P. Mackintosh, *The British Cabinet*, Stevens & Sons Ltd., London, 1962, p. 436.
[6] Earl Attlee, Letter, *Daily Telegraph*, 9 August 1960.

An approach to one-man government is in my view a mistake. The job of a prime minister is to lead and co-ordinate a team, not to seek to be an omnicompetent minister . . .

It's a good maxim that if you have a good dog you don't bark yourself. I had a very good dog in Mr Ernest Bevin and on only one occasion did I at his request visit the American president in order to discuss major policy . . .

There was a time when Foreign Affairs was regarded as something esoteric left to the judgement of a foreign secretary and but rarely discussed. Nowadays there must be close co-ordination with the minister of defence and the chancellor of the exchequer. It is unwise for a prime minister to supersede his foreign secretary. The example of Neville Chamberlain is a warning.

Even placing the Suez crisis aside, Eden is not regarded as a good chairman of Cabinet. Aside from his frequent outbursts (he was highly strung), he disliked Cabinet discussions and kept many matters within a tight circle. Here he explains how he was first attracted to this model.[7]

I have sat in Cabinets or attended them under four Prime Ministers, MacDonald, Baldwin, Chamberlain and Churchill. I thought Baldwin's method of frequent consultation alone with each of his principal colleagues was good and I followed it. His failing lay in not always supporting the result with sufficient authority, but that is another matter. My colleagues knew that I was always available to each one of them and we saved the Cabinet some extra stress of business that way.

---

[7] Sir Anthony Eden, *Full Circle*, Cassell, London, 1960, pp. 269–70.

In 1957 Mackenzie and Grove described how the increasing use of Cabinet committees meant that ever more of the decisions brought to Cabinet required little more than a rubber stamp.[8]

The practice of careful preparation means that much Cabinet business is now almost formal. Many items of great importance are dealt with by the presentation of a paper agreed in advance by all concerned, generally after discussion in a Cabinet committee: the matter can then be disposed of quickly, by agreement to record the Cabinet's approval of the action recommended.

Suez, and Eden's eventual resignation, revealed the intense pressures a prime minister sometimes faced, even if self-imposed. Yet he was not the only one – throughout the post-war period, the Chancellor of the Exchequer was also put under frequent and intense pressure, even as the power of the Treasury had become a popular cause for complaint (amongst both those studying, and serving in, the Cabinet). In his memoirs, Lord Woolton considered the powers and pressures of the office and its effects on the Cabinet.[9]

In the world of commerce it is common for a group of men to share confidential and secret information and, in the process, to share the burden of responsibility and the wisdom they have learned from experience. Under successive governments we have been faced with financial crises and a damaging level of taxation. I wonder whether financial decision, among men of such high rank and responsibility as cabinet ministers, need be made into a personal burden on any chancellor of the exchequer. Incidentally, other members of the

---

[8] W. J. M. Mackenzie and J. W. Grove, *Central Administration in Britain*, Longman, London, 1957, p. 339.

[9] Lord Woolton, *The Memoirs of the Rt. Hon. The Earl of Woolton*, Cassell, London, 1959, p. 375.

Cabinet are placed in considerable difficulty by this problem, since they become politically committed to financial decisions with which they may not agree; the decision to resign, and so disturb all the other work of the government, is a hard one to take unless some vital national principle is involved.

Eden's resignation left the Cabinet and Conservative Party in crisis. When Harold Macmillan (1984–1987) was appointed Prime Minister in January 1957, he was by no means certain that he would be able to hold the Cabinet together. This is his recollection of his conversation with the Queen when he met to kiss hands.[10]

I could not disguise from her the gravity of the situation. Indeed, I remember warning her, half in joke, half in earnest, that I could not answer for the new government lasting more than six weeks.

Macmillan is regarded as a commanding premier. As a former Foreign Secretary, for example, he took a particularly close interest in foreign affairs. Yet he was also careful to manage the Cabinet, and many also regard him as a collegial premier. Richard Lamb, in a biography after the Macmillan-era archives had been opened, argued that this aspect of his style may have been exaggerated.[11]

The archives show that even more than generally believed Macmillan ran his government on the lines of an American president rather than a traditional British prime minister. In this he was considerably influenced by Winston Churchill's methods during the Second World War. Like American presidents Macmillan

---

[10] Harold Macmillan, *Riding the Storm, 1956–1959*, Macmillan, London, 1971, p. 185.
[11] Richard Lamb, *The Macmillan Years, 1957–1963: The Emerging Truth*, John Murray, London, 1995, p. 1.

favoured the use of personal policy advisers; as a result his Principal Private Secretaries, Tim Bligh and Philip de Zulueta, played important roles in deciding government policy. Macmillan consulted Bligh on Treasury matters and de Zulueta on foreign affairs, often in preference to the ministers responsible and their departments; Burke Trend of the Treasury and Cabinet Offices was frequently asked for his personal view, chiefly on colonial and economic affairs. The practice must have been galling for ministers.

Intellectually Macmillan towered head and shoulders above his Cabinet colleagues and, often mistrustful of their judgement, he insisted on full control . . . There is a surprising weight of minutes and memoranda in the archives written by Macmillan himself; they show not only that he fussed greatly sometimes over small matters, and interfered continuously with his colleagues' conduct of their departmental affairs, but that he had a great command of detail and an impressive capacity to absorb at once the implications of any problem facing the government.

In his memoirs, Macmillan maintained that he took Cabinet seriously.[12]

The Cabinet must continue as it had always been, collectively responsible for all great decisions. This practice I was scrupulous in observing, as, for example, in the Middle East crisis over Lebanon and Jordan. In addition we must continue to work partly through a small inner group of ministers, meeting occasionally, but chiefly through committees of ministers dealing with particular groups of subjects. That it was possible to operate the system and yet retain the confidence of the Cabinet as a whole was due partly to the generosity of my colleagues and partly to the skill of Sir Norman Brook and my private secretaries in gaining their confidence.

[12] Harold Macmillan, *Pointing the Way, 1959–1961*, Macmillan, London, 1972, pp. 22–23.

While the Prime Minister appeared to be getting more powerful – and Harold Macmillan during his 'Supermac' period was one of the more influential – Macmillan himself was surprised at the lack of support the Prime Minister received, in comparison to that available to departmental ministers. To Dame Evelyn Sharp (1903–05), his former Permanent Secretary at the Department of Housing and Local Government, this prompted questions about whether that support should be beefed up.[13]

One day . . . Mr Macmillan, then Prime Minister (whom I had known well at [the Ministry of] Housing and Local Government) asked me to lunch . . . One thing he said was: 'It's a strange thing that I have now got the biggest job I ever had and less help in doing it than I have ever known'. And that clicked with my growing notion that there was a gap in the machinery of government at the centre. Should there be a prime minister's department? Or a staff to serve the Prime Minister and Cabinet ministers?

In a conversation with his Press Secretary, Harold Evans (1911–83), Macmillan put his relative political impotence in a more constitutional context.[14]

While he was being made up and waiting to go on, we talked about the role of prime minister – a theme of current debate and of a forthcoming *Gallery* programme. It was absolute nonsense, he said, to argue that we were moving to a presidential system. That was about the point of evolution we had reached at the time of Charles II. The president had his own court. He appointed ministers who

---

[13] Tessa Blackstone and William Plowden, *Inside the Think Tank: Advising the Cabinet 1971–1983*, Heinemann, London, 1988, p. 7.
[14] Harold Evans, *Downing Street Diary: The Macmillan Years, 1957–1963*, Hodder & Stoughton, London, 1981, p. 248.

were not elected, might be either Whig or Tory and might not even have met each other. He did not need to take the advice of his Cabinet. It had no collective responsibility. The only check on his power – as it had been with Charles II and his successors – was the need to go to the Legislature for funds. In the British system the Cabinet had collective responsibility. You could not ignore it. Even Winston had made sure that he could carry the Cabinet with him in major decisions. As for himself, had it escaped notice that before completing the agreement about Polaris with President Kennedy he had thought it necessary to put the agreement to the Cabinet. So, too, at Key West in 1960 when Vietnam was discussed with the President.

Still, there were areas where prime ministerial power was growing. Just as the First and Second World Wars had seen powers deposited with the prime minister and never fully restored afterwards, so the new realities of the nuclear age saw others tranferred to the premier. One such was the decision to use nuclear weapons. This is from a 1962 memorandum within the Air Ministry about coordination of a nuclear strike.[15]

The decision to use nuclear weapons is reserved to the Prime Minister or his designated deputy. Adequate arrangements have been made for the Prime Minister or his designated deputy to be continuously available in a period of tension to receive information on the need for the release of nuclear weapons and to give decisions.

---

[15] PRO AIR 20/10056, *Co-ordination of Nuclear Strike Forces, 1960, 1961 & 1962, Initiation and Control of Nuclear Strikes in Overseas Theatres*, letter 21 December 1962, p. 3.

Despite this, Macmillan generally succeeded in getting what he wanted from Cabinet. And he used all manner of means to do so. This is the famous story of how he smoothed agreement on the approval of the Concorde project.[16]

The story of the second and final Cabinet has passed into Whitehall folklore. The Prime Minister was in a reminiscent mood. He told his colleagues about his great aunt's Daimler, which had travelled at 'the sensible speed of thirty miles an hour', and was sufficiently spacious to enable one to descend from it without removing one's top hat. Nowadays, alas! People had a mania for dashing around. But that being so Britain ought to 'cater for this profitable modern eccentricity'. He thought they all really agreed. No one seriously dissented. It was all over in a few minutes.

In his memoirs Lord Home (1903–95) recounted an incident which shed light on the sometimes very personal nature of Cabinet government. Even Macmillan, it seems, could be put off his stride![17]

One morning I came into the Cabinet room rather early and found the Cabinet Secretary, Sir Norman Brook (later Lord Normanbrook) changing all our places. I asked what had happened – Had there been a shuffle? – or had one of us died in the night? 'Oh no,' said Sir Norman, 'it's nothing like that. The Prime Minister cannot stand Enoch Powell's [(1912–98); Minister of Health]steely and accusing eye looking at him across the table any more, and I've had to move him down to the side.'

---

[16] Jock Bruce-Gardyne and Nigel Lawson, *The Power Game: An Examination of Decision-Making in Government*, Macmillan, London, 1976, p. 29.
[17] Lord Home, *The Way the Wind Blows*, Collins, London, 1976, p. 192.

The Plowden Committee, set up to consider public expenditure, recommended regular four-year surveys of public spending in relation to resources, stability of public spending decisions, improved tools for measuring and handling public spending problems, and a more effective machinery for collective decision-taking by ministers.[18]

Under the traditional system it is natural that a departmental minister should be primarily concerned with the expenditure charged to his own vote and that the control of expenditure in aggregate should tend to be regarded as merely another sector of departmental administration, constituting the responsibility of the chancellor of the exchequer alone. But if, as we believe, the attitudes of Parliament and public opinion no longer apply as a systematic a restraint to public expenditure as they did in the past, it is for consideration whether some modification of present practice in this respect is required.

This would not imply any change in the personal responsibility of the chancellor of the exchequer, within the Cabinet, for fiscal and economic policy. The [social, political and economic] changes of the last twenty years, particularly the developing concept of the role of the Budget in relation to the national economy, make this unity of responsibility more indispensable than ever. But, without any infringement of this principle, it should be possible to find means of providing the chancellor of the exchequer with a greater measure of support and of ensuring that departmental ministers are enabled to discharge more effectively, in relation to the totality of public expenditure, the collective responsibility which is allied and complementary to the individual responsibility which each of them bears for the expenditure of his own department.

---

[18] Cmnd. 1432, *Control of Public Expenditure*, HMSO, 1961, p. 12.

SUEZ AND AFTER, 1956–1964

In 1958 John Mackintosh was asked to update Arthur Berriedale Keith's classic work on Cabinet government. As he began his work, it became increasingly clear to him that there had been such change that an entirely new assessment needed to be made. In 1962, he published his own work, The British Cabinet, *which argued that the prime minister, rather than the Cabinet, was now the central figure in British politics, although he also noted the growing significance of Cabinet committees.*[19]

A successful, strong and opinionated prime minister can put his impress on a whole government. His ideas will be worked out either by himself or with a few colleagues. If there is an 'inner ring' the qualification for entry is not seniority, office or ability but possession of the prime minister's confidence. It is easiest for such a premier to conduct affairs with the aid of the departmental minister concerned, and the Cabinet falls into place as a forum for informing his colleagues of decisions that have been taken. In these circumstances it is very hard for a minister who begins to have doubts to intervene with effect. He has insufficient knowledge, he is always too late, and is contending with the prime minister and the men whom the latter has elevated to a position of trust. Also, when decisions have been taken, there is little that can be done other than protest in the secrecy of the Cabinet or resign. Normally such divergences are avoided because policies take time to mature, and the views of the prime minister, if he is a positive leader, either permeate his colleagues or the latter react and leave office. On the other hand the premier will make adjustments to meet changes of attitude among those who normally agree with him, so that if trouble does arise it will usually be confined to one or two men at the bottom of the table.

* * *

---

[19] J. P. Mackintosh, *The British Cabinet*, Stevens & Sons Ltd., London, 1962, pp. 420, 451, 452.

While British government in the latter half of the nineteenth century can be described simply as Cabinet government, such a description would be misleading today. Now the country is governed by the Prime Minister who leads, co-ordinates and maintains a series of ministers all of whom are advised and backed by the civil service. Some decisions are taken by the premier alone, some in consultations between him and the senior ministers, while others are left to heads of departments, the Cabinet, Cabinet committee, or the permanent officials. Of these bodies the Cabinet holds the central position because, though it does not often initiate policy or govern in that sense, most decisions pass through it or are reported to it and Cabinet ministers can complain that they have not been informed or consulted. The precise amount of power held by each agency and the use made of the Cabinet depends on the ideas of the premier and the personnel and situation with which he has to deal. Lloyd George, Neville Chamberlain, Mr Churchill during the War, Mr Attlee and Sir Anthony Eden all adapted the machinery to suit their own tastes and purposes. Bonar Law, Ramsay MacDonald, Stanley Baldwin (and, it appears, Mr Macmillan) on the other hand have tended to accept the existing pattern, but they have all imposed their stamp on the governments they have led.

* * *

However, the real sphere in which Cabinet ministers in charge of the less important offices can act is not in the Cabinet itself but in the committees covering their field of interest and in their own departments. This is not presidential government because the premier can, in exceptional circumstances, be removed and he will collapse if deserted by his colleagues or by his party. There is no single catchphrase that can describe this form of government, but it may be pictured as a cone. The Prime Minister stands at the apex supported by and giving point to a widening series of rings of senior ministers, the Cabinet, its committees, non-Cabinet ministers, and departments. Of these rings, the only one above the level of the civil service that has formal existence and acts as a court of appeal for lower tiers is the Cabinet.

In July 1962 Macmillan, facing pressure after a series of political reverses, sacked seven Cabinet ministers and dramatically reconstructed his government. The event became known as the 'Night of the Long Knives', and in theory it exhibited the Prime Minister's ultimate power to 'hire and fire' his Cabinet ministers. In reality, it undermined his position by showing him to be panicked, and by picking on politically weak colleagues – especially Chancellor Selwyn Lloyd – it undermined his position further. This was particularly damaging for Macmillan, who had cultivated an image of 'unflappability' and when he was first appointed wrote out the phrase 'Quiet calm deliberation disentangles every knot' and had it framed on his wall.[20] This is from the memoirs of Lord Kilmuir, one of those who was sacked, and begins on the evening of 11 July, 1962.[21]

Macmillan took me aside and said, 'The Government is breaking up,' and murmured something about 'You don't mind going?' I was startled, but merely replied, 'You know my views.'. . .

The result of the Leicester by-election was declared at midnight on Thursday, July 12th. Labour held the seat with a majority of 1,948 over the Liberal, the Conservative once again being a poor third. On the following morning, when I was attending another committee of the Cabinet, I was handed a message that the Prime Minister wished to see me. Our interview began at 11.15 and lasted about three-

---

[20] Harold Macmillan, *Riding the Storm, 1956–1959*, Macmillan, London, 1971, p. 198.
[21] Lord Kilmuir, *Political Adventure: The Memoirs of the Earl of Kilmuir*, Weidenfeld & Nicolson, London, 1962, p. 324.

quarters of an hour. What was said must remain confidential, but the results are well known. Seven Cabinet ministers were to go, and there was a corresponding shake-up among junior ministers, and the reconstruction was to be immediate and dramatic.

I got the impression that he was extremely alarmed about his own position, and was determined to eliminate any risk for himself by a massive change of government. It astonished me that a man who had kept his head under the most severe stress and strains should lose both nerve and judgement in this way.

This quip from Liberal Leader Jeremy Thorpe (1929–) neatly summarised contemporary opinion about Macmillan's butchery.[22]

Greater love hath no man than this, that he lay down his friends for his life.

Still, belief in prime ministerial omnipotence was widespread. In 1962 Lord Home, the Foreign Secretary, gave an interview to Kenneth Harris of the Observer. *In it he made some claims about the role of Cabinet Ministers* vis-á-vis *the Prime Minister which, when later Prime Minister himself, he was to find painfully far from the mark.*[23]

Harris: To what extent is the Foreign Secretary a creative influence on foreign policy and to what extent is he the Prime Minister's – well, agent?

Home: Every Cabinet minister is in a sense the Prime Minister's agent – his assistant. There's no question about that. It is the

---

[22] Anthony Jay (ed.), *The Oxford Dictionary of Political Quotations*, Oxford University Press, Oxford, 1996, p. 364.

[23] Kenneth Harris, 'The Foreign Secretary opens up', *Observer*, 16 September 1962.

Prime Minister's Cabinet, and he is the one person who is directly responsible to the Queen for what the Cabinet does.

If the Cabinet discusses anything it is the Prime Minister who decides what the collective view of the Cabinet is. A minister's job is to save the Prime Minister all the work he can. But no minister could make a really important move without consulting the Prime Minister, and if the Prime Minister wanted to take a certain step the Cabinet minister concerned would either have to agree, argue it out in Cabinet, or resign.

The following year Home found out what it was really like to be Prime Minister. His succession to the premiership after Harold Macmillan's illness (temporary, as it turned out), in October 1963, was controversial because he was a peer, and two senior Ministers – Enoch Powell and Iain Macleod (1913–70) – refused to serve under him. The latter later wrote this damning indictment of the tightness of the process of consultation by which he was appointed.[24]

It is some measure of the tightness of the magic circle on this occasion that neither the Chancellor of the Exchequer nor the Leader of the House of Commons had any inkling of what was happening.

In 1963 Richard Crossman (1907–74), at the time a Labour shadow minister, was asked to write an introduction for a new edition of Bagehot's The English Constitution. *Crossman, a leading socialist intellectual, used the occasion to argue that Britain had now moved from Cabinet to 'prime ministerial' government. In an often-critical assessment of Bagehot, Crossman endorsed the earlier conclusions of John Mackintosh, and expressed his wonder at the extent to which the*

---

[24] Iain Macleod, 'The Tory Leadership', *Spectator*, 17 January 1964.

'institutions and the behaviour of voluntary totalitarianism' had been retained since the war.[25]

The post-war epoch has seen the final transformation of Cabinet government into prime ministerial government. Under this system the 'hyphen which joins, the buckle which fastens, the legislative part of the state to the executive part' becomes one single man. Even in Bagehot's time it was probably a misnomer to describe the premier as chairman, and *primus inter pares*. His right to select his own Cabinet and dismiss them at will; his power to decide the Cabinet's agenda and announce the decisions reached without taking a vote; his control, through the Chief Whip, over patronage – all this had already before 1867 given him near-presidential powers. Since then his powers have been steadily increased, first by the centralisation of the party machine under his personal rule, and secondly by the growth of a centralised bureaucracy, so vast that it could no longer be managed by a Cabinet behaving like the board of directors of an old-fashioned company.

Under prime ministerial government, secondary decisions are normally taken either by the department concerned or in Cabinet committee, and the Cabinet becomes the place where busy executives seek formal sanction for their actions from colleagues usually too busy – even if they do disagree – to do more than protest. Each of these executives, moreover, owes his allegiance not to the Cabinet collectively but to the prime minister who gave him his job, and who may well have dictated the policy he must adopt. In so far as ministers feel themselves to be the agents of the premier, the British Cabinet has now come to resemble the American Cabinet . . .

It has often been observed that when they were plunged into total

---

[25] Richard Crossman, Introduction to Walter Bagehot, *The English Constitution*, Fontana, London, 1963, pp. 51–52, 56.

war in 1940, the British people readily put their democratic Constitution into cold storage, and fought under a system of centralised autocracy. The Nazi totalitarian state was defeated because we were ready to accept a more far-reaching system of voluntary totalitarianism. What is not so often noticed is the extent to which the institutions and the behaviour of voluntary totalitarianism have been retained since 1945.

Hans Daalder's 1963 book on the Cabinet was unusual in providing some idea of what he felt a Cabinet should do rather than simply what it did. It is notable for continuing to place the Cabinet at the centre of decision-taking, a far cry from Mackintosh's analysis – that Cabinet now merely implemented decisions taken elsewhere.[26]

1. The Cabinet should be able to decide the most important policy questions encountered by the central government both in day-to-day practice and in long-term perspective. This implies that ministers should have the time to concentrate on such questions; that they should have at their disposal the best expert advice available from departmental and non-departmental advisers; and that they must remain aware of the more important ideas and social movements found in the country at large.

2. The Cabinet should supervise the machinery and processes of administration and make sure that the bureaucracy functions effectively and in unison. To do this, the Cabinet must have adequate insight into actual administrative procedures. It must be able to intervene in specific issues and to ensure coordination where necessary. But it must not be burdened to such an extent that the normal flow of administration becomes hampered and insufficient

---

[26] Hans Daalder, *Cabinet Reform in Britain, 1914–1963*, Stanford University Press, Stanford, 1963, pp. 264–65.

attention is given to long-term policy considerations. Decisions must be effectively prepared, and once taken they must be fit for execution *and* be recognised as such by the departmental and other official organs that will have to implement them.

3. The Cabinet should be able to make valid its claim to represent the political desires of at least the majority of politically articulate groups in the population. This requires that the relations between the Cabinet and the parliamentary party and its constituent groups be so close that steady support is secure; that enough voters continue to view the government as effectively promoting their articulate or inarticulate interests; that the nation as a whole (notwithstanding group and party differences) be willing to abide by the leadership of the Cabinet; and that the internal relations within the government allow a softening of political and personal conflicts to such an extent that external homogeneity can be preserved and a constant clearance of political, policy, and administrative decisions can be effected.

4. In all its functions – as decider of policy, administrative coordinator, and focus of political desires – the Cabinet should be able to proceed without impairing the legal and political responsibility of individual ministers and of the government as a whole toward Parliament. This requires that Parliament remain able to hold individual ministers responsible for the efficient discharge of their duties; that collective responsibility remain intact; and that, in addition, Parliament be able to judge the more general question of whether the process of decision-making is that of an efficient and responsible government.

8
Technocracy, 1964–1970

Harold Wilson became Labour Party Leader in 1963, after the death of Hugh Gaitskell. The following year he became Prime Minister, having campaigned on a platform of modernisation and technological progress in that year's general election. In this interview with Norman Hunt, a Politics Fellow at Exeter College, Oxford,[1] in 1964, he set out some of his expectations for how he would manage the office in relation to his Cabinet colleagues.[2]

Hunt: Whatever the size of your Cabinet Secretariat, what sort of jobs will they be doing?

Wilson: Well, the traditional job of the Cabinet Secretariat is, of course, to brief – to service the Cabinet committees, provide secretaries for the Cabinet committees and see that the papers are properly circulated and a certain amount of co-ordination done by those means. I think they will also have to do much more in the way of briefing the prime minister, not only briefing him on the machinery of government and briefing him on the work of any Cabinet committee, but also providing a briefing agency, so that he is right up to date and on top of the job in respect of all these major departments of state. My conception of the prime minister

---

[1] Wilson later appointed him to the Fulton Committee.
[2] Norman Hunt, 'Harold Wilson: Pre-experience: Harold Wilson interviewed by Norman Hunt', in Anthony King (ed.), *The British Prime Minister: A Reader*, Macmillan, London, 1969, pp. 86, 90, 91.

is that if he's not a managing director, he is at any rate and should be very much a full-time executive chairman.

* * *

Hunt: I'm just wondering whether, with your emphasis on Cabinet Secretariat, your emphasis on experts and so on, the Cabinet itself really will be the hub of your government, if you're prime minister? Or will the decisions really be taken for the most part by yourself in conjunction with the minister and the experts concerned?

Wilson: Heavens, no! The decisions must be in the Cabinet. It is the prime minister's duty to ensure that any major questions of policy, particularly where there are inter-departmental disagreement, should be taken by the Cabinet itself. But I think the prime minister can help by, as I've said, ensuring an adequate secretariat for the digestion of those problems that can be pre-digested at other Cabinet committees. I think it can also help if, for example, he's maintaining pretty close contact with his minister, on a scheme which is germinating, by pointing out to that minister that perhaps he hadn't realised that 'this is a matter on which we ought at an early stage to consult the Secretary of State for Scotland', – certainly that he ought to consult the Treasury. I think a great deal of the efficiency of government does depend on what authority is given to junior ministers. Except where there's a case for real urgency, papers coming up to the minister from the civil servant should come via the Parliamentary Secretary so that he can express a view on it, and it does mean that the minister then does get the advice not only of a good colleague but one who has a good political approach. I think this is a better answer for him than the idea of a separate *cabinet*.

* * *

Hunt: Would you also expect to have in effect an inner Cabinet as well?

Wilson: An inner Cabinet? No, I don't think that this is a very good idea, but of course the prime minister keeps in very close touch with the leader of the House and, of course, the chief whip; with the chancellor, with the foreign secretary, with the first secretary or deputy prime minister (if there is a deputy prime minister), with the head of your economic planning organisation, and this is, in a sense, the list of the prime minister's closest advisers – the lord chancellor too – but whether they should ever meet as an inner Cabinet I'm doubtful.

Once in government, Wilson fell for the inner Cabinet idea, and eventually tried several – the later Parliamentary Committee and Management Committee were formal 'inner Cabinets'. One early experiment was his attempt to have the government's four senior Ministers, including George Brown (1904–85) at that point Deputy Prime Minister and Secretary of State for Economic Affairs, constitute a 'permanent nucleus' on all Cabinet MISC (ad hoc) committees. This is Wilson's memo to Brown, suggesting the idea.[3]

In the light of our talk the other day I have been thinking over our arrangements for handling our affairs in general, particularly the sort of business we conduct in MISC meetings. I think there is great value in these meetings. But they cover a great range of subjects and involve, in total, a considerable number of ministers; and I think that there would be advantage in putting them on a rather more formal and systematic basis. Many of them raise issues which may affect government policy as a whole; and I should like to feel that the senior

---

[3] PRO, PREM 13/530, *Personal Minutes from Prime Minister to Ministers*, Wilson to Brown, July 8 1965, Prime Minister's Personal Minute M56/65.

members of the Cabinet, whose duties cover between them the whole range of the government's responsibilities, are continuously associated with them. What I have in mind; therefore, is that you, the Lord President, the Chancellor of the Exchequer and the Foreign Secretary might form a sort of permanent nucleus of the MISC meetings, on the basis that you would be free to attend any particular meeting or not, as you saw fit, but that you would be present in a personal, rather than a departmental, capacity and would not, therefore, necessarily need to be represented if you were prevented from being present, unless, of course, the subject under discussion happened to concern your department. To this permanent nucleus other ministers, and officials, would be added as the nature of the meeting required; but the nucleus would ensure continuity of general government policy and, from time to time, might well meet on its own to discuss major problems or general issues, to take stock of the way our affairs are going and to act as a kind of clearing-house and progress chaser of our business as a whole.

George Wigg (1900–83), Paymaster General in the new government, described the difficulties Wilson faced on forming his first Cabinet.[4]

Another chilling fact was that, perhaps to a greater extent than any of his modern predecessors in office, Wilson was engaged in a perpetual balancing act to ensure that on foreseeable Cabinet issues he would not be left in a minority. Almost every senior minister had voted against him in the election for the party leadership. In accordance with custom, he mulled over the selection of his junior ministers with Bowden, Short, Brown and Callaghan, to get the right balance of party influence. Selection with a pin might have been preferable!

[4] Lord Wigg, *George Wigg*, Michael Joseph, London, 1972, p. 312.

Shortly after the general election, the Cabinet Secretary, Sir Burke Trend (1914–87), sent Wilson a note with a copy of the latest version of 'Questions of Procedure for Ministers', suggesting that it should be sent to new ministers as soon as possible.[5]

I attach a memorandum on 'Questions of Procedure for Ministers', which is customarily circulated to all ministers on first appointment, whether at the outset of a new Administration or on the occurrence of individual policy changes during an Administration's lifetime. It is an entirely non-party document, which codifies the general principles of ministerial conduct as they have evolved over many years. It has the authority of a good many prime ministers, of different party complexions; and it is revised, in the light of changes in practice, at regular intervals. The most recent modification is the arrangement whereby a new minister, after signing a declaration that he has read the relevant provisions of the Official Secrets Acts, is given a briefing by the Security Service on the threat to our security.

There is considerable advantage in ensuring that new ministers study this memorandum as soon as possible; and you may feel, therefore, that, in accordance with the normal practice, it should be sent to each member of the government with a covering note by yourself on the lines of the attached draft. It would also be helpful if you would mention it briefly at your first Cabinet meeting and would ask members of the Cabinet to ensure that, in so far as it is relevant to junior ministers, parliamentary secretaries, personal staffs and so forth, its provisions are brought to their attention.

---

[5] PRO, CAB 21/5199, *Cabinet Questions of Procedure for Ministers*, Trend to Wilson, 16 October, 1964.

In this interview in 1965 with Norman Hunt, Lord 'Rab' Butler disputed the notion that Cabinet committees were taking more decisions than previously. He drew on his wartime experience of the 1944 Education Act, and substantial post-war experience as Home Secretary, Foreign Secretary, Chancellor and Deputy Prime Minister.[6]

Hunt: But wouldn't it be true to say that more and more Cabinet committees are taking more and more decisions that in previous times would have come before the Cabinet?

Butler: Most of my work when I was Minister of Education was done outside the Cabinet, and hardly referred to the Cabinet at all, and that was a major reform in our social affairs . . .

Hunt: In this general context could we look at one or two specific issues illustrating the role and power of the Prime Minister and the Cabinet – first in your 1944 Education Act?

Butler: It was rather exceptional, being war time, so the War Cabinet certainly would not have considered it. It used to go before a body called the Lord President's Committee, but I must tell you that the greater part of the negotiation and preparation for this huge measure, which is still unimplemented – this shows the size of it – today, was done outside the Cabinet, and outside the Lord President's Committee.

* * *

Hunt: But in a sense, as you were saying, on all these questions that we have been discussing the Cabinet was really faced with a pretty well unanimous recommendation to move in a certain direction. And so, even on political issues like these, the Cabinet really wasn't in a position freely to take a decision?

---

[6] Norman Hunt, 'Lord Butler interviewed: Reflections on Cabinet Government', in Valentine Herman and James Alt (eds.), *Cabinet Studies: A Reader*, Macmillan, London, 1975, pp. 193, 196, 207.

Butler: I think if you take the Cabinet as covering the Cabinet committees and the committees of ministers under it, you get a rather better conception of what the Cabinet is. If you just take the Cabinet meeting itself, you have to come to the conclusion that unless the people are very alive that day, and very political, much of the decision has already been taken before it reaches them. That is the conclusion I would come to.

The difference between a Cabinet and non-Cabinet minister was considerable. Here Roy Jenkins (1920–2003), the Minister for Aviation who had just turned down a move to the Department of Education (and into the Cabinet), described it.[7]

I did however have to be disabused of my foolish view that I ought to have the best of both worlds, that is to be treated like a Cabinet minister even though I had declined to become one. In the following week Churchill died and at his great state funeral in St Paul's the Cabinet had some sort of special *entrée* which was denied to lesser ministers and through which I saw the Croslands gliding. Equally, I recall that when I was next summoned to be 'in attendance' at the meeting of the Cabinet I was slow to leave when my item was over and half expected Wilson to invite me to stay on. Quite rightly, he did not.

There was a separate hierarchy within the Cabinet, with the Treasury at the top. Treasury power has been an ongoing concern over many years, particularly in the Labour Party. This is Edward Short (1912–), Wilson's Chief Whip and later Education Secretary, from 5 April 1965.[8]

---

[7] Roy Jenkins, *A Life at the Centre*, Papermac, London, 1991, p. 171.
[8] Edward Short, *Whip to Wilson*, Macdonald, London, 1989, p. 142.

On the following Monday Jim[9] revealed all, or nearly all, to the Cabinet, where it was reasonably well received. Of course, such is the strength of the Chancellor's position in the Government that whether the Budget met with approval or not, it was too late for any changes. This made some of our less docile ministers begin to chafe. The pre-Budget meeting once again demonstrated the utter unassailability of the No. 10–No. 11 solar alliance in which George Brown was still a partner. But later in the government's life, he was to find that he also had to knuckle under when he fell foul of Downing Street. The rest of the Cabinet were either the inveterate sycophants who always supported the alliance in the hope of preferment, or the slightly, but always politely, rebellious.

Some Labour figures found this unassailability unacceptable. This is from the memoirs of Joe Haines (1928–), from 1969 Wilson's Press Secretary and one of his closest advisers.[10]

I find it astonishing that a Labour Cabinet can still tolerate a situation where the Chancellor of the Exchequer only acquaints them with the content of his Budget some twenty-eight hours before he presents it to Parliament. On that time scale, only a massive spontaneous revolt against the Budget can make a fundamental change in it. I have no strong opinions about whether the annual Budget ritual should continue, but the secrecy in which the Budget is drawn up is not only absurd and anti-democratic, it is a powerful buttress to the supremacy of the Treasury mind over that of the elected Government's.

---

[9] James Callaghan (1912–) Chancellor 1964–67.
[10] Joe Haines, *The Politics of Power*, Jonathan Cape, London, 1977, p. 66.

In 1968, the Royal Institute of Public Administration's Study Group on central government reported, and offered a clear and concise contribution to the debate about the power of the Treasury.[11]

The Treasury is, however, itself only a department, and it is in the last resort only as strong as the desire of the government as a whole to put financial considerations first, or the man who holds the office of chancellor of the exchequer. But the Treasury is responsible, under the Cabinet, for controlling expenditure, and it is on this that its influence and its position as a 'central' department is primarily based. Most actions of government have financial aspects which automatically bring them into the Treasury's orbit, and in 1914 the supervision of departmental expenditure by the Treasury was already complete. Whatever the full reasons may be, the Treasury was – and has remained throughout our period – at least *primus inter pares* in Whitehall.

The meetings of the 1964–70 Labour Cabinet were notably long and the discussion sometimes circuitous. In these diary entries, two years apart, Barbara Castle gives a fascinating insight into why.[12]

Thursday, 4 March 1965
Tony Crosland complained to me, 'There are twenty ministers debating this. If only there had been as much heat generated over Vietnam.' I retorted acidly, 'The Parkinson's Law of words operates

---

[11] F. M. G. Willson and D. N. Chester (eds.), *The Organization of British Central Government, 1916–1964, A Survey by a Study Group of the Royal Institute of Public Administration* (second ed.), George Allen & Unwin Ltd., London, 1968, p. 284.
[12] Barbara Castle, *The Castle Diaries, 1964–1976*, Macmillan, London, 1990, pp. 10, 151.

in this Cabinet. Words expand to fill the time available to them. The length of these Cabinet meetings is purely dictated by the PM's engagements.' He grinned agreement.

Thursday, 28 September 1967
I passed a note to Peter Shore next to me: 'Speak up! Assert your rights as a *full* member of the Cabinet.' He scribbled back: 'Not yet.' That is the trouble with Cabinet meetings. There is something paralysingly anodyne about the atmosphere. It isn't 'done' to have any concerted move by like-minded men – unless, of course, Harold has organised it. Tony Greenwood sat in total silence and Peter was obviously inhibited by his own newness from speaking up. I know just what he is suffering from – a sense that he has been brought in for economic affairs and shouldn't intrude on some other departmental preserve. This is the creeping disease of Cabinet government and Dick [Crossman] himself once suffered from it. There is only one cure for it (as long experience on the NEC[13] taught me). You must just speak your mind and ignore the sneers.

This extract from Susan Crosland's fond biography of her husband Tony (1918–77), appointed Secretary of State for Education in 1964, similarly illustrates some of the dynamics within the early Wilson Cabinets.[14]

When Tony first entered the Cabinet he was uncertain how it worked and initially said very little: 'I cannot offer comment because I haven't given the matter serious thought.' Jim Callaghan said to him after the first few weeks that while he might regard himself as 'knowing nothing about it', he was considerably more informed

[13] National Executive Committee of the Labour Party.
[14] Susan Crosland, *Tony Crosland*, Jonathan Cape, London, 1982, p. 152.

than most of his colleagues: 'You're too modest, Tony.' A couple of days later Callaghan pushed a note across the Cabinet table for the SoS Education: 'Splendid. You see how right you were to start joining in. In one bound you become an Opinion-former (and in this Cabinet that's a bloody marvel!). Jim.'

Although the later diaries and memoirs hardly bore out the description, during the 1960s Wilson was criticised for adopting a Kennedy-esque presidential style. This is his description of the role and scope of the Cabinet Office, in an interview with the BBC on 6 April 1967.[15]

In the first place the Cabinet Office exists partly to service the Cabinet and Cabinet committees, to provide accurate records of discussion so that a Cabinet decision is a decision understood by all departments and not just an account of a discussion; and so that papers are prepared adequately. Ministers fully briefed and issues brought to a clear point of decision. But, in addition, the Cabinet secretariat is the private department of the Prime Minister. Each member of the Cabinet Office staff services and serves the whole Cabinet but they are also my own staff. If you take, for example, the Permanent Secretary of the Cabinet – he is the servant of the whole Cabinet and attends all its meetings, but he is also my Permanent Secretary / Chief Adviser. He advises me, briefs me, not only for Cabinet meetings and other Cabinet committees over which I preside, but on the general running of the government so far as policy is concerned.

---

[15] R. K. Mosley, *The Story of the Cabinet Office*, Routledge, London, 1969, p. 78.

Crossman is one of the most interesting Cabinet ministers of the post-war era, because he had very firm views about Cabinet government when he was appointed, and set out to test them against reality by keeping a detailed diary of his time in office. Each weekend, he would take his notes and papers back to his house to record his impression of the week's events. The publication of the diaries, after he had left office, was intensely controversial, both within government and outside. Here are the key sections from the first of the three volumes, covering Crossman's time as Minister of Housing.[16]

Thursday, 22 October 1964

As for Cabinet as a decision-taking body, my first impression is that it's a much more genuine forum of opinion than I had been led to expect or than I had described in my Introduction to Bagehot. On the other hand it's quite clear that the preparations for dealing with the economic crisis, the item which followed the Queen's Speech, had been entirely done by Harold Wilson himself with the help of James Callaghan, George Brown and – I imagine – Douglas Jay at the Board of Trade. The crisis programme was just imposed on the rest of us. I didn't much like that. We were given the draft of the statement due next Monday on the crisis and the measure to meet it. Personally, I didn't think very highly of the draft but Cabinet as a whole had no advance notice so we simply had to accept the *fait accompli* or resign. To judge from this first meeting the Prime Minister can consult whoever he likes in a crisis and once he has been consulted, Cabinet must really go along. The contrast between this and the way Harold handled the steel issue was interesting. There is, I think, more possibility of decision in Cabinet than I realised as well as more possibility of prime ministerial dictatorship.

[16] Richard Crossman, *The Diaries of a Cabinet Minister, Volume One: Minister of Housing 1964–66*, Book Club Associates, London, 1977, pp. 28–29, 47, 198–99, 202–203, 591–92.

Thursday, 5 November 1964
Reading my papers early in the morning I suddenly realised that the White Paper which accompanied a Bill for the underground storage of gas would actually increase the alarm it was supposed to allay. I made this point at the Home Affairs Committee and as a result poor Fred Lee, the Minister in charge, had to withdraw the White Paper. Well, I won. But did I gain by it? On reflection I realise that all I've done is to make an enemy. Why should I sit there and do this? I realise now something about Cabinet government: one should always be looking for friends and allies, not making enemies. That's why a Cabinet minister is reluctant to weigh in on too many things. I dare say Aneurin Bevan used to and Manny Shinwell used to. Should I be the sort of minister who weighs in on everything and doesn't calculate on friends and enemies? Or shall I be the careful kind of calculating man who puts up papers so as to get himself on the map, supporting or opposing not on the merits of the case but on the effect on his allies or his enemies? It seems to be clear that two-thirds of my colleagues here, as on the NEC, are going to act in the second way. I hope I shall act in the first fashion but with a great deal more caution and restrain than I would have done, say, five years ago.

Sunday, 18 April 1965
Broadly speaking, the analysis I made in the Introduction to Bagehot is being confirmed. Certainly it is true that the Cabinet is now part of the 'dignified' element in the constitution, in the sense that the real decisions are rarely taken there, unless the Prime Minister deliberately chooses to give the appearance of letting Cabinet decide a matter. I was also right to recognise the importance of Cabinet committees. I am a permanent member of two, the Home Affairs Committee and the Economic Development Committee. In addition, I attend the Immigration Committee and the Broadcasting

Committee as well as the Legislation Committee. But I am not a member of the Social Services Committee. Nor, of course, am I a member of the two really important committees, on Defence and Foreign Affairs. From these I am totally excluded. So I am very much a home-front Cabinet Minister.

The really big thing I completely failed to notice when I wrote that Introduction was that, in addition to the Cabinet committees which only ministers normally attend, there is a full network of official committees; and the work of the ministers is therefore strictly and completely paralleled at the official level. This means that very often the whole job is pre-cooked in the official committee to a point from which it is extremely difficult to reach any other conclusion than that already determined by the officials in advance; and if agreement is reached at the lower level of a Cabinet committee, only formal approval is needed from the full Cabinet. This is the way in which Whitehall ensures that the Cabinet system is fairly harmless.

Another big surprise was the discovery that Cabinet minutes are a travesty, or to be more accurate, do not pretend to be an account of what actually takes place in the Cabinet. The same applies to the minutes of Cabinet committees. Normally, what they record is not what was actually said but a summary of the official brief which the minister brought with him, the official papers on the original policy, and the official conclusions. The minutes never describe the real struggle which took place. That struggle is only abstracted in the form of 'in the course of discussion the following points were made . . .'. And in this summary the name of the minister who made the point is rarely mentioned.

The combination of this kind of Cabinet minute (which provides the main directive for Whitehall) and official committees enormously strengthens the civil service against the politicians.

... Has the Cabinet changed during these first six months? On the economic crisis Cabinet didn't do anything in the so-called Hundred Days except rubber-stamp. The only decisions we were allowed were on prescription charges, pensions and MPs' salaries. And the decision in which I was involved, with George Brown, to stop all office building in London, was largely arranged after a telephone conversation between Harold and myself at breakfast-time. But even since the Hundred Days, Cabinet hasn't really become a collective decision-taking body – we have been mainly dealing with secondary disagreements which have to be resolved. We were promised a discussion of general economic policy before the budget, but that discussion never took place. Instead, we had endless leaks in the press about disagreements between Callaghan and Brown which were apparently being fought out partly at Chequers and partly in the special economic group Harold Wilson had established. All I knew of this was what I learned from Tommy Balogh and from the press. Cabinet only heard about the budget on the day before it was presented to Parliament. So we were completely excluded from the general economic planning.

This was equally true with regard to defence policy. I admit that before he went to Washington the Prime Minister did give us an account of his view of the independent nuclear deterrent. But there was no paper and he spoke his piece very rapidly in Cabinet and got it agreed to. After that, two defence issues were brought to Cabinet: the future of the HS-681 – brought to Cabinet too late to reverse – and the future of the TSR2. On the TSR2 I have described how each of us was made to make up his mind on three alternatives formulated by the PM.

The other big issue brought up to Cabinet was my housing programme. The reason it came to Cabinet was of course because there was a disagreement between the Chancellor and myself. I got the policy through as a result of the firm support of the PM and an alliance with George Brown. But even so we had some difficulty, because all the other departmental ministers resented seeing Housing get more money at the cost of their own budgets. That is why Barbara Castle is against me, for instance.

I think I have listed the main decisions which were the result of genuine collective Cabinet action. Harold Wilson, at the centre of things, has certainly allowed some of us a great deal of Ministerial freedom in forging our own departmental policies. Nevertheless, I would say that he has completely dominated foreign affairs and defence, as well as all the main economic decisions. Here the Cabinet has been excluded and the PM has played the formative role by arbitrating the struggle between George Brown and Callaghan.

However, even in the areas in which he runs his prime ministerial government a few formal occasions have been interspersed on which he has chosen to have a demonstration of Cabinet government in action. On these occasions he hasn't 'taken the voices'. He has added up the opinions and listed them on a piece of paper. Indeed, I have seen him take pleasure in getting a tie and then forcing us to resolve a closely fought-out decision by a personal vote from each of us.

Thursday, 28 July 1966
This incident also reveals something about Cabinet government. The Prime Minister has suddenly become weak and the ministry with big departments, like George Brown and Callaghan, are now stronger than he is. So he must try to square them and the whole Cabinet on every minor issue. Sometimes he is tossed about like a cork on the water.

The Mackintosh and Crossman argument about overweening prime ministerialism was controversial. One academic in particular, Professor George Jones, wrote a sharp response, arguing that every example claimed and every argument made by the proponents of prime ministerialism was far less clear-cut than they presented it, and that ultimately a prime minister could be 'only as strong as [his colleagues] let him be'.[17]

It has become part of the conventional wisdom expressed by some academics and journalists that the position of the prime minister in the British system of government has altered significantly in recent years. No longer, they assert, is he merely *primus inter pares* or just the leading member of the Cabinet, but he has been transformed into something quite new, perhaps a quasi-president, or an elected monarch or even an autocrat. The prime minister's predominance, attained by Churchill during the Second World War, is said to have persisted in peace-time during the administrations of Attlee, Churchill again, Eden, Macmillan and Douglas-Home and now Wilson. If this view is correct then Cabinet government is a dignified façade behind which lurks the efficient secret of prime ministerial power...

* * *

But even with the scanty evidence at present before us, there are grounds to argue that the prime minister's power has been exaggerated and that the restraints on his ascendancy are as strong as ever, and in some ways even stronger.

* * *

The prime minister has no executive powers vested in him. To achieve anything he must work with and through his ministers who have executive power vested in them. These men have powerful and independent departments to brief them and possess significant followings in their party who hope to see their man one day leader. To

---

[17] G. W. Jones, 'The Prime Minister's Power', in Anthony King (ed.), *The British Prime Minister: A Reader*, Macmillan, London, 1969, pp. 168, 169, 183, 186, 187, 189–90.

become and remain prime minister a man must carry these major colleagues, who are his rivals, with him. He cannot dictate to them, but must co-operate, consult and negotiate with them and even at times defer to them. Cabinet government and collective responsibility are not defunct notions. Shared responsibility is still meaningful, for a prime minister has to gain the support of the bulk of his Cabinet to carry out his policies. He has to persuade it and convince it that he is right. Its meetings do not merely follow his direction. Debate and conflict are frequent. It cannot be by-passed and he cannot be an autocrat. To attempt to become one presages his political suicide.

The prime minister is the leading figure in the Cabinet whose voice carries most weight. But he is not the all powerful individual which many have recently claimed him to be. His office has great potentialities, but the use made of them depends on many variables in the personality, temperament, and ability of the prime minister, what he wants to achieve and the methods he uses. It depends also on his colleagues, their personalities, temperaments, and abilities, what they want to do and their methods. A prime minister who can carry his colleagues with him can be in a very powerful position, but he is only as strong as they let him be.

* * *

The two instances always quoted to show the great scope of prime ministerial power, the decision to produce atomic weapons and to carry out the Suez venture, have been presented in a very biased way. The decision to produce atomic weapons was taken after thorough discussion in the Defence Committee of the Cabinet;[18] it was circulated in the Cabinet agenda, but not discussed in the Cabinet because the decision was accepted by Cabinet ministers; the decision

[18] In fact, two Cabinet committees – GEN75 and GEN163 – did the work on atomic weapons, and not the Defence Committee. This only became known when the files were declassified.

was also announced to Parliament, and again no discussion took place because at that time in 1948 there was no significant opposition to the manufacture by Britain of such weapons. The Suez affair was not the personal policy of the Prime Minister. The policy was discussed and initiated in a committee of the Cabinet, comprising the chief men in the Cabinet; the full Cabinet was kept informed about the committee's decisions, and objections seem to have been raised by a few members; but clearly the majority of the Cabinet was behind the policy of the committee. Thus in neither case were these decisions taken solely by the Prime Minister. He had to carry with him his chief colleagues and the majority of the Cabinet.

* * *

None of the ministers who were dismissed or retired after disagreement with the Cabinet in the post-war years were men of sufficient standing in their parties to present a significant challenge to the Prime Ministers, with the exception perhaps of Aneurin Bevan. No Prime Minister threw out or forced the resignation of a man who had support enough to displace him. Even in the July purge of 1962 no serious contender for the leadership was removed. The Prime Minister took care to keep in the Cabinet his main rivals. His display of butchery illustrated further the limitations of his freedom of action. It did not enhance his position, rather it damaged an already fading reputation.

* * *

The only Prime Minister who claimed that he was more than *primus inter pares* and acted as such by for example interfering and fussing with ministers and their departments was Sir Anthony Eden. His activities did not gain him the support of his colleagues, and he can hardly be called one of the more successful prime ministers of Britain.

In the second volume of his diaries, Crossman had been moved out of a department, and become Lord President of the Council and Leader of the House of Commons. His new role put him on more Cabinet committees and allowed him to take a broader view over government policy, but his interest in the mechanics remained undiminished.[19]

Sunday, 25 September 1966
The only central direction this government has consists of the PM surrounded by a few staff – Marcia Williams, George Wigg, Tommy Balogh, and Burke Trend from the civil service. But the whole of Whitehall has revolted against this idea of strong prime ministerial government. Central coherent purpose was, after all, the main thing which Harold laid down as the characteristic which distinguished our method of government from the spasmodic drooling of the Tories; now we are drooling in a not very dissimilar way. I've got another personal anxiety. When I think about life now, when I think that here I am, Lord President of the Council, in Harold's Labour government, I feel no relief. I don't feel I'm part of a government pledged to fundamental change, with any idea of where it's going. When I'm in Cabinet I'm just sitting with a number of men who are running their departments. And, strangely enough, just because we won an election, these men now feel that they can relax because they have five years ahead of them as ministers. Personally, I don't feel very good just being a senior Minister unless I'm a member of a team determined to substitute central purposive direction for the old easy-going muddle-through. Though I'm devoted to Harold I know I'm working with a Prime Minister who has no more purposive direction than Macmillan had – rather less, I suspect – perhaps the same as Douglas-Home. He's enormously skilled and clever but he

[19] Richard Crossman, *The Diaries of a Cabinet Minister, Volume Two: Lord President of the Council and Leader of the House of Commons, 1966–68*, Hamish Hamilton, London, 1976, pp. 51, 324–25.

hasn't an idea how to construct the vital central machine of control. The strange thing is that the Cabinet would be entirely willing to accept central direction from No. 10 because this will make the Cabinet system work and also because my colleagues want to survive and feel that they can't go on muddling through. They shared Harold Wilson's illusion that all that was necessary was for him to get into No. 10 instead of a Tory prime minister and then everything would automatically change. But of course since 1964 nothing has really changed. We're still working from hand to mouth trying to overcome the immediate short-term problems. It's true that departmentally in Housing and Education and Social Security things are not going too badly. It's at the centre, where strong strategic purpose is essential, that the failure lies.

Sunday, 23 April 1967
I'm interested enough in politics this weekend to put down some reflections about the problem of leaks from the Cabinet. These have now become an important fact in our Cabinet behaviour. Harold often says he can't discuss things in Cabinet because of the leaks. When he does so, four members out of five in the Cabinet would reply that 'the leaks are chiefly the result of your setting the example'. Certainly in his early days in No. 10 Harold set a new standard of press relations – talking and feeding out to the press and discussing his new ideas with them. When I became Lord President he'd cut himself off from the press. He held no Lobby conferences but only had selected pressmen occasionally down to Chequers. Now he does a lot more. He still has Trevor Lloyd-Hughes running his prime ministerial press service from No. 10, he still has Gerald Kaufman, and he still has George Wigg operating in the background. In addition he now has me running my weekly press conference on Thursday and doing quite a number of jobs for him as well.

This is keenly felt by the rest of Cabinet and I'm sure that many ministers talk to the press in order to counter the influence of No. 10. Sometimes they do it to counter the influence of another ministry. Recently, for example, we have had weeks on end when the press has been full of leaks and counter-leaks from the Ministry of Labour and the D.E.A.[20] about the prices and incomes policy which was being discussed in a Cabinet committee. This has given Harold the excuse for keeping vital issues out of Cabinet and that brings me to the fight about devaluation. Devaluation had never been discussed in Cabinet since last July. In order to have some discussion of the subject, at least by the inner Cabinet, S.E.P.[21] was created but we've never discussed devaluation in S.E.P. We were due to discuss it time after time but it's always been postponed. Harold actually told me when I was talking to him on Friday that I had been expected to raise the issue at the last S.E.P. and that he and the Chancellor had agreed that if I did so Jim would take a sealed envelope out of his pocket in order to discuss it with me. In fact I had no idea of what I was expected to do so I didn't raise the issue and he didn't need his sealed envelope. This shows how careful and calculating Harold is in avoiding unpalatable discussions. He only revealed all this when on Friday I'd asked him about how devaluation could best be raised at the Chequers' conference on the Common Market. He told me to raise it when the officials were not present on the Sunday and then went on to tell me that he and the Chancellor had looked at the problem very carefully and at the moment there wasn't any necessity. On the other hand, there may well have to be a degree of devaluation before we go in and there was a certain risk that even the announcement of our intended entry would produce a run on the pound. He made it perfectly clear that these are things he felt perfectly entitled to keep from Cabinet and discuss with the Chancellor alone.

[20] Department for Economic Affairs.
[21] Steering Committee on Economic Policy.

One of the most controversial claims in Crossman's diaries was that the Cabinet minutes did not always accurately represent either the discussion, or agreements reached.[22]

Thursday, 17 November 1966
Cabinet. Before we got back to our PESC[23] discussion the Prime Minister had decided to take my procedure package of parliamentary reform. Actually it took nearly two hours and was a ghastly discussion. How ghastly you certainly wouldn't get an idea from the Cabinet minutes. Discussing how to handle our colleagues, John and I had decided that the order of presentation was extremely important and I would start with morning sittings, then deal with Standing Order No. 9 and finally discuss the Specialist Committees. The Cabinet minutes merely attribute to me the brief which I took with me of which I didn't read a single word because I knew it was unsuitable. The official minutes even change the order of the items on the agenda so that they agree with the brief. According to the minutes Specialist Committees come first and then morning sittings. I record this because it's important to remember how little historians can trust Cabinet minutes to tell what really went on. What they do tell is what went on according to the officials and the official briefs.

In his biography of Crossman, his former Parliamentary Private Secretary Tam Dalyell (1932–) supported the claims about Cabinet minutes.[24]

---

[22] Richard Crossman, *The Diaries of a Cabinet Minister, Volume Two: Lord President of the Council and Leader of the House of Commons, 1966–68*, Hamish Hamilton, London, 1976, p. 129.
[23] Public Expenditure Survey Committee.
[24] Tam Dalyell, *Dick Crossman: A Portrait*, Weidenfeld & Nicolson, London, 1989, pp. 235–36.

There was another delicate matter, a supremely delicate matter, which caused Crossman a kind of sotto-voce deep-felt concern that is unusual in ministers, who have so many worries that they do not want gratuitous trouble. This was the accuracy of the Cabinet minutes. Crossman used the word 'travesty' about them. They did not, according to him, even attempt to be an account of what actually took place in Cabinet. I was not in Cabinet, but from March 1965 until the fall of the Labour government in 1970, I saw a great many, though not all, Cabinet minutes. From what other members of the Cabinet said to me and to other members of the PLP, the minutes did not tally with what had taken place in the Labour Cabinet. The minutes, submitted by the Cabinet Secretary, the late Lord Trend, were an amalgam of the official brief which a minister took along to Cabinet, the official papers on the original policy, and the official conclusions. The minutes failed to describe the real struggle which, according to Callaghan, Barbara Castle and George Brown off the record, had in fact taken place. The abstracts anaesthetized the ministers' contributions and usually did not identify who had said what. This had the effect of enormously strengthening the civil service against the politicians. Though Crossman was to make little progress against an increasingly Burke Trend / civil-service-orientated Prime Minister, the *Diaries* did expose this situation. I believe that after the *Diaries* were published, the Conservative opposition studied what Crossman had said, and vowed to take action against the civil service.

In the third volume of his diaries, Crossman began to reflect on the downside to being a minister – the exhaustion and detachment from everyday life. Back in a department, initially as an 'overlord' responsible for bringing together the Ministries of Health and Social Security, he remained fascinated by machinery of government issues. The excerpt from January 1970 refers to a meeting where the Cabinet agreed on regional reorganisation outside local government; according to Crossman, Barbara Castle had been verbose and unprepared.[25]

Tuesday, 29 October 1968

It happened again this morning at Cabinet, where it was felt that if the inner group chaired by the PM had decided Cabinet could only accede. Here we see another interesting constitutional development, the setting-up of these inner groups. The first two that I went for, S.E.P. and the Parliamentary Committee, were attempts at an inner Cabinet that, because they were official Committees, rapidly extended themselves to include more than half the Cabinet. So we moved back to the old situation where there are small groups of ministers close to Harold, groups that are not even given names. It is 'the ministers most closely affected have been meeting'. There are four of these: a little group who meet about the economic situation, certainly an inner defence group smaller than O.P.D.[26], the informal group on Rhodesia, which is now never discussed, as it used to be, at the special O.P.D. committee but is dealt with by the PM and his closest friends and then presented as a *fait accompli* to the Cabinet, and now this inner group on the constitution.

Tuesday, 10 June 1969

We are supposed to be drifting near the edge of disaster but at these meetings where we chat together we are borne along by the structure of Whitehall politics and Whitehall administration. It isn't of course only Whitehall. It's the black cars, the departments, the standing in Parliament, buoying us up and insulating ministers against shocks to an extraordinary degree. Every now and again the real world

---

[25] Richard Crossman, *The Diaries of a Cabinet Minister, Volume 3: Secretary of State for Social Services, 1968–70,* Hamish Hamilton, London, 1977, p. 243, p. 511, p. 567, p. 784.
[26] Overseas Policy and Defence Committee.

impinges on us but only when Whitehall and Westminster politics require it to do so. And this means that although we have ceased to be an effective government or to have any authority we are quietly carrying on in this quiet atmosphere, feeling ourselves, as we did this morning, secure and relaxed.

Sunday, 13 July 1969
I personally feel very much that five years in government as a top Cabinet minister is long enough for anybody. I am not browned off but I am certainly not as alert as I was. I drive hard at the Ministry, I have gained by experience but, heavens alive, the excitement of the first eighteen months isn't there any more and I have ploughed into the Cabinet Minister's routine. This is where I think there is a lot to commend the British system, where five or six years is a government's normal life and it has to struggle hard and be very lucky to have a second term.

Thursday, 15 January 1970
Afterwards Harold ran into me and said, 'In twelve minutes you got the biggest change in the Health Service for twenty years and you did it because you prepared well.' It is also clear to me now how important a factor it is in a Cabinet struggle to have the Cabinet Secretariat on your side. The reason is very simple. The Cabinet Secretariat briefs the PM on these things. They brief him on Barbara and me and, if you get Burke on your side by doing your homework, being conscientious in committee and getting a good reputation in Whitehall, the PM's brief is favourable. I am rather pleased to find my reputation is good on this particular difficult work on the reconstruction of the Health Service. It gives me an enormous advantage in the battle for power.

In early 1968 major cuts had to be made to public expenditure. In the end, the Cabinet backed a delay in raising the school leaving age. The decision was controversial in itself, but was made even more so by Education Secretary Patrick Gordon Walker's decision to support the Chancellor's cuts. This extract from the diaries of Tony Benn (1925–), the Minister of Technology, gives some indication of how visceral that anger was. In answer to a question, Gordon Walker (1907–80) had just said he'd prefer to delay raising the school leaving age to cutting funding to universities.[27]

Friday, 5 January 1968
George Brown exploded, 'May God forgive you. You send *your* children to university and you would put the interests of the school kids below that of the universities.' It took some time to restore order. George then continued his attack, in which he said that education was the basis of class in Britain and if we denied these kids the opportunity of staying in school for an extra year, we would be perpetuating class distinctions.

In his 1973 book about the Cabinet, Patrick Gordon Walker defended his decision on education cuts, arguing that he was simply behaving collectively rather than departmentally. But the book was a more academic exercise than that, and he sought to dismiss allegations that an inner Cabinet of powerful ministers had effectively replaced the full Cabinet during the Wilson government. Arguing that decisions over the A-bomb and Suez had been misused by proponents of prime ministerialism, he said they were instead cases of 'partial Cabinets'.[28]

---

[27] Tony Benn, *Office Without Power, Diaries 1968–72*, Hutchinson, London, 1988, p. 6.
[28] Patrick Gordon Walker, *The Cabinet* (revised ed.), Heinemann Educational Books, London, 1973, pp. 32, 44, 99–101.

As Secretary of State for Education I did not conceive it as my sole or prime duty to fight all out and at all costs in defence of my departmental estimates as they stood. Each department in my view had to try and forward the government's collective policy by agreeing to accept economies as great as were compatible with the maintenance and, in due course, the renewed advance of the social service concerned. Having secured a considerable scaling down of the original proposals for a four-year postponement of the raising of the school-leaving age and for cuts in capital investment in the universities, I agreed to lesser reductions in both these expenditures as being on a par with those made in defence and the other social services as necessary, with those other savings, to reach the desired target of economies. This attempt to take a governmental and not merely a departmental line was not popular amongst all departmental ministers and was attacked by some of them. About half the ministers in charge of spending departments took a line similar to mine. The proportion, I understand, was about the same in post-war Conservative Cabinets, when similar issues arose.

* * *

The term 'inner Cabinet' is a misnomer. It is in no sense a Cabinet and must be distinguished from a Cabinet committee. An inner Cabinet has no organic or set place in the Cabinet structure: it is no more than an informal, small group of friends, or confidants of the Prime Minister drawn from members of his Cabinet. It is not formally set up; it has no papers and records; it is not served by the Cabinet Secretariat. An inner Cabinet as such has no power, no place in the hierarchy of political authority. It may, amongst other things, discuss questions coming before the Cabinet; but only to cement the advice the members of the inner Cabinet will tender to their colleagues. An inner Cabinet does not and cannot predigest the business of the Cabinet; nor set it aside or duplicate its work.

* * *

The cases of Attlee and Eden were not therefore startling departures: they fit into a pattern that started earlier and continued later.

I myself knew about the decision to make the atom bomb. The use of the Woomera range in Australia was involved and as Commonwealth Secretary I was a member of the Cabinet Committee dealing with the matter. We were making decisions that were continuous, highly technical and which related to military and scientific secrets of other countries besides our own. There was no question of the Prime Minister alone making decisions. A number of senior ministers shared in every decision. When the minutes of the committee were before the Cabinet, the Prime Minister (as Mr Crossman puts it) 'did not feel it necessary to call attention to this item'. Why should he? The minutes had been circulated to Cabinet ministers, any one of whom could have raised the matter. Ministers receive many such papers or items in the Cabinet agenda. Owing to the composition of the Cabinet committees there can be little doubt, had the matter been raised, that the outcome would have been no different...

Thus the two concrete examples cited as proof of prime ministerial government (and other later examples that could be prayed in aid) turn out to be instances of partial Cabinets – which is something wholly different; for in a partial Cabinet a prime minister cannot act independently and in virtue of his office.

A partial Cabinet contains influential members of the Cabinet who can be said to represent it in the sense that collectively they carry very great influence within it. These members must be unanimous or nearly so before a partial Cabinet can function as such: otherwise there would be no certainty, and indeed little hope, of carrying the Cabinet. Dissenting ministers might well insist on taking the issue straight to the Cabinet. In a partial Cabinet the prime minister's views might be rejected. Where there have been protests in the Cabinet against a partial Cabinet, these have been in reality directed against a particular policy rather than against the method by which it has been reached: this was so in 1911 and over Duff Cooper's resignation in 1938.

A partial Cabinet is the very opposite of prime ministerial government: it presupposes that the prime minister carries influential Cabinet colleagues with him, and that these will, with the prime minister, convince the Cabinet if policy is questioned when the Cabinet is informed. In fact Cabinets of all parties have accepted partial Cabinets as necessary, in proper circumstances, to the conduct of the affairs of the state: just as they accept, for the same reason, the selective distribution of telegrams.

Partial Cabinets, but not prime ministerial government, have become an accepted and established part of the Cabinet system.

George Brown, the brilliant but flawed Deputy Leader of the party, and successively Secretary for Economic Affairs and Foreign Secretary, resigned in 1968. He did so after heated late-night discussions about the decision to grant the US administration its request for a bank holiday the following day. The US made the request in order to make changes to the Gold Pool. This required the currency exchanges to be closed, and the only way to do so was to call a Bank Holiday. Brown protested that the decision had been taken without proper Cabinet consultation. He used his resignation statement to the House of Commons on 18 March 1968 to produce a broader critique of Wilson's style.[29]

I do not propose today to go into the history of my various disagreements with government decisions, and, even more, with the way in which they have been increasingly made and the con-

---

[29] George Brown, *In My Way: The Political Memoirs of Lord George-Brown*, London, Victor Gollancz Ltd., 1971, pp. 180–81.

siderations on which they were so often based. There will be time enough for all that. But in view of some of the wilder speculations and exaggerations over the week-end, I feel I owe it to the House and to my right hon. friends on this side of the House, in particular, and, if I may say so, to myself, to say why I decided to resign at this time.

It was not despite the gravity of the situation; it was, in a sense, because of it. It is in just such a situation that it is essential for Cabinet government to be maintained if democracy is to be assured, and equally it is in just such a situation that temptation to depart from it is at its greatest. Power can very easily pass not merely from Cabinet to one or two ministers, but effectively to sources quite outside the political control altogether.

It is open to anyone to challenge my judgement of the situation on Thursday night, when it was learned that the Prime Minister and two other Ministers were already at the Palace, or to feel that I exaggerated the dangers in it. But I am very conscious of past parallels in my own political lifetime, and felt strongly enough on the issue to gather some of my colleagues together and to protest then. When that protest was virtually brushed aside on the basis that what I had done was in itself irregular, I felt that the time had come to leave the government.

But for what I have read over the weekend, I would feel it quite unnecessary to say that, of course, my purpose in the action I have taken is not to challenge the Prime Minister or to set out to lead a left-wing revolt against the Cabinet.

I had a feeling that that suggestion might have amused and surprised some of my hon. friends, as it did me.

I do, however, feel most strongly that if the authority and success of this government is to be re-established, as, indeed, it must be, then the basis on which they take their decisions must be changed and their communications within the government and with those outside must be greatly improved. Just making what are called tough decisions on occasions, valid as they may be, is not enough. There must be a thread of continuity evident in all that is done.

Barbara Castle's White Paper on industrial relations, In Place of Strife, *provided one of the most contentious episodes of the 1964–70 government. Developed in near-secrecy precisely because it was controversial, the lack of consultation infuriated many Cabinet ministers and one, James Callaghan, voted and spoke against it at a Labour NEC meeting. Tony Benn described the Cabinet meeting immediately following the NEC.*[30]

Thursday, 3 April – Friday, 4 April 1969

The main item was of course the row over Jim Callaghan's behaviour at NEC over Barbara's White Paper. Harold was much more moderate with Jim than I had expected and allowed Jim to get away with an explanation which was simply not true. I am afraid I was rather sharp with him. Barbara was vague and woolly and didn't want any action taken, although if I were her I would have been absolutely furious with Jim. Harold then asked the Cabinet to reaffirm their belief in the White Paper. Jim objected to this and Harold said it was all subject to consultation. We left the meeting without knowing more about where we were than at the beginning. I am afraid Jim is winning.

After the Cabinet Harold leaked the whole thing to the press – about how tough he had been and had warned ministers they would get fired if they didn't stay in line. It was a perfect example of instant politics. It was so disrespectful of Harold to suggest he had kicked his ministers into line.

---

[30] Tony Benn, *Office Without Power, Diaries 1968–72*, Hutchinson, London, 1988, p. 158.

This is the note in the Cabinet minutes of the statement Wilson made to that Cabinet, the substance of which was released to the press.[31]

The Prime Minister said that there had for some time been a growing tendency for some Ministers to act in ways which called in question the collective responsibility of the Cabinet, in so far as they had apparently felt free, in their personal dealings both with members of the PLP and with the press, to dissociate themselves from certain of the government's policies and to allow this to be known to outside bodies particularly the Trade Unions, with whom their colleagues were often conducting difficult and delicate negotiations in the name of the government as a whole. Before a decision was reached on any item on government policy a minister was entitled to defend his own point of view within the Cabinet as strongly and persuasively as he wished. But once a decision had been taken the principle of collective responsibility required every member of an Administration to endorse it and to defend it to any outside body on any occasion, whether private or public. This remained true even if the minister was himself a member of the outside body concerned. There was no objection in principle to ministers retaining affiliations of this kind provided that no conflict of interest or allegiance resulted. But this proviso was especially important in the case of ministers who were members of the National Executive Committee of the Labour Party (NEC), where any clash of loyalties was liable to be particularly embarrassing. It had to be recognised that the NEC's concept of its relationship to the Parliamentary Party had changed since the Labour Party became the government party. During the Labour government of 1945–51 the Executive would never have sought to enforce a decision of the annual conference of the party on

---

[31] Sir Harold Wilson, *The Governance of Britain*, Weidenfeld & Nicolson, London, 1976, pp. 191–92.

the government. And even in 1960, when the Labour Party were in Opposition, the Executive had refused to try to impose the decisions of the conference on the PLP. Now, however, it was seeking to assert a right to withhold support from the government on issues on which the annual conference had not yet expressed a view.

It would be unfortunate if circumstances developed, perhaps later in the year, in which it proved impossible to deal with this situation except by means of a ruling that no member of the Cabinet might offer himself for election to the NEC. He himself would greatly regret it if he were forced to give such a ruling, since the result would be not only to weaken the links between the government and the NEC but also to reduce the latter to a body which was competent merely to discuss and to protest but not to exercise influence or to accept responsibility. Nevertheless, this situation could be avoided only if ministers themselves recognised and accepted that, where any conflict of loyalties arose, the principle of the collective responsibility of the government was absolute and overriding in all circumstances and that, if any ministers felt unable to subscribe to this principle without reservation, it was his duty to resign his office forthwith.

In his official biography of James Callaghan, historian Kenneth O. Morgan argued that the outcome of the In Place of Strife *crisis demolished Crossman's thesis about overweening prime ministerialism.*[32]

In the event, Wilson lost control of his parliamentary supporters, and his Cabinet; he could never remotely claim to have control over the unions. It was all a remarkable demolition of Crossman's thesis, outlined in a republication of Walter Bagehot's *English Constitution*,

---

[32] Kenneth O. Morgan, *Callaghan: A Life*, Oxford University Press, Oxford, 1997, pp. 341–42.

to the effect that Cabinet government had been replaced by prime ministerial government, and that the Cabinet was joining the House of Lords and the monarchy as 'dignified' rather than 'efficient' parts of the constitution. It was a view publicised also by Professor Mackintosh, in a lengthy work on *The Cabinet* . . . Callaghan's demonstration that, at a time of crisis, a senior figure could have more authority over the Cabinet than the Prime Minister himself emphatically disproved both authors.

Wilson was normally able to handle Cabinet with skill, though. This is how Bruce-Gardyne and Lawson described the first (and only) meeting formally to consider devaluation, and how he allowed it to get sidetracked by a demand from Richard Crossman for an inner Cabinet.[33]

Wilson seized on the second leg of the argument, insisting that, if a wider circle were drawn in, there would be 'leaks'. Crossman was played with great finesse; and when Wilson eventually conceded the committee (having, as we have seen, already privately assured Callaghan that, so far from broadening the economic policy power centre, he would narrow it from the triumvirate to a duumvirate), Crossman was convinced that he and his friends had won a famous victory. The Strategic Economic Policy Committee (SEP) was duly constituted, packed with such luminaries as the Secretaries of State for Scotland and Wales, and disappeared from sight. (From time to time in the year that followed Crosland valiantly attempted to raise the issue devaluation in SEP, but no one took any notice.)

Wilson frequently used constitutional fixes for dealing with political

---

[33] Jock Bruce-Gardyne and Nigel Lawson, *The Power Game: An Examination of Decision-Making in Government*, Macmillan, London, 1976, pp. 136–37.

problems. The In Place of Strife *debacle prompted another: he wound up one inner Cabinet, the Parliamentary Committee, and set up another, the Management Committee. The intention was to exclude James Callaghan from membership, but Wilson felt himself unable to do so until the Committee had been meeting for several weeks. This is a note from Roger Dawe, the Private Secretary for Economic Affairs in Number 10 to Michael Halls, Wilson's Principal Private Secretary, reporting what Wilson had told reporters about the new committee.*[34]

At his meeting with the Lobby this afternoon the Prime Minister said that he had found the Parliamentary Committee very valuable since it had been set up. He had now decided to constitute a smaller group of 'political heavyweights' who would be concerned with the general political and strategic direction of the government's work. No doubt it would become known as the 'inner Cabinet', although he himself was not calling it this. He would let them know when he thought of a better name!

In answer to supplementary questions on this the Prime Minister made the following points:

1 The Parliamentary Committee would be wound up.
2 The new Committee would number about 7 people.
3 Members of the new Committee would be on the Committee in a personal capacity rather than representing Ministerial offices.
4 The Secretaries of State for Scotland and Wales would be invited for items of interest to them, and the Chief Whip would also be invited for particular items of interest to him. Similarly other Ministers would be invited to attend if any items came up of interest to their departments.
5 The new Committee had not yet met but, informally, had been 'functioning in a sort of way for some time'.

[34] PRO, PREM 13/2512, *Cabinet Committees*, Dawe to Halls, 29 April 1969.

Another reason these experiments with inner Cabinets had relatively short lives was the difficulty Wilson had in keeping people out of them. Here Lord Armstrong of Ilminster (1927–), later a Cabinet Secretary but in the 1960s a civil servant in the Cabinet Office and the Treasury, recalled the institutional and political reasons why such a body was bound to fail.[35]

Mr Wilson at one stage sought to create an inner Cabinet. He called it the Economic Strategy Committee and it was rather a small committee of senior ministers. It started off well, but the trouble was, if you have a formal inner Cabinet like that, it becomes a matter of disgrace to a minister who is not on it and therefore a matter of intense manoeuvring to get on it, and as successively Mr Wilson conceded membership of the Economic Strategy Committee to people to whom it ought never to have been conceded, it ceased to have the virtues and values that an inner Cabinet undoubtedly can have.

It wasn't just inner Cabinets with which Wilson experimented. Like Lloyd George before him, Wilson was heavily criticised for the purported influence of what the press dubbed his 'kitchen cabinet'. One member of this coterie, the Hungarian economist/adviser Tommy Balogh (1905–85), was singled out for particular attention. Yet when the memoirs began appearing, his role was frequently downplayed. This is Marcia Williams (1932–), later Lady Falkender, Wilson's Political Secretary and a hugely controversial figure herself.[36]

---

[35] Nigel Lawson and Lord Armstrong of Ilminster, 'Cabinet Government in the Thatcher Years', *Contemporary Record*, Vol 8, Winter 1994, Number 3, p. 451.
[36] Marcia Williams, *Inside Number 10*, Weidenfeld & Nicolson, London, 1972, p. 52.

The story was that Thomas somehow dominated No. 10 and Harold's economic thinking in a sinister, Rasputin-like fashion. It is true that his contribution in economic thinking at No. 10 was invaluable and his analyses were extremely accurate. But what is equally true is that Thomas was never as fully integrated in the team surrounding the Prime Minister as people imagine he was.

Although it calmed down later, at the start of his premiership, Wilson's 'kitchen cabinet' fought running battles with the civil service over matters large and small. For example, Whitehall had put up formidable resistance to some of Wilson's early appointments. He did not always, or easily, roll over: this is an early minute he wrote to Sir Lawrence Helsby (1908–78), Head of the Home Civil Service, about the employment of Michael Halls as Principal Private Secretary.[37]

If I am told that this is a question of patronage and challenged to choose between prime ministerial patronage and patronage exercised by a small, self-perpetuating oligarchy of permanent secretaries, I have no alternative but to say that patronage, if patronage it be, must be exercised by me.

I certainly cannot accept the implied suggestion that such an appointment would imply a deterioration of standards since the arrival of the present administration. I do not know whether the system you extol was responsible, or whether there was at work a system not merely of prime ministerial patronage, but prime ministerial *political* patronage, but the fact remains that of four secretaries in post up to October 1963, the two most senior are now on the short list for adoption as candidates in safe Conservative seats, a third, recruited direct from Conservative Central Office to Mr Macmillan's Private

---

[37] Philip Ziegler, *Wilson: The Authorised Life of Lord Wilson of Rievaulx*, Weidenfeld & Nicolson, London, 1993, pp. 213–14.

Office, now takes the Conservative whip in the Upper House. My suggested appointment has no political implications, I have not the slightest idea of the political views, if any, of the five I saw.

But I do not regard the appointment as patronage, reward for past services, or as a promise for the future, still less an intellectual accolade comparable to a Fellowship of All Souls. I regard it as the means of ensuring that my office will work . . . as efficiently, smoothly and agreeably as possible. What I want is a private secretary, actual or in embryo. No. 10 is an office, not a government department; it is also a small and necessarily intimate community – it is also a home.

Despite his experience as a civil servant and Cabinet Minister and the thought he evidently gave the matter before his accession to the office, Wilson's administrative reputation as Prime Minister is as poor as his political reputation. Peter Hennessy provides a fairly typical assessment.[38]

Wilson bids fair to be the untidiest of all the postwar premiers in administrative terms despite his pride in his housetraining. This really was quite extraordinary for someone who had sat at the feet of Edward Bridges in the War Cabinet Office and it sustains the justice of that still vivid political folk-memory, observed by Peter Riddell even in the mid 1990s, 'of the confusion and incoherence which so undermined Harold Wilson's government'. It was as if he were the bureaucratic equivalent of an experiment-crazed boffin. He reckoned 'overlords' were 'a system which I believe, in general, to be unworkable under our administrative parliamentary system'. Yet he made Douglas Houghton an 'overlord' in all but name for both Health and Social Security in July 1965 as Chancellor of the Duchy[39]

---

[38] Peter Hennessy, *The Prime Minister: The office and its holders since 1945*, Penguin, London, 2000, p. 310.
[39] of Lancaster.

and, in effect, that is what he made himself when he 'took control' of the DEA in particular and the economy in general in September 1967. And in 1968 Wilson privately described Crossman as '"overlord" for the social services' when he began the process of merging Health and Social Security into a single DHSS.

As for reshuffles, he made the practice so frequent that Roy Jenkins later referred to them as Wilson's 'annual gymkhana'. The fun-filled pains he took over these exercises is evident from the files of his earliest ones, which have reached the Public Record Office.

Seven years after he had first aired his thoughts on Cabinet government, and after six years in the Cabinet, Richard Crossman was asked to give the 1970 series of Godkin lectures at Harvard University. Crossman was ideally placed to add an expert insider's account to the observer's analysis he had previously offered. It is hard to find dramatic differences, particularly when Crossman was answering a question about the Prime Minister's power to sum up after a Cabinet meeting.[40]

Crossman: So the moral of this is that prime ministers must sum up properly. Once the prime minister has summed up, though it may not represent the discussion at all, once he sums up, the secretary to the Cabinet will record it in the peculiar style evolved for Cabinet minutes – impersonal, dry, flat, and precise, duly divided into conclusions and decisions – translated in fact from the prime minister's own words into the language of a civil service directive. So what it comes to is this: if the prime minister lost his nerve and failed to formulate the conclusion and decision required and then wanted to have it recorded that he had done so, the secretary might very well say, 'I must have a minute instructing me to correct.'

---

[40] Richard Crossman, *Inside View*, Jonathan Cape, London, 1972, pp. 50–51, 46, 64–65.

Q: ... In this process, am I right in understanding that the prime minister does not run things by the formality of motion, amendments and votes, but by interpreting a consensus, and this gives him a lot of flexibility?

Crossman: In our system there are no formal votes, amendments or resolutions at all. There is an agenda which is decided by the prime minister. There are papers but there are no motions.

Now, if you ask me, does the PM sometimes insist that everybody declare themselves, I should guess he probably does if he wants to make sure where each man stands on a difficult issue.

But it is always understood in British Cabinet life that the prime minister can define the consensus as being what he thinks fit. Even though a majority of the opinions expressed were against him, that would not necessarily prevent him from deciding as he wishes – if he can get away with it. How much he uses this power is up to his own discretion, his estimate of how far he can take his colleagues with him. But he certainly does not rely on formal voting, written resolutions or amendments.

* * *

I remember Aneurin Bevan once saying to me, 'You know, Dick, there are only two ways of getting into the Cabinet. Once way is to crawl up the staircase of preferment on your belly; the other way is to kick them in the teeth. But,' he said, 'for God's sake, don't mix the two methods.' That remark contains a great truth about the way a British Cabinet is chosen. It contains within it quite a number of enemies of the prime minister and rivals who would be too dangerous outside. As Bagehot said, 'the first ten people in the Cabinet pick themselves'; they have got to be there, either because they are indispensable, or because they are political enemies. After that the prime minister will draw the teeth from the back benches as far as he can by bringing the talent available into the Cabinet.

* * *

Collective responsibility now means something totally different. It means that everybody who is in the government must accept and publicly support every Cabinet decision, even if he was not present at the discussion or, frequently, was completely unaware the decision had been taken. As we have seen, collective decision-taking is now fragmented, and many major decisions may be taken by two, three, four or five ministers. But the moment they have been taken, *and minuted*, they have the force of a decision taken by the whole Cabinet, and are binding on a hundred-odd members of the government.

This is an interesting transformation of the old notion of collective responsibility, and it enormously increased prime ministerial power. There is all the difference in the world between a prime minister who had to carry twenty colleagues with him when anything of importance was being decided, and a new-style prime minister who has appointed some eighty members of his government, each with a specific job to do, each permitted to hear only after the event nine-tenths of the decisions for which he shares collective responsibility. It is by this transformation that Cabinet government, in my view, has been evolved into what I call prime ministerial government.

When Crossman gave his lectures, he was still a member of the government, and had to submit them for approval. They spurred an interesting debate within the civil service. This is from a note by Sir Burke Trend, the Cabinet Secretary, to Wilson, about the section about Prime Minister and Cabinet.[41]

[41] PRO, PREM 13/3352, Trend to Wilson, 2 April 1970.

I think that we are bound to ask Mr Crossman to revise these passages and to give greater emphasis both to the role of the prime minister as an independent chairman of the Cabinet, with the responsibility of securing a balanced decision, and to the role of the Cabinet Secretariat as objective recorders of the course of any particular discussion. In this connection, it is curious that, although the text contains one – rather perfunctory – bow towards the concept of collective ministerial responsibility, it makes no reference at all to the complementary principle of individual ministerial responsibility. As a result it greatly exaggerates the importance of Cabinet minutes, since it fails to point out that, although those minutes provide ministers and departments with a useful means of confirming that they are doing the right thing, it is nevertheless the responsibility of ministers themselves, as soon as they leave the Cabinet room, to give whatever instructions are necessary to ensure that the Cabinet's decisions are carried out . . . It is also curious that Mr Crossman does not once refer, throughout this lecture, to the significant difference that a British prime minister can choose the date of a general election whereas an American president cannot. But I do not think that it is for me to put that point to Mr Crossman!

William Armstrong (1915–80), Head of the Home Civil Service, had this to say about Crossman's comments on the role of the Cabinet Office.[42]

The general tone of pages 21–23, which imply that the Cabinet Office sticks at nothing in its sole loyalty to the Prime Minister (even to the extent of fudging Cabinet conclusions) could bear some revisions.

---

[42] PRO, PREM 13/3352, Ministers, Armstrong to Andrews, 1 April 1970.

In this passage, first published in 1969, David Butler, the most authoritative post-war psephologist, explained in electoral terms the growth of prime ministerialism described by Crossman.[43]

A large part of modern British electioneering displays the personalities of the two main leaders. The prime minister or, to a lesser extent, the alternative prime minister are now seen as very much more than the 'first among equals' of the traditional textbooks. The increasing complexity of government and the extension of the system of Cabinet committees have made the premier appear more and more presidential. His share in the moulding of his party's image is much enhanced by the coming of new styles of journalism and even more by the advent of television. It is understandable that pre-eminent electoral importance should often be attributed to the rival leaders.

Harold Wilson published a memoir of the 1964–70 Labour government very shortly after leaving office. In it, he responded to George Brown's accusations about dictatorial personal government, and set out his case for an inner Cabinet, reversing the position he had taken before becoming PM.[44]

George Brown's explanation of his resignation related his decision to complaints of a presidential, indeed dictatorial, government. When Michael Stewart arrived at the Foreign Office and met George there he rebuked him, in his crispest pedagogical manner, for these references. They were, indeed, a little hard to understand since George, only a few days earlier, had in a private talk criticised my

---

[43] David Butler and Donald Stokes, *Political Change in Britain: The Evolution of Electoral Choice* (second ed.), Macmillan, London, 1974, p. 351
[44] Harold Wilson, *The Labour Government 1964–1970: A Personal Record*, Weidenfeld & Nicolson, London, 1971, pp. 512, 523–24.

style of government. He had been pressing me to take more decisions myself and not to refer so many issues for collective decision by the Cabinet or Cabinet committees. Every prime minister sitting in that chair, he said, would run No. 10 in a different way; were he there he would take more of the decisions. 'Alone,' I asked, 'or in consultation with the Deputy Leader?' George found that an embarrassing question. But throughout my premiership he had found my desire to refer major issues for collective discussion irksome.

* * *

I had often been attracted, as is every prime minister, by the idea of a smaller Cabinet, not just marginally smaller by one or two, but something not much larger than half the average size of a post-war Cabinet. On this occasion I made a real effort to see whether I could appoint a Cabinet of no more than eleven or so – with other departmental heads outside the Cabinet – along the lines of the two, very differing, War Cabinets in two world wars. But when I drew up such a list, the impossibility became clear. A Cabinet as small as eleven is possible only if it consists almost exclusively of two or three key departmental heads, such as the foreign secretary and chancellor, together with non-departmental ministers and 'overlords' (in the first Churchill Cabinet even the chancellor was not a member). But all experience was against the appointment of 'overlords', with the divided responsibility between an ivory tower chief on the one hand and, on the other, ministers with statutory duties responsible to Parliament. There is another problem. Prime ministers who have tried to keep numbers down by leaving out of the Cabinet the minister ultimately responsible for, say, education, agriculture or transport, have alienated very important interests, indeed essential components of our society – as witness Sir Winston Churchill's exclusion of Education from the Cabinet in 1951. Equally, I felt that the Board of Trade, with its responsibility for exports, could not be omitted. Trying to work to a list of eleven or twelve, which I prepared as an experiment, proved conclusively that my hopes must remain unrealised.

Instead I set up the equivalent of an inner Cabinet, or Parliamentary Committee as it was officially called. It was not intended in any way to replace the Cabinet. It did not take decisions, but it was to give a more coherent political direction to the work of the government and to ensure that decisions taken with insufficient thought of parliamentary reactions were more carefully worked out in their political context, not least so far as timing was concerned.

Under their new leader, Edward Heath (1916–), the Conservative opposition had been working hard on policies for the next general election, due in 1970 or 1971. A chance conversation between Crossman and Heath just months before Heath became Prime Minister indicated how radically the Conservatives had been looking at reform of central government, and within months Heath would be in a position to put his ideas into practice.[45]

Tuesday, 4 November 1969
I went back to the House and ran into Heath walking along the passage. For once we got into conversation and I said, 'Back at school. I always feel one can manage the department nicely until Parliament starts.' 'Yes,' he said. 'Why on earth haven't you taken the opportunity to relieve yourself of that problem?' 'What do you mean?' I said. 'Why haven't you arranged to have ministers outside the House of Commons?' I really was surprised. Ministers outside? 'Oh, no,' I said, 'I don't want that at all. I find it a strain but I wouldn't lose my position in the Commons for anything.' Heath

---

[45] Richard Crossman, *The Diaries of a Cabinet Minister, Volume 3: Secretary of State for Social Services, 1968–70*, Hamish Hamilton, London, 1977, p. 716.

pursed his lips and I suddenly realized he had let out something he really meant. He would like an American presidential system with ministers outside the House and suddenly he had let his guard down and said something true about himself.[46] He won't say anything to me again for five or six months, I know that very well.

---

[46] Heath did not pursue the matter further when he became Prime Minister.

9
Seventies stress, 1970–1979

When he entered Number 10 after the 1970 general election, in administrative terms Edward Heath was arguably the best-prepared Prime Minister ever. He believed that the problem of 'overload' had become acute, and had used the period in opposition to consider changes he wished to make to the functioning of central government. Out of this review came changes to the civil service and the creation of a Central Policy Review Staff. In this memorandum to his most senior colleagues, Heath outlined what he expected their contribution would be.[1]

Now that the main Cabinet committees have been constituted I should like to remind my colleagues of the importance of ensuring that all the main issues of government policy are fully examined by the appropriate committees before they are submitted to the Cabinet. Where possible they should be decided by the committee concerned; and questions should only be referred upwards to Cabinet if they are of major importance or involve sensitive political issues. The right of all ministers to appeal to the Cabinet will, of course, remain unimpaired. But I hope that they will use this right sparingly; and I shall normally be guided by the view of a committee chairman in deciding whether an appeal to the Cabinet should be

[1] PRO, PREM 15/11, Setting up and structure of Cabinet committees under new Administration, CP (70), Note by the Prime Minister, July 1970.

allowed. Once we have taken a decision we must stick to it. We must also ensure that it has the maximum impact on public opinion; and I ask my colleagues, therefore, to take particular care to make certain that the Lord President's Office is informed in adequate time of all forthcoming announcements of policy in order that the Lord President may consider both their presentation and their most appropriate timing.

It is understandable that under pressure of our first few days of office it should have been necessary to take, and sometimes to announce, policy decisions without full consultation with colleagues. But this should no longer be so, and I must ask all ministers to ensure that issues of policy are not henceforward decided without thorough discussion in the relevant committee. I should like them also to remember that this Administration will not normally introduce legislation with retrospective effect unless it is advantageous to the ordinary citizen. I am sure that it is important that we should be seen from the outset to observe this principle.

The 1970–74 Conservative government is not generally regarded as a success in policy terms – with the sole exception of the entry into the EEC in January 1973 – but Heath is regarded as a gifted administrator. Despite his autocratic style, his practice of Cabinet government and the remarkable unity it retained throughout are notable.[2]

In terms of carrying a united Cabinet and party through spectacular policy u-turns, Heath proved a remarkable leader. The high esteem in which he was held by his Cabinet colleagues was reflected in the

---

[2] Dennis Kavanagh, 'The Heath Government, 1970–1974', in Peter Hennessy and Anthony Seldon (eds.), *Ruling Performance: British Governments from Attlee to Thatcher*, Basil Blackwell, Oxford, 1987, p. 232.

large number of them who voted for him on the first ballot in the leadership election in 1975. In spite of the u-turns, there were no resignations from the Cabinet on the grounds of policy disagreement. There were also very few leaks from the Cabinet – probably an indication of high morale and solidarity. The contrast with the well-publicised divisions in the Cabinet governments of 1964–70 and 1974–79 and the Thatcher government is remarkable.

Heath's dominance of his government was attributed by journalist David Watt to the agreed set of policies produced by the Conservative Party before the 1970 election. This is a contemporary view of how that dominance was consolidated and extended in government.[3]

Mr Heath is not only making the fullest possible use of the [strictly constitutional] sources of power but, as I would argue, is also extending them in the process. Civil servants, who are acutely aware that the public is frightened of extensions of anyone's powers – at any rate in theory – reply that what gives Mr Heath his pull is not really the exploitation of mechanical advantages but the overwhelming personal dominance he has over his colleagues.

This unity came despite the existence of an informal inner Cabinet, an often detached leadership style, and the Prime Minister's frequent preference for the company of civil servants to that of his fellow politicians. In an interview with Peter Hennessy in April 1999, Heath's Political Adviser Douglas Hurd (1930–), himself later Home Secretary, Foreign Secretary and a candidate for the Conservative Leadership in 1990, described those relationships.[4]

---

[3] David Watt, 'The power of the Premiership', *Financial Times*, 5 May 1972.
[4] Peter Hennessy, *The Prime Minister: The office and its holders since 1945*, Penguin, London, 2000, pp. 342–43.

Hennessy: Would you have a Cabinet committee, whether you called it an 'inner Cabinet' or not, that was a kind of strategic committee of the big hitters . . . ?

Hurd: I think it would depend so much on the personalities. I think one would probably do it as Ted did with a supper at Prunier's occasionally and that would enable you to ring the changes a bit.

Hennessy: So it would be informal?

Hurd: Yes.

Hennessy: And the Prunier's group was essentially Carrington, Prior, Whitelaw . . .

Hurd: Well, it wasn't definite. It varied very much and sometimes it was just the inner folk.

Hennessy: By the 'inner folk' you mean people like you and Robert Armstrong as well?

Hurd: And Michael Wolff [the Prime Minister's senior political adviser and speech writer] and so on, and Jim Prior, yes certainly. But then other people would be brought in as needed. And it was also a recreation for the Prime Minister. There's a great deal to be said for getting a certain amount of the discussion and the thinking done out of No. 10 – away, physically. It could be Prunier's; could be Chequers; it could be somewhere else. Geography is quite important.

Hennessy: Ted did that more than perhaps outsiders realised?

Hurd: Oh much more. He kept it all very private.

Hennessy: Yes, things didn't leak in your days. Things leaked very seldom in Ted's Cabinet.

Hurd: No, we wouldn't have dared! No, of course not. We hugged the secret of these things to ourselves because it made it more fun. No, it was quite a different world . . . absolutely different in that kind of respect.

As Hurd suggested, many of Heath's closest advisers were not politicians, but his civil servants. John Campbell, his biographer, argued that this eventually became a problem.[5]

[Heath] came to lean increasingly, and in the end dangerously, on officials who could pose no threat to him. Although his political colleagues were outstandingly loyal, they all had careers and constituencies and interests of their own, whereas his officials were devoted exclusively to serving him. Heath's greatest satisfaction was the sense of having the government machine at his command . . . senior civil servants felt that he was at heart one of them, a permanent secretary *manqué*. He in turn appreciated their intellectual calibre – unequalled by any of his close colleagues – and enjoyed working with them. As problems mounted up and political nostrums failed he turned increasingly to the civil service to come up with new policies and new mechanisms to carry them out.

One of Heath's most interesting, although not, as it turned out, longest-lasting, innovations was the creation in government of a 'think tank'. Named the Central Policy Review Staff (CPRS), it was intended to review collective government policies, with an eye in particular for strategic and longer-term thinking that was hard given the day-to-day grind of politics. This is how the new government presented its rationale for the creation of the CPRS and described its functions.[6]

---

[5] John Campbell, *Edward Heath: A biography*, Pimlico, London, 1994, p. 490.
[6] Cmnd. 4506 (1970), *The Reorganisation of Central Government*, pp. 13–14.

In recent years, however, it has become clear that the structure of inter-departmental committees, each concerned with a separate area of policy, needs to be reinforced by a clear and comprehensive definition of government strategy which can be systematically developed to take account of changing circumstances and can provide a framework within which the government's policies as a whole may be more effectively formulated. For lack of such a clear definition of strategic purpose and under the pressures of the day-to-day problems immediately before them, governments are always at some risk of losing sight of the need to consider the totality of their current policies in relation to their longer term objectives; and they may pay too little attention to the difficult, but critical, task of evaluating as objectively as possible the alternative policy options and priorities open to them.

The government recognise that the task of producing a strategic definition of objectives, in the sense described above, is a new and formidable one and can only be approached gradually. They therefore propose to begin by establishing a small multi-disciplinary central policy review staff in the Cabinet Office.

This staff will form an integral element of the Cabinet Office and, like the Secretariat and other staffs in the Cabinet Office, will be at the disposal of the government as a whole. Under the supervision of the Prime Minister, it will work for ministers collectively; and its task will be to enable them to take better policy decisions by assisting them to work out the implications of their basic strategy in terms of policies in specific areas, to establish the relative priorities to be given to the different sectors of their programme as a whole, to identify those areas of policy in which new choices can be exercised and to ensure that the underlying implications of alternative courses of action are fully analysed and considered.

The CPRS had come, unofficially, to be known as the 'Think Tank'. Burke Trend here describes the wonderful (and impeccable) logic behind its official name.[7]

It became known as the Think Tank, but they weren't quite the words you could see on the front of a White Paper. I remember scratching my head and sucking my pencil and thinking, 'What on earth are we going to call this thing?'

And then it seemed to me that if you took the words which we finally did adopt, they came as near as I could come to being accurate about it. It *was* central, it *was* concerned with policy; and it *was* concerned with reviewing policy centrally and it consisted of a staff, not a political unit.

According to Simon James, the role of Lord Rothschild, the first head of the CPRS, was crucial in developing its independent ethos.[8]

Lord Rothschild's best gift to his staff was to impart to it the 'CPRS style' of investigation and reporting: independent, radical and terse, it was the deliberate antithesis of Whitehall circumspection, reflecting Rothschild's stated concept of policy analysis: political impartiality and intellectual honesty, analysing all evidence without concession to ministerial preoccupations, always reaching firm conclusions, never fudging a compromise.

---

[7] Conversation with Lord Trend, 7 November 1983, for BBC Radio 3's *Routine Punctuated by Orgies*, quoted in Peter Hennessy, *Whitehall*, Pimlico, London, 2001, pp. 221–22.
[8] Simon James, *The Central Policy Review Staff, 1970–1983*, Political Studies, Number 34, 1986, p. 425.

The CPRS put non-elected outsiders into the very heart of Whitehall for the first time since Lloyd George's Garden Suburb. Yet it was not rejected outright by the civil service bureaucracy. Sue Pryce, in her analysis of advisory mechanisms in Whitehall, explained why.[9]

A major factor explaining its acceptance in Westminster may have been that it was not perceived to be an alternative advisory system serving the Prime Minister that might strengthen him *vis-à-vis* his Cabinet.

When two of its former members wrote its obituary, after its 1983 abolition, they emphasised not its collective role, though, but its relationship with the Prime Minister.[10]

The prime minister was formally responsible for the CPRS and answered questions on it in Parliament. The CPRS's relationship with the prime minister was always closer than with the other ministers. The relationship was not the same throughout the CPRS's life: it varied between prime ministers and within the period of office of individual prime ministers. However, each prime minister saw the CPRS to some extent as his or her own instrument as well as a body which worked collectively for all ministers. The CPRS also tended to see itself as having a common interest with the prime minister in trying to create a coherent policy out of the often disparate policies of the other ministers. It felt itself to be 'on the side' of the prime minister even though it might differ with him/her on specific issues of policy.

At the same time – as events ultimately showed – the CPRS's

---

[9] Sue Pryce, *Presidentializing the Premiership*, Macmillan, Basingstoke, 1997, p. 95.
[10] Tessa Blackstone and William Plowden, *Inside the Think Tank: Advising the Cabinet 1971–1983*, Heinemann, London, 1988, pp. 53–54.

survival was entirely dependent on the prime minister, the one person who could abolish it at a stroke. The fact that it survived under four very different prime ministers was due to its usefulness to four very different individuals and partly to its own ability to adapt to change. If it had lacked that ability it might have gone much earlier.

However, the CPRS's formal role was to work for ministers collectively. This made its relationship with the prime minister slightly ambiguous and one which needed sensitive handling *vis-à-vis* other ministers. For example, for whom did the CPRS speak in interdepartmental meetings of officials? Should its representatives speak on behalf of the prime minister, as departmental officials speak on behalf of their ministers? In practice, CPRS members spoke at such meetings for the CPRS; only in rare cases where it was asked to do a specific job by the prime minister was there any departure from this. In any case, under both the Wilson/Callaghan and Thatcher governments, the Prime Minister's Policy Unit was often represented separately on official (and sometimes ministerial) committees.

When Labour returned to office in 1974, the Cabinet was far more experienced than it had been in 1964. For Harold Wilson, this meant he could occupy a very different role, as he explained to the Parliamentary Labour Party shortly after the election.[11]

In the 1964 government, I reminded them, I had to occupy almost every position on the field, goalkeeper, defence, attack – I had to take the corner-kicks and penalties, administer to the wounded and bring on the lemons at half-time. Now, I said, I would be no more than what used to be called a deep-lying centre-half.

---

[11] Harold Wilson, *Final Term: The Labour Government 1974–76*, Weidenfeld & Nicolson, London, 1979, p. 17.

Wilson's new role did not stop him from introducing two key innovations: a Downing Street Policy Unit and the widespread use of ministerial 'special advisers'. The 'special advisers' were brought in to help ministers cope with the political aspects of their work; Bernard Donoughue (1934–), the first head of the Policy Unit, explains its significance.[12]

These are the three characteristics which distinguished the Policy Unit from what had existed before: it was systematic, it was separate from the Whitehall machine and it was solely working to the Prime Minister. This strengthening of the supportive mechanisms serving the Prime Minister has proved an important reform among the several contributions which Harold Wilson made to the effectiveness of British central government. It is significant that not only did James Callaghan retain the Policy Unit, but his Tory successor, Margaret Thatcher, continued and strengthened it.

Donoughue explained the new Unit's remit in a memorandum to its staff, and made clear the Prime Minister's role in the strategic direction of the government which it entailed.[13]

The Unit must ensure that the Prime Minister is aware of what is coming up from departments to Cabinet. It must scrutinise papers, contact departments, know the background to policy decisions, disputes and compromises, and act as an early warning system. The Unit may feed into the system ideas on policy which are not currently covered, or are inadequately covered ... The Unit should feed in 'minority reforms' which departments may overlook, or

---

[12] Bernard Donoughue, *Prime Minister, The Conduct of Policy under Harold Wilson and James Callaghan*, Jonathan Cape, London, 1987, p. 20.
[13] Ibid., pp. 21–22.

which fall between departmental boundaries, or which are the subject of worthy but unsuccessful Private Members Bills. This is especially the case with issues which concern ordinary people (and of which Whitehall may be unaware). [The political dimension in its work was underlined:] 'The Prime Minister has assumed responsibility as custodian of the Labour manifesto. The Unit must assist in that role, making sure that the manifesto is not contravened, nor retreated from, without proper discussion and advance warning . . . Throughout its policy work the Unit will clearly be aware of the political dimension in government. It must maintain good relations with the party organisation. The individual ministries must not become isolated from the government as a whole and lapse into traditional "departmental views".'

Richard Crossman's criticisms of the civil service and of the role of the Cabinet Secretary, which became public when his diaries were published in the mid-1970s, had thrown a spotlight on the work of civil servants and their relationships with political leaders. Bernard Donoughue's observations, from his Downing Street perch, are interesting.[14]

The Cabinet Secretary is the only person who institutionalises and reconciles the legitimate departmental conflicts of interests and differences of policy view which inevitably exist in Whitehall . . .

A similar ambiguity arose concerning whether the Cabinet Secretary's prime responsibility lay to the Cabinet as a collective whole or personally to the Prime Minister, on whose right hand he always sits in Cabinet. It can be argued that there should be no problem here since the Prime Minister is both chairman and part of the Cabinet. However, political life is not as simple as that. At times

[14] Ibid., pp. 27, 29.

the Prime Minister has personal interests which do not necessarily coincide with those of all his Cabinet colleagues. The Prime Minister might wish to restrain the policy activities of certain Cabinet colleagues, in which case he would want to influence the pace and way in which these were handled by the Whitehall machine. He might even wish to keep these issues from coming to Cabinet and also to influence which departments were or were not represented on the Cabinet Committees which discussed them. He would then use the Cabinet Secretary to achieve this – as Tony Benn periodically complained of during 1974–9. The Cabinet Secretary is, of course, supposed to serve the whole Cabinet but, in practice, where there is a conflict between the Prime Minister's interests, he is always tempted to give priority to his final master and centre of power, the Prime Minister, who in any case might be said to be ultimate definer of what is in the Cabinet's true interest.

In opposition from 1970–74, Labour's internal disagreements over Europe had become deeper, and begun to bleed into other areas of policy. By 1974 Roy Jenkins, the highest profile pro-European, who had resigned as Deputy Leader in 1972 over Europe, was feeling increasingly detached, leading to this odd exchange after the Prime Minister had made him Home Secretary for the second time, an appointment Jenkins did not particularly welcome.[15]

As soon as he could get away from these awkward questions of personnel, Wilson turned to more general conciliatory points. He said that now that we were in government again he had reverted to his 1960s' belief that I would be his natural successor. And he reiterated his intention not to stay for very long. He then ended with one of the oddest remarks that a prime minister can ever have made

---

[15] Roy Jenkins, *A Life at the Centre*, Papermac, London, 1991, p. 371.

to a colleague in a new Cabinet. Maybe the Home Office was the best solution after all, he suggested. If, as was perhaps inevitable for a time, I wanted to be a semi-detached member of the government, it was the most suitable department from which to play such a stand-off role.

Yet it was another Cabinet Minister, Tony Benn, who was to be isolated for much of the 1970s. But his isolation in the Cabinet did nothing to diminish his popularity in the wider Labour Party – Benn was on its left, and opposed continued British membership of the EEC. Protagonists tend to regard his experience either as just desserts or the result of the civil service's innate conservatism and inability to cope with a radical Minister. As early as 1974, Benn described this isolation in his diary.[16]

Friday, 14 June 1974
I had a candid talk to Roy Williams.[17] 'Look. This is what is really happening. All my industrial and regional policy in respect of Europe is being taken away and put under the Foreign Secretary's control. My Green Paper is being blocked by the Treasury, by the Chancellor's minute. My day-to-day business is now being watched by Harold Lever and Joel Barnett. All my speeches are controlled, and indeed I have been told by the Prime Minister not to speak or broadcast. And as regards appointments, the Prime Minister has said I am not to proceed even by letting it be known there are vacancies. This is the position I am in and do you wonder that, frustrated within Whitehall, I turn outside, where my support is?'

---

[16] Tony Benn, *Against the Tide: Diaries 1973–76*, Hutchinson, London, 1989, p. 176.
[17] Roy Williams was Benn's Parliamentary Private Secretary.

Shortly afterwards, in a difficult conversation with Wilson, who had a whole series of issues to raise with him, Benn went so far as to refuse to accept that he was bound by Questions of Procedure for Ministers.[18]

17 June 1974
He said, 'I notice that you have been disobeying all my rules of Procedure for Ministers.'

'I didn't reply to any of them but I do not accept them. They have never been published. They have never been collectively discussed with me and I do not accept them.'

Very shortly after it returned to office in March 1974[19]*, the Labour government began renegotiating the terms on which Britain had entered the EEC, and the Cabinet eventually voted to recommend the new terms in the subsequent referendum campaign. Yet because of some Cabinet ministers' deep-seated opposition to continued British membership of the EEC, collective responsibility was suspended for the duration of the campaign, allowing dissenting ministers to speak out honestly. These decisions – to recommend remaining in the EEC and to suspend collective responsibility – were arguably the most significant, and potentially the most divisive, taken by the 1974–76 Wilson governments. Here Bernard Donoughue describes Wilson's approach, and how the Cabinet came to make the decision to recommend accepting the renegotiated terms that would keep Britain in the EEC.*[20]

---

[18] Ibid., p. 177.
[19] Although election day was 28 February, the government did not take office until March.
[20] Bernard Donoughue, 'Harold Wilson and the renegotiation of the EEC terms of membership, 1974–75: a witness account', in Brian Brivati and Harriet Jones (eds.), *From Reconstruction to Integration: Britain and Europe since 1945*, Leicester University Press, Leicester, 1993, pp. 194, 201, 199–200.

Wilson was primarily concerned to secure enough concessions to satisfy his manifesto and party conference commitments. As always, his was primarily a party and not a policy concern. As for myself as his Senior Policy Advisor, this could at times be frustrating and irritating. But it was not a dishonourable position for a party leader – especially the leader of a party which was really a coalition of so many disparate elements – to have as a prime priority, that of keeping his party together.

* * *

A welcome instrument of truly Wilsonian flexibility. He believed that it was acceptable to suspend normal cabinet collectivity and allow ministers to campaign how they wished for four reasons: because of the uniqueness of the situation, because it was an issue of great constitutional importance; because it cut deeply across all normal party lines; and because the adoption of the referendum itself was unique in British history.

* * *

The Cabinet met to discuss the Dublin agreements over two days, 17–18 March 1975. It was potentially a very dangerous situation for the Prime Minister, not only because his Cabinet was deeply divided, but because on the issue he had to chair some very dogmatic and uncompromising individuals. On the pro side, Roy Jenkins was believed to be committed to resign from the Cabinet if it decided not to recommend the terms for continuing membership of the EEC. Shirley Williams had stated in the election campaign that she would leave politics altogether if the Cabinet said no. Therefore on the pro side were Cabinet ministers – and some junior ministers – who were prepared to put this issue above the survival of the government or their own ministerial careers. On the other side were Tony Benn, Michael Foot, Peter Shore and Barbara Castle who were equally passionately opposed to Europe. The Cabinet was in danger of being torn apart. The tension within Number Ten at this time was tangible and unforgettable.

Wilson handled that long Cabinet meeting on 17–18 March with consummate skill. Every member was given an opportunity to speak. Yet, in a classic Wilsonian way, he prevented it from developing into a confrontation. He hated confrontations of all kinds.

Some of the first morning was deliberately devoted to a long and balanced report by Callaghan on the development of the negotiations. That blunted the edge of the discussion and afterwards Wilson was openly pleased that there had been no fireworks. That evening the junior ministers were summoned to Downing Street, to the state dining room, to air their views on the EEC. Wilson had deliberately and cleverly arranged to hold the meeting in the middle of the Cabinet so there could be no discussion of the Cabinet's final decision. The speakers were roughly evenly divided. Those against included Frank Judd, Stanley Clinton Davies, and Margaret Jackson (Beckett). The pro speakers were mainly minor figures. Prominent pro campaigners, such as William Rodgers and Denis Howell, had decided not to perform at this meeting.

On the second day of the Cabinet, the early part of the morning was again defused by a long presentation, this time on the referendum arrangements by Edward Short, the Deputy Leader. After that the Prime Minister went around the table asking each minister in turn his view of the terms. To begin, both he and James Callaghan stated formally that they were in favour of a positive recommendation – though Wilson seemed to indicate that he had been in doubt until recently. He also suggested this in speeches and interviews. Whether true or not, it was certainly a useful device to gather in doubters to his position: by implying that he had shared and understood their doubts, but then suggesting that a reasonable doubter would, like himself conclude in a pro position. At the count the majority in favour of recommending the terms was 16–7.

Wilson then suggested a rare Cabinet innovation – coffee break. This hopefully would allow tensions to subside – and he wished especially to create a break after ministers had declared their position. It was then proposed that after coffee the dissenting ministers would be asked whether they wished to register formally as dissenters who would actually campaign against the Cabinet's decision. This was at Callaghan's suggestion and the hope was that some dissenters who had satisfied their consciences and their constituencies ahead of the national executive elections by declaring against in the main vote, would be dislodged from the minority at the second count. It did not work. But the coffee break was a small example of a typical Wilson approach – to cushion and smooth the sharp edges of argument and always to leave people feeling that they had room for manoeuvre and were not up against a wall. (The opposite, for example of Mrs Thatcher's handling of Michael Heseltine over the Westland helicopter affair.)

The majority of 16–7 was satisfactory to the Prime Minister and greater than many would have predicted at the opening of the negotiations. This certainly owed much to the skilful handling by the Wilson-Callaghan team. In fact five of the 16 majority had been publicly committed against staying in the Community when Labour took office in March 1974. Three of them – Merlyn Rees, John Morris and Fred Peart – were very close to Callaghan and his influence on their change of position was certainly very important, possibly decisive. Lord Shepherd, the Leader of the Lords, was basically a loyalist and unlikely to oppose the Prime Minister. The fifth switcher, Reg Prentice, was in the course of a profound evolution of political views which ended with him as a member of a later Conservative administration.

If these five had remained hostile then the vote would have been

12–11 against staying in the EEC. Wilson and Callaghan deserve the credit for swinging the Cabinet vote to a comfortable majority.

Wilson's announcement that the principle of collective responsibility would be suspended for the duration of the campaign was made in an effort (ultimately successful) to keep his party together during the referendum campaign. This is how Barbara Castle, one of the anti-marketeer minority in the Cabinet, recorded his statement in her diary.[21]

Tuesday, 21 January 1975
Then Harold came in quietly: 'As soon as we have made our decision on the terms I am going to recommend that the minority should be free to campaign in the country on their own point of view.' And he added, 'This is unprecedented'. But in his long-winded way he proceeded to justify it, qualifying his proposal with the implied rebuke: 'But this must apply only after the campaign starts.' And he thought we should issue some guidelines to prevent the argument from becoming unruly and personalised. There was a long silence when he asked for comments. I think the reason was that people like Mike [Michael Foot], Wedgie [Tony Benn] and me were secretly jubilant, while the pro-marketeers were reluctant to accept openly the course of action they knew was inevitable.

This management of the decision to remain in the EEC is well regarded by all but some of those commentators who wish the opposite decision had been taken. Peter Hennessy's is a neat summary.[22]

---

[21] Barbara Castle, *The Castle Diaries, 1964–1976*, Macmillan, London, 1990, p. 550.
[22] Peter Hennessy, *The Prime Minister: The office and its holders since 1945*, Penguin, London, 2000, p. 365.

His management of the European question bids fair to be both Wilson's finest exposition of collective Cabinet government and his final gift to the party whose unity he placed above all other considerations.

During the first Wilson government Tony Crosland had been the recipient of a note from then-Chancellor Jim Callaghan congratulating him on speaking up in Cabinet.[23] *By the time Callaghan had become Prime Minister, though, Crosland had adopted a much less constructive attitude towards new Cabinet members. Bill Rodgers (1928–), the Secretary of State for Transport, spoke briefly to him after one Cabinet meeting during this period, and recorded his later disillusion in his memoirs.*[24]

As I walked out of Number 10 with Tony Crosland after one of my early Cabinet meetings, I plainly showed my disappointment about how things had gone. 'You're not surprised, are you,' he asked, 'at the unsatisfactory nature of Cabinet?' I had already noticed that his own contributions to discussion were often thin and inconsequential, but Tony had a habit of dismissing as unimportant matters that he did not want to understand or that presented him with an awkward political choice. What I had not previously recognised was that much routine cabinet business involved only four or five ministers and a good deal of boredom for the rest. To pass the time I learnt to decorate my Cabinet agenda with the most elaborate and complex designs, all inviting rather obvious Freudian analysis, although the objects of my frustration were the events around me ... except in the closing months, frustration rather than exhilaration marked much of my time at Cabinet meetings and I often returned to my office in Marsham Street to lie flat on the floor to unwind, assisted by my favourite drink, an outsize gin and Italian.

[23] Chapter 8, p. 137.
[24] Bill Rodgers, *Fourth Among Equals*, Politico's, London, 2000, p. 162.

Crosland was not, though, unprepared to offer insights into how Cabinet could be made to work. This is what he told Maurice Kogan, who was working on a book about educational politics. A minister could win in Cabinet, Crosland said:[25]

By persuading, arguing, cajoling, exploiting his political position, being a bloody nuisance in Cabinet ... Above all, by being persistent. Obviously success depends on a whole mixture of factors, a lot of them a matter of luck – your relations with the Chancellor; your standing in the Cabinet; the way the rest of the Cabinet feels towards the education service; whether you can exhaust your colleagues before they exhaust you. It's an endless tactical battle which requires determination, cunning and occasional unscrupulousness. In an ideal world it would all no doubt be settled by some omniscient central unit, but this is the way it happens in our crude democratic world.

Wilson resigned in 1976, unique amongst prime ministers in so doing before he faced significant political pressure to leave office. He very soon turned his hand again to writing, and produced several books. One, in particular, was notable for the insight it offered into Wilson's views of Cabinet government in general, and on how it operated during his premiership in particular. His analysis highlighted his own essentially technocratic approach to government.[26]

Commentators who have rightly quoted Neville Chamberlain's personal foreign policy before and after Munich, and Anthony Eden's preoccupation with Egypt after the nationalisation of the Suez Canal, do not in my view affect the main argument so much as

---

[25] Susan Crosland, *Tony Crosland*, Jonathan Cape, London, 1982, p. 163.
[26] Sir Harold Wilson, *The Governance of Britain*, Weidenfeld & Nicolson, London, 1976, pp. 8, 8–9, 49–50.

draw attention to the personal characteristics of two recent prime ministers. In Chamberlain's case there must be strong criticism of the Cabinet's collective pusillanimity – though Anthony Eden, and later Duff Cooper, resigned – and it is fair to say that Chamberlain in forming his Cabinet deliberately picked the least able and courageous among the leading Conservatives available to him. It is also clear that his partnership with Sir Horace Wilson at times amounted to a conspiracy to deceive the House of Commons, and even any members of his Cabinet showing a disposition to independence or criticism . . . My own conclusion is that the predominantly academic verdict of overriding prime ministerial power is wrong. It ignores the system of democratic checks and balances, in Parliament, in the Cabinet, and not least in the party machine and the party in the country. The checks and balances operate not only as long-term safeguards, but also, in one way or another (often unpredictable), almost every day.

* * *

Cabinet is a democracy, not an autocracy; each member of it, including the prime minister, seeks to convince his colleagues as to the course to follow. The Cabinet bears his stamp, it is true, on each and every policy issue, but it is the Cabinet not the prime minister who decides.

* * *

The prime minister may then wish to indicate how the discussion should be handled and decisions taken. He may, for example, say that the question raises, say, three issues, and it might be helpful to discuss each separately, without prejudice to the decision to be taken at the end. Or interim decisions on each of the three may be taken, and the viability of the package as a whole considered at the end, when it will be necessary to deal also with a fourth question, handling and presentation. Alternatively, particularly on a major or new issue, he might suggest that the Cabinet begins with a 'second reading' debate, which enables members to make their set-piece contribution, which must be short, possibly raising fundamental or long-term issues. This averts the need for wide-ranging oratory when the meeting comes to decide detailed practical questions requiring a clear decision. Again, at the first meeting on a major issue – e.g. devolution, the EEC negotiations in 1967 and 1974–5, the EEC referendum, House of Lords reform or pay policy – a wide ranging second reading debate is virtually mandatory, and saves much time in the end. Even without such cases, a great deal of preparatory work will have been done in clearing the ground and identifying points for decision at high-level Cabinet committee meetings, usually with the prime minister in the chair.

It would be usual for the prime minister to open such a discussion. On other issues, where papers had been submitted by departmental minister, he would be unlikely to speak first, but would be ready to steer and guide the discussion to the point of taking the required decision. Very occasionally he opens the discussion, usually on a procedural point. For example, he may feel it right to remind the Cabinet that they have not met to review a broad policy decision – that has been taken – but one concerned with this or that point of implementation. Alternatively, he will point out that they are not this morning taking the major decision on subject X – that will be the subject of a further meeting separately documented – but that an interim decision on a narrower aspect must be taken now. Or if he feels, from the papers submitted and his knowledge of the strength of different ministers' feelings, that there is a danger of perhaps unnecessary polarisation, he may suggest at the outset that there is a possible third course which might be more productive, and on which agreement might be possible.

The prime minister must be ever-alert to issues which raise

fundamental, doctrinal or theological passions on the part of one or more ministers, and do all he can to avert an unnecessary clash without sacrificing principle, and without fudging an issue on which a clear decision has to be reached, binding the Cabinet.

Jim Callaghan won the race to become Prime Minister after Wilson's retirement. The new premiership provided the opportunity for journalists to survey the political and constitutional landscape, and in some cases to offer suggestions for reform. Michael Wolff, in this 1976 article in The Times, *first suggested then ruled out the idea of a Prime Minister's Department. Here he describes how attempts to consolidate power in Number 10 can flounder.*[27]

[The Prime Minister] is certainly a good deal worse off than a departmental minister, who has everything streamlined and everyone under control, a well-oiled machine working along well-established lines. And when a prime minister seeks to make up for his lack of engine-power by creating what Lord Armstrong[28] describes as his 'anti-machine' and bringing in an outsider or a distinguished civil servant or even the Cabinet Secretary to be his principal confidant then it only exacerbates what is anyway an inherent conflict between No. 10 and Whitehall.

In 1976, Britain's economic position worsened so far that the government had to go, cap in hand, to the International Monetary Fund (IMF), a body which Britain had helped found as part of the post-war effort to regularise the international financial system, for an emergency loan. As part of the loan agreement, the IMF demanded a package of politically painful spending cuts, which several members of the

---

[27] Michael Wolff, 'The power of the Prime Minister: Should he pick up the ball and run with it?', *The Times*, 24 May 1976.
[28] William Armstrong.

government vehemently opposed. At a series of meetings between 23 November and 2 December James Callaghan invited the whole Cabinet to consider the various different plans for meeting the IMF strictures, a process which eventually led to the endorsement of the package proposed by his Chancellor, Denis Healey (1917–), but which prevented a fatal Cabinet split. Peter Hennessy explains its significance.[29]

It is Callaghan's attempts to manage the currency, spending and confidence crises of that year while maintaining the niceties and processes of collective Cabinet government *and* managing a simultaneous and highly secret operation involving personal economic diplomacy at the highest level, which have become a hotly debated and classic case-study of the practice of premiership as well as an intrinsically important benchmark in the (so far) 130-year long march away from economic and financial superpowerdom.

Edmund Dell (1921–99), who at the time of the IMF crisis was Secretary of State for Trade in the Cabinet, takes a different and very sceptical view of those long meetings, arguing that far from being a high point they in fact represented an unnecessary diversion; that a small cabal of policy-makers was in fact desirable and that collective responsibility has already dissolved so far that it is now little more than a myth. He did not take a positive view of later developments, either, arguing in particular that the 1980s 'Star Chamber' was a mechanism for compromise where none was needed.[30]

Collective responsibility is a myth. Myths may serve a useful

---

[29] Peter Hennessy, *The Prime Minister: The office and its holders since 1945*, Penguin, London, 2000, p. 382.
[30] Edmund Dell and Lord Hunt of Tanworth, 'The Failings of Cabinet Government in Mid to Late 1970s', *Contemporary Record*, Vol. 8, Winter 1994, Number 3, pp. 458–59, 460–61, 464.

purpose, but to serve that purpose they have to be believed and this one is not believed. I am aware of only one sense in which ministers are collectively responsible according to any definition of the term which I have heard, and that is that they are responsible for giving cover to their colleagues by remaining in government with them. But that is really not very much different from the responsibility of Members of Parliament in the House of Commons who maintain a government by their votes. In a vote of confidence in the House of Commons you do not say 'I agree with the government', you say 'I prefer them to the other lot'. And this view of the situation justifies my argument that what actually holds governments together in this country is not collective responsibility, it is something I call 'collective tolerance'. That is the concept which governs the relationship between ministers. That is the concept which governs the relationship between a government and the party that supports it in Parliament. When collective tolerance breaks down, governments are in trouble. Collective tolerance also takes account of the fact that whether or not we have formal coalitions in this country, all parties are coalitions and some of them are quite remarkable coalitions.

* * *

Now, should Callaghan have managed the 1976 crisis the way he did? He says he had to do it that way to prevent his colleagues resigning. I have never noticed among Labour ministers the least enthusiasm to resign. I have in my time described the 1976 Cabinet meetings as a farce and a dangerous farce at that. Nine Cabinet meetings while the market was impatiently waiting for a decision. In a sensible system of government Callaghan would, after discussing with Healey and Foot and possibly, as a matter of *amour propre*, with Tony Crosland, have told the Cabinet 'It is my responsibility. We have to cut public expenditure. Do not be so stupid as to resign, which actually I know you are not going to do anyhow and bring the government down and let Thatcher in. The party would never forgive you.' If he had said that after a couple of Cabinet meetings I am sure the Cabinet would have accepted it.

* * *

... the 'Star Chamber' ... was very far from being a 'Star Chamber' because Wise Willie [that is, Whitelaw[31]] was in the chair and Wise Willie was in favour of compromise and not making too harsh decisions. Of these attempts, the present method is probably the best. There is the Cabinet committee EDX chaired by the Chancellor of the Exchequer, not by a neutral wise man like Whitelaw. But there is always a danger if ministers can go to Cabinet. That is why I say these decisions should be made by the Chancellor and by the Prime Minister.

Lord Hunt of Tanworth (1919–), Cabinet Secretary at the time, disagreed with Dell, arguing both that collective responsibility was a reality, and a desirable one.[32]

I do not believe that those nine Cabinets were purely tactical in terms of a rather cynical operation that had to be gone through, in order to keep the lads together and to stop them resigning. It is perfectly true that he felt that in this Cabinet there were very different views on what should be done, ranging from the sort of siege economy which Mr Benn was putting forward and a rather more modified position of import controls from Peter Shore. There was the Tony Crosland

---

[31] William Whitelaw (1918–99) was an influential member of Margaret Thatcher's early Cabinets.

[32] Dell, Edmund and Lord Hunt of Tanworth, 'The Failings of Cabinet Government in Mid to Late 1970s', *Contemporary Record*, Vol. 8, Winter 1994, Number 3, pp. 467–8, 470.

view which was more orthodox but much less extreme than going the whole way with Denis Healey. And then there was the Healey view. I think Jim Callaghan felt that he had to establish a Cabinet consensus even if, though it did not happen, one or two members were to go. Edmund Dell has said that in the end he was bound to back the Chancellor, but I think that he was also seeing if there was not some other way out. I think at heart he would have liked very much to go along with what I call the Tony Crosland school and he also placed a lot of weight on getting some help from his friends Gerald Ford and Helmut Schmidt, which might ease the problem for the government. So that I do not think he was committed to supporting Denis Healey. To some extent he was testing the Treasury view and was looking for what other solution could be found. But, as Edmund has said, when at the end of the day and after these tortuous Cabinets, he decided to come down in favour of Healey, and I remember the moment when that happened, that was the end of the discussion.

So I do not think collective responsibility is a myth. I think it is a reality. It is cumbersome. It is difficult. It has all sorts of disadvantages, and it is possible it may need change . . .

* * *

I think that probably under any of these systems it is going to be a bit of a shambles. But I do think it has got be, so far as possible, a democratic and accountable shambles.

Denis Healey, Chancellor during the IMF discussions, reflected on the difficulties of the job.[33]

The Chancellor of the Exchequer's is a lonely job, particularly in a

---

[33] Denis Healey, *The Time of My Life*, Penguin, London, 1990, p. 388.

period like mine, when he is obliged to disappoint the hopes of his party and the aspirations of his colleagues – not to speak of his own. Without the support of the Prime Minister it is impossible.

Bill Rodgers described the IMF discussions as an unexpected lurch towards open government.[34]

On this occasion, eight meetings of the full Cabinet were needed to settle matters; and alternative courses of action were explored in a process closely followed by observers outside Parliament. It was open government by accident.

Meanwhile, new Conservative Leader Margaret Thatcher (1925–) was thinking along radically different lines as she contemplated how she would form her first administration. This is from an interview she gave the Observer *in February 1979.*[35]

If you're going to do things you want to do – and I'm only in politics to *do* things – you've got to have a togetherness and a unity in your Cabinet.

There are two ways of making a Cabinet. One way is to have in it people who represent all the different viewpoints within the party, within the broad philosophy. The other way is to have in it only the people who want to go in the direction in which every instinct tells me we have to go. Clearly, steadily, firmly, with resolution. We've got to go in an agreed and clear direction. As Prime Minister I couldn't waste time having any internal arguments.

It's the same with the Shadow Cabinet. We've got to be together as a team. A football manager wouldn't put anyone, however

---

[34] Bill Rodgers, *Fourth Among Equals*, Politico's, London, 2000, p. 163.
[35] Kenneth Harris, 'My Kind of Conservatism: Mrs Thatcher talks to the Observer', *Observer*, 25 February 1979.

brilliant, in the team if he believes that player couldn't work together with the rest. I've got to have togetherness. There must be dedication to a purpose, agreement about direction. As leader, I have a duty to try to inspire that.

If you choose a team in which you encounter a basic disagreement, you will not be able to carry out a programme, you won't be able to govern. I think that's probably what's wrong with the present Labour government: there are two basic parties in it, two basic philosophies. We, on the other hand, have a Shadow Cabinet with a unity of purpose.

When the time comes to form a real Cabinet I do think I've got to have a Cabinet with equal unity of purpose, and a sense of dedication to it. It must be a Cabinet that works on something much more than pragmatism, or consensus. It must be a 'conviction' Cabinet.

The worsening conflict between the Labour left and right manifested itself in ever more bitter exchanges in Cabinet.[36]

In another exchange in Cabinet on 1 February, the Prime Minister summed up what many of us wanted to say, when he put a question to Tony Benn: 'What do you say about the thuggish act of a walk-out, without notice, from a Children's Hospital?' Tony replied that: 'When decent people become irrational, something else must be wrong if they are driven to such desperate acts.' Jim Callaghan's response was that he 'had never in fifty years been so depressed as a trade unionist'. Denis Healey, more pointedly said: 'We should not allow middle-class guilt to blind us to what's going on.'

---

[36] Joel Barnett, *Inside the Treasury*, Andre Deutsch, London, 1982, p. 175.

Benn recounted the same discussion in his diaries.[37]

I have always worked on the principle that, where large numbers of people behave irrationally, something else is usually wrong. People feel a deep sense of injustice and they don't feel properly represented. We have to be careful not to fall for this idea that everybody has just gone mad. David Owen says that what is happening is pure thuggery, but I doubt that. It can't be easy for people to go on strike. They lose their income and they have a deep feeling of anxiety. When I was in Newcastle recently, I heard an NUJ man deliver the most violent attack on the management of his paper and he swore that he would die in the last ditch with the printers. I discovered that he was a Tory candidate for a north-east constituency.

I talked about picketing and the reasons for not crossing picket lines, and Jim said, 'What about intimidation? Strikers are intimidating people.'

'The people of Grunwick were intimidated,' I replied, 'and, if I may say so, some Cabinet ministers give the impression that they really support what Mrs Thatcher is saying. The trade unions have no interest in penalising the public – they just want to be in a position to develop their arguments in an effective way.'

It was a bitter exchange but at least they listened.

Occasionally, Benn's stance caused him real difficulties with his fellow ministers, and indeed the Prime Minister. Shortly after one of several cuts packages was agreed by the government, Callaghan had to rebuke Benn for trying to reserve his position.[38]

---

[37] Tony Benn, *Conflicts of Interest: Diaries 1977–80* (ed. Ruth Winstone), Hutchinson, London, 1990, pp. 449–50.
[38] Bernard Donoughue, *Prime Minister, The Conduct of Policy under Harold Wilson and James Callaghan*, Jonathan Cape, London, 1987, p. 92.

Tony [Benn] telephoned to say that he had a problem. He explained that he must consult with his constituency activists over whether he should now resign completely from the Cabinet or merely continue to campaign in public against the Cabinet's decision on cuts in public expenditure. The Prime Minister replied, 'Tony, why don't you make up your own mind? And if you do stay in the Cabinet but continue campaigning against a collective Cabinet decision, you will be sacked immediately.' I do not know what the small elite group of Bristol activists advised, but Tony Benn remained, and relatively quietly.

David Owen (1938–), then Foreign Secretary, came from the opposite end of the political spectrum to Benn (he later left the Labour Party to found the Social Democratic Party), yet was not entirely unsympathetic to Benn's plight, at least insofar as his treatment by the permanent civil service was concerned.[39]

I think the Cabinet was a very happy Cabinet, but the one exception was Tony Benn. He just wasn't on the main wavelength of the majority of the Cabinet ... You just felt that a lot of his contributions were for his own record of what he had said in Cabinet and not actually for the benefit of the Cabinet ... The civil service, sensing this disagreement amongst ministers, and the fact that Tony Benn was really an outsider in the Cabinet, did tend to conspire against him, and you would find, in briefing notes for a Cabinet meeting, 'Mr Benn is expected to say the following, and you should argue against it ...' Well, how the hell did they know what he was going to say? Obviously they'd been told along some sort of mafia.

[39] Quoted in Phillip Whitehead, 'The Labour Governments, 1974–79', in Peter Hennessy and Anthony Seldon (eds.), *Ruling Performance: British Governments from Attlee to Thatcher*, Basil Blackwell, Oxford, 1987, pp. 249–50.

In late 1978 there was a widespread expectation that Callaghan would hold an autumn election. Here Bill Rodgers recalled the Cabinet meeting at which the Prime Minister announced that it would not be. It proved a costly mistake: trade union strikes during the 1978–79 'Winter of Discontent' brought much of the country to a standstill and effectively destroyed the Labour Party's chances of winning the election which followed the next spring.[40]

As we assembled for Cabinet after the holidays in the lobby outside the Cabinet room, we might have been the Cup Final team waiting to take the field. Elbows were grasped in self-conscious greeting and slightly nervous jokes eased the tension. At the TUC earlier in the week the trade unions had overwhelmingly rejected 5 per cent, but when the Prime Minister's speech had alerted them to the political battle ahead, they had rallied to give him a standing ovation. In advance of Cabinet, Jim Callaghan had canvassed individual views and I took for granted this had shown a clear majority for an early election. As the Prime Minister described how he had seen the Queen that morning, then rehearsed his government's achievements, this seemed the prelude to a formal announcement. When he said that, to the contrary, he proposed to carry on, we almost rose from our chairs in astonishment. 'May we consider for a moment the economic consequences?' asked Peter Shore. 'You may', came the reply, 'but I have no intention of making a second visit to the Palace today with a different message'. Shirley Williams also tried to intervene, but the Prime Minister brushed her aside, saying that he would like to turn to Cabinet business. And that was that.

---

[40] Bill Rodgers, *Fourth Among Equals*, Politico's, London, 2000, p. 179.

No surprise, perhaps, that in his memoirs Callaghan rejected calls for new prime ministerial powers.[41]

... from time to time there is discussion about the need for a formal Prime Minister's Department and such talk frequently overlooks the instruments he already has. He is able to provide himself with his own sources of information; he can send up a trial balloon or fire a sighting shot across a ministerial bow without directly involving his own authority or publicly undermining that of the minister; and he has the necessary facilities to take a decisive hand in policy-making at any moment he chooses to intervene.

The establishment of a formal Prime Minister's Department, with the prime minister's representatives attending Cabinet committees, would not only add an unnecessary layer of administration, but could have the political disadvantage, when contentious issues were under discussion, that his or her representatives would be forced to take a line too early and thus restrict room for manoeuvre later on. For, despite current fashion, reconciliation and compromise between contending groups in a well-ordered system of Cabinet government will continue to be an important function of the prime minister, as well as the need to give a clear lead when the occasion demands.

Lord Hailsham (1907–2001) was one of the twentieth century's most experienced ministers, having served in a variety of functions under five prime ministers over forty years. In the 1976 Richard Dimbleby Lecture, he called the current state of British government 'elective dictatorship'.[42]

---

[41] James Callaghan, *Time and Chance*, Collins, London, 1987, p. 408.
[42] Lord Hailsham, 'Elective Dictatorship', *The Listener*, 21 October 1976.

The whole absolute powers of Parliament, except in a few matters, like divorce or abortion, are wielded by the Cabinet alone, and sometimes by a relatively small group within the Cabinet.

The 1970s saw one crucial development in the study of the Cabinet, too – the evolution of 'core executive studies' as an alternative to study of a single institution at the heart of government, which had been the dominant mode up to that point. Professor Rod Rhodes, a practitioner of that discipline, describes it here.[43]

The 'core executive' is the heart of the machine, covering the complex web of institutions, networks and practices surrounding the prime minister, Cabinet, Cabinet committees and their official counterparts, less formalised ministerial 'clubs' or meetings, bilateral negotiations and inter-departmental committees. It also includes coordinating departments, chiefly the Cabinet Office, the Treasury, the Foreign Office, the Law Officers and the security and intelligence services. The label 'Cabinet government' was the overarching term for (some of) these institutions and practices but it is inadequate and confusing because it does not describe accurately the effective mechanisms for achieving coordination. At best it is contentious, and at worst seriously misleading, to assert the primacy of the Cabinet among all organisations and mechanisms at the heart of the machine.

---

[43] R. A. W. Rhodes, 'Introducing the Core Executive, Surveying the Field', in R. A. W. Rhodes and Patrick Dunleavy (eds.), *Prime Minister, Cabinet and Core Executive*, St. Martin's Press, Basingstoke, 1995, p. 12.

Government has grown dramatically since Bagehot wrote The English Constitution, *and with it the number of ministers needed to oversee and control its behaviour. The 1970s as a decade saw a high and growing percentage of national income spent by the state, and as such was an appropriate time for Richard Rose to examine the growth of ministerial offices.*[44]

The number of persons styled ministers has been growing primarily because of the increase in the number of ministers outside the Cabinet. In recent years, the number of ministers of Cabinet rank outside the Cabinet has been about as numerous as those in the Cabinet. Some of these officeholders are in charge of autonomous but minor departments, e.g., the Solicitor General; others hold subordinate posts in large departments, e.g., Ministers of State in the Foreign and Commonwealth Office. Another tier of official appointees – parliamentary secretaries and under-secretaries – are unambiguously junior ministers. Their status, as measured by salary or departmental authority, is usually well below that of the highest ranking civil servants in a department, and their effective influence is usually very limited too. Collectively, these individuals form the government. i.e., the ministry of the day. The lowest stratum of political appointees – parliamentary private secretaries of individual ministers – is unpaid and not formally recognized by legislation. Informally it is well established, and increasingly, the PPS is expected to be bound by conventions regulating the behaviour of ministers.

---

[44] Richard Rose, 'The Making of Cabinet Ministers', in Valentine Herman and James Alt (eds.), *Cabinet Studies: A Reader*, Macmillan, London, 1975, pp. 5–6, 10.

The growth of ministerial appointments – 1900–70

	1900	1910	1917	1920	1930	1940*	1950	1960	1967	1970†
Cabinet Ministers	19	19	5	19	19	9	18	19	24	18
Non-Cabinet Ministers	10	7	33	15	9	25	20	20	27	25
Junior Ministers#	31	36	47	47	30	40	43	43	58	38
MPs in paid posts	33	43	60	58	50	58	68	65	92**	68**
Total paid posts	60	62	85	81	58	74	81	82	115	79
PPSs	9	16	12	13	26	25	27	36	30	32
Total MPs appointed	42	59	72	71	76	83	95	101	122	98

* Chamberlain
† Heath
\# Includes political appointments in the Royal Household
** Includes paid assistant whips

As part of the same study, Valentine Herman looked at ministerial tenure.[45]

We have undertaken a comparative analysis of the stability of British Cabinet ministers in the postwar years. Our major conclusions can be summarised as follows. (1) Although British governments have remained in office for relatively long periods of time, the same cannot be said for the holders of key portfolios in these governments. Whether comparisons are made with either Commonwealth or European countries, the tenure of office of British ministers has been noticeably short. One of the most distinctive features of British

[45] Valentine Herman, 'Comparative Perspectives on Ministerial Stability in England', in Valentine Herman and James Alt (eds.), *Cabinet Studies: A Reader*, Macmillan, London, 1975, pp. 73–75, 22.

Cabinets is the rate at which ministers come to and leave office, a rate which is matched by no other Commonwealth country and very few of the European ones. (2) The pattern of ministerial government in Britain is not only distinguished by the limited tenure of office of ministers, but also by the fact that these ministries are subjected to more governmental reorganisations than their counterparts in any other Commonwealth or European country. The high incidence of within-government changes experienced in Britain is not experienced elsewhere. (3) Although the British patterns of structural and personnel continuing across successive administrations compares unfavourably with those of other Commonwealth countries, they compare quite favourably with the European patterns. In Britain, ministers are both unlikely to remain in office for the duration of a government or (even if the party base of the government remains the same) to be in the same office at the formation of a new government.

At this stage in our analysis we must ask what, if any, are the consequences of the low tenure of office of British Cabinet ministers? It does not appear to be the case that ministerial instability has a detrimental effect on the policy-making process. By and large government policies are continuous and lasting and are not unduly affected, at least in the short and medium runs, by a high rate of ministerial turnover. Notwithstanding the comings and goings of Cabinet ministers, the fact that senior civil servants remain attached to specific ministries for lengthy periods ensures a large amount of policy continuity. Innovative policies are much more likely to be brought about by changing social and environmental conditions than by a particular minister entering or leaving a department. Given the whole variety of political, social and economic restraints on the policy-making process, it appears most unlikely that the formulation and implementation of policies in Britain would be different in nature if ministerial stability were greater. When comparisons are made with either Commonwealth or European countries, it seems that there are few, if any, major policy discontinuities of any consequence which can be attributed to the kinds of ministerial instability we have been focusing on in this chapter.

Duration in ministeral offices 1900–1914 and 1955–70

Office	Ministers 1900–14	Average months per minister	Ministers 1955–70	Average months per minister	Difference in months
Foreign Secretary	2	82.5	8*	22.5	−60.0
Chancellor of the Exchequer	5	33.0	7	25.7	−7.3
Home Secretary	5	33.0	6	30.0	−3.0
Defence	5**	33.0	7	25.7	−7.3
Local Goverment and Housing	4	41.2	6	30.0	−11.2
Education	6	27.5	10*	18.0	−9.5
Board of Trade	6	27.5	8	22.5	−5.0
Scottish Secretary	5	33.0	4	45.0	+12.0
Agriculture	5	33.0	5	36.0	+3.0
Postmaster General	6	27.5	6	30.0	+2.5
Public Building and Works	4	41.2	9	20.0	−21.2
Averages	4.8	34.4	6.9	26.1	−9.7

*A minister who held the same post with other appointments intervening is counted twice.
** This figure averages turnover rates for the Admiralty and the War Office, each of which had five men in charge in the period, 1900–14.
(Time spans calculated from November 1900–July 1914 inclusive, 165 months; and from June 1955–May 1970 inclusive, 180 months.)

Resignations over policy have become rarer, but the politics of a threatened resignation are very interesting, and go to the heart of prime ministerial versus ministerial power. This is Peter Madgwick's assessment of the politics of resignation.[46]

Usually, however, resignations mean much more than honourable withdrawal; they are part of political strategy, the attempt to win over colleagues. In the Cabinet, the threat to resign secures consideration by the full Cabinet, under some pressure to make concessions. If this works, there is no resignation and incidentally no public knowledge of the situation for several years. Most of the time Cabinets argue and bargain for a consensus: this arises from their political nature rather than from an implied threat of resignation. But occasionally, an explicit threat lies, so to speak, on the table. This seems to have been particularly true of the Lloyd George and Attlee Cabinets. But the threat of resignation is a dangerous weapon, for the bluff may be called, as Randolph Churchill discovered in 1886. Few men are indispensable, and a Cabinet will not often be called to heel by a sudden threat of resignation, even from a senior minister. Like military deterrents, resignation works only if it can inflict unacceptable damage. Normally, this is beyond its capacity.

---

[46] P. J. Madgwick, 'Resignations', in Valentine Herman and James Alt (eds.), *Cabinet Studies: A Reader*, Macmillan, London, 1975, pp. 87–88.

In their 1976 book, Jock Bruce-Gardyne and Nigel Lawson used several examples of government decision-taking to examine the operation of power. Their conclusions would be unsustainable just ten years later, and in a sense offered a eulogy to a system in which the prime minister was still, just, primus inter pares. *And as the post-war consensus ended with Jim Callaghan's last days in Number 10, traditional understandings of Cabinet government would be shaken sharply by the new resident of that famous address.*[47]

The common theme that emerges is one of the prime minister as arbiter of choice in government, rather than the preselector of decisions. His acquiescence is a necessary (though not a sufficient) condition for decision on major policy issues – even if that acquiescence has sometimes to be extracted by something akin to *force majeur*. Hence a strong prime minister is not an indispensable precondition for decisive government in Britain. The lack of a dominant lead from the top results in paralysis of government in genuine presidential constitutions such as those of France or the US (or even in hybrids such as that of Federal Germany). In Britain the Queen's government was carried on effectively enough under Sir Alec Douglas-Home; and history may well conclude that the relaxed – not to say negligent – style adopted by Harold Wilson during his second term of office proved more rewarding than the frenetic activism of his first tenure of the premiership.

---

[47] Jock Bruce-Gardyne and Nigel Lawson, *The Power Game: An Examination of Decision-Making in Government*, Macmillan, London, 1976, p. 154.

10

Cabinet by Handbag, 1979–1990

Margaret Thatcher (1925–) became a dominant Prime Minister and sought a radical transformation in British politics, dismantling the post-war consensus and replacing it with monetarist economics and conviction politics. Also clear was her disdain for the traditional processes of British government and collective decision-taking. She believed she should take decisions with others merely consulted. This passage is from the memoirs of James Prior, the Conservative Employment Secretary, and a prominent 'wet' – opposed to the monetarism and desire for a sharp confrontation with the unions which characterised its approach.[1]

In the early days I think Margaret was worried that we would not accept her authority and would not do what she wanted. I dare say she was right since most of the powerful voices were ranged against her. She decided that in those circumstances she must control economic policy, and in Geoffrey Howe[2] she found someone whom she could both control and trust.

It was really an enormous shock to me that the budget which Geoffrey produced the month after the election of 1979 was so extreme. It was then that I realised that Margaret, Geoffrey and Keith[3] really had got the bit between their teeth and were not going to pay attention to the rest of us at all if they could possibly help it.

[1] James Prior, *A Balance of Power*, Hamish Hamilton, London, 1986, p. 119.
[2] Geoffrey Howe (1926–), then Chancellor of the Exchequer.
[3] Keith Joseph (1918–1994), then Secretary of State for Industry.

*Geoffrey Howe accepted as much in his memoirs.*⁴

It must be acknowledged that, at least in the early years of the Thatcher era, the Budget Cabinet had almost joined the previous evening's Palace audience on the 'dignified' rather than the 'efficient' side of Bagehot's constitutional analysis. By then all the decisions had been taken and the speech written; Cabinet on that morning was little more than a chance for colleagues to wish the Chancellor well. This was particularly the case from 1979 to 1981, in which years there was no significant prior discussion of the Budget in Cabinet. Colleagues were, of course, always consulted about changes concerning their own departments, and, except in 1979 when we were in effect implementing the manifesto, I discussed my main themes with senior colleagues. I should have wished to do more than this to extend internal understanding of our plans. But Margaret was always, and with increasing reason, preoccupied by fear of leaks. So Budget secrecy had acquired a new dimension.

That non-collegial approach was to change markedly when the Falklands War, the result of Argentina's invasion of the Falkland Islands, began. Former Prime Minister Harold Macmillan is widely credited with having advised the Prime Minister on how to set up the machinery for running a war. That credit is largely the result of his own claim, in an interview here with Ludovic Kennedy⁵, and Thatcher's own later recollection.⁶

---

⁴ Geoffrey Howe, *Conflict of Loyalty*, Macmillan, London, 1994, pp. 133–34.
⁵ From *Reflections*, BBC1, 20 October 1983, quoted in Peter Hennessy, *Cabinet*, Basil Blackwell, Oxford, 1986, p. 118.
⁶ Margaret Thatcher, *The Downing Street Years*, HarperCollins, London, 1993, p. 188.

Macmillan: I did try and help her about how to run a war because it's such a long time since anybody's run a war – I mean the technical methods of running a war – which she did very well.

Kennedy: What were you able to draw on there in your own experience?

Macmillan: Well, I mean that you have to have a War Cabinet, you have to have a Committee of Chiefs of Staff, that the Secretary of the Committee of Chiefs mustn't be the Secretary of the War Cabinet. It must be the nearest thing you could get to Lord Ismay . . . it was just the tip how to run it, how to manage it from the government point of view. All of which I'd learned from Churchill, of course.

Macmillan was not the only veteran whose advice she sought, though. In his book on the prime ministers, Peter Hennessy revealed that Sir Frank Cooper (1922–2002), at that time Permanent Secretary of the Ministry of Defence and a former Spitfire pilot who had been in Whitehall since 1948, had also been consulted, and had given very similar advice to Macmillan's.[7]

'What nobody knows,' he [Cooper] said, 'is that I told her at a private lunch on the Sunday. I was ushered up to her little flat on the top floor. Carol [Thatcher] took lunch out of the fridge – a bit of ham and salad. We had a gin and she [Mrs Thatcher] asked me "How do you actually run a war?"'

I [Hennessy] asked if he had written anything down.

'No, I didn't write it down. I knew it and I said, "First, you need a small War Cabinet; second, it's got to have regular meetings come hell or high water; thirdly, you don't want a lot of bureaucrats hanging around." Then we talked about its composition.'

[7] Peter Hennessy, *The Prime Minister: The office and its holders since 1945*, Penguin, London, 2000, pp. 104–05.

I wondered in which sense did Sir Frank 'know it'?

'One had seen it so often in a funny sort of way . . . I knew about Berlin, Korea, Malaya. We'd had Suez, which was a monumental cock-up. Cuba was different – very much a No. 10/Kennedy thing. And we'd long had this Transition to War Committee [In 1956 it was called the Defence (Transition) Committee. It became TWC in 1961.] which actually met at the time of Suez and was the biggest shambles of all time. The one thing I was quite clear about was that you couldn't have this bloody thing where people weren't going to take decisions.'

In a later interview, Cooper elaborated still further upon his conversation with Mrs Thatcher on 'Falklands Sunday'. He stressed to her that 'the chain of command should be kept as simple as possible'.

In return Mrs Thatcher 'raised some ideas of her own . . . she didn't, for example, want to have too many ministers on the core group and she didn't want the Chancellor [of the Exchequer] . . . She thought that the money could be too much of a distraction.' Sir Frank's evidence is significant here as the idea of keeping the Treasury out of the Falklands 'War Cabinet' is usually attributed to Harold Macmillan who, as is well known, called on Mrs Thatcher just after Prime Minister's Questions the following Tuesday (6 April 1982) to be asked the same question she had asked Cooper: 'Harold, how do you run a war?'

Peter Hennessy described the change which the war wrought in Mrs Thatcher's behaviour.[8]

The first few months of the Falklands conflict were very illuminating of the Prime Minister's character but with Mrs Thatcher under

---

[8] Peter Hennessy, *The Prime Minister: The office and its holders since 1945*, Penguin, London, 2000, p. 413.

severe stress they were also, in a way, counter-cultural. For they revealed her as a punctilious traditionalist in her dealings both with her Cabinet and with Parliament even where her Boadicea qualities were most in demand.

The resignation of Lord Carrington (1919–), Foreign Secretary, for the diplomatic failures which lead to the Falklands War, is sometimes seen as self-sacrificial. But not by everyone: this is Peter Madgwick's view.[9]

Though this was regarded as a sacrifice on Carrington's part, taking the blame on his shoulders at the outset of a war, there is a good case for regarding it as a genuine case of resignation under the convention of ministerial responsibility for clearly demonstrable ministerial and departmental fault.

Shortly after the Falklands War, Colin Seymour-Ure examined the role of War Cabinets in limited, as opposed to all-out, wars. These are his conclusions.[10]

In crises leading to a limited war, the Cabinet assigns responsibility for its detailed management to a 'War Cabinet'. For Korea the standing Defence Committee was used; the Cabinet's role was effectively limited to parliamentary and public relations. Smaller, *ad hoc* committees were used in the Suez and Falklands crises. At times of greatest pressure the Cabinet in each case had the formal opportunity to take major decisions; but in practice, especially during Suez, this amounted to an opportunity for a veto which was unlikely to be used. Two dangers facing a War Cabinet are those of

[9] Peter Madgwick, *British Government: The Central Executive Territory*, Philip Allan, Hemel Hempstead, 1991, p. 223.
[10] Colin Seymour-Ure, 'British "War Cabinets" in Limited Wars: Korea, Suez and the Falklands', *Public Administration*, Volume 24, summer 1984, p. 181.

tunnel vision and of the undue influence of military or technical considerations. The full Cabinet, best suited in principle to relate the problems of the war to the Government's other problems and goals, risks finding itself flanked by a War Cabinet too close to the war and by a Parliament which is too far away and too excitable.

Despite the new-found usefulness of the collective approach during the Falklands, in June 1983, just days after the general election, Mrs Thatcher announced the abolition of the CPRS. A collective body which had come to serve few other than the Prime Minister, it had found itself increasingly trying to make headway against the political tide during the Thatcher years, and its dependence on her ultimately cost its existence. This was the Prime Minister's announcement notice.[11]

The CPRS has been a valuable source of policy analysis and collective advice to Ministers in successive governments since it was established in 1971. In the meantime, however, departments have established or expanded their own policy units for long-term planning, and the Cabinet Office Secretariat's role in preparing issues for collective ministerial discussion has grown considerably. A policy unit has also been established in the Prime Minister's office.

In the light of these developments, and of the development of the role of special advisers as a source of general advice to ministers, the Prime Minister has decided, after consultation with her Cabinet colleagues, that the purposes for which the CPRS was set up are now being met satisfactorily in other ways and it should therefore be disbanded at the end of July.

---

[11] Tessa Blackstone and William Plowden, *Inside the Think Tank: Advising the Cabinet 1971–1983*, Heinemann, London, 1988, pp. 179–80.

Tessa Blackstone and William Plowden, in their monograph on the CPRS, published in 1988, drew some lessons from its successes and failures to provide guidance on how a future CPRS might operate rather more successfully. In some of the structures introduced under Tony Blair a decade later, it is possible to see that some of their advice was heeded, even if one crucial component – the collectivity – is still hard to come by.[12]

If our view is accepted that the 'strategy' function is important and should be performed, a future reconstructed CPRS ought to ensure that this function is formally written into its job specification. This might perhaps commit the CPRS to report once or twice a year to a special meeting of the Cabinet, perhaps followed by meetings with junior ministers, on the government's strategy in the medium to longer term. This commitment might be more acceptable to a future prime minister, and easier to sell to Cabinet colleagues, if a future CPRS were slightly more political, with its head and some of its members known to be sympathisers of the party in power. Without a formal commitment, all the pressures of the day-to-day government are likely to have the effect of pushing some future CPRS into fire-fighting and away from strategy . . .

It is a difficult question whether this central capability should serve the prime minister as head of the government and chairman of the Cabinet. The question raises the issue of the balance of power between the prime minister and his or her Cabinet. William Rodgers, a member of the Cabinet during the Callaghan government, has argued that the CPRS was bound to suffer the fate that eventually overtook it; that is, to become the short-term instrument of the prime minister rather than the long-term instrument of the Cabinet. It may also be the case that given Mrs Thatcher's style of Cabinet government, in which

---

[12] Ibid., pp. 215, 218–19.

she leads from the front and takes many decisions in small *ad hoc* groups of ministers rather than through the Cabinet and its system of committees, the expanded Policy Unit can fill the hole in the centre satisfactorily. But we do not believe that the characteristics of the CPRS under Thatcher derive from some inherent features of British Cabinet government. With a return to a more collective Cabinet decision-making process there would be a need for collective advice to ministers of the kind given by the CPRS. There would also be a need for a prime minister's Policy Unit. The simultaneous existence, between 1974 and 1983, of the CPRS and the Policy Unit, playing different but complementary roles, demonstrated that they could work alongside each other and occasionally together. Since 1983 the Policy Unit under Mrs Thatcher has served her needs as a radical Prime Minister more effectively partly because it has been more in tune with her political beliefs than the CPRS, which sometimes found it difficult to give the kind of committed advice she wanted.

Nigel Lawson (1932–) was a hugely influential Chancellor of the Exchequer and a 'true believer' in Thatcherism from the off. From his perspective, the weekly meeting of Cabinet mattered little – most decisions were taken instead in Cabinet committees, and much of their business was effectively bypassed by bilateral agreements between the Prime Minister and departmental ministers – what he called 'creeping bilateralism'[13] *preventing other ministers from building coalitions of interest against a proposal. Here he explains the importance of both, and uses the example of the poll tax, 'the most disastrous single decision which the Thatcher government took', to show how this castration of effective scrutiny could produce poor public policy.*[14]

---

[13] Nigel Lawson and Lord Armstrong of Ilminster, 'Cabinet Government in the Thatcher Years', *Contemporary Record*, Vol 8, Winter 1994, Number 3, p. 443.
[14] Ibid, p. 440, pp. 442–43, 445.

What most people think of as the Cabinet is, as everybody in this room knows, really the least important part of being a member of the Cabinet and of Cabinet government. I am referring here to the pictures they see on television of ministers trooping in for the weekly Cabinet meeting on Thursday mornings, and trooping out again. When I was a minister I always looked forward to the weekly Cabinet meeting intensely because it was, apart from the summer holidays, the only period of real rest that I got in what was a very heavy job. Cabinet meetings are, 90 per cent of the time, nowadays rather part of the dignified, rather than the efficient, part of Cabinet government.

* * *

... over a period of time, and this can happen remarkably soon, ministers can cease thinking as members of Cabinet with the collective responsibility for everything that is done, and function solely as heads of their own departments with their own departmental interests, with a departmental agenda and departmental issues that they feel particularly strongly about. If that is so, then it is very convenient for them, if on an issue which they consider to be particularly important, to do a deal with the Prime Minister in the confident expectation that it will go through, and they do not have to worry too much about the collective discussion. Again, when an issue comes to be collectively discussed, in a Cabinet committee where real decisions are taken, in a Cabinet committee, say, chaired by the prime minister of the day (as a number of them are), then a minister who is involved in some running battle with the prime minister over a matter where he has departmental responsibility may well feel reluctant to spend too much of his political capital, arguing a case against the prime minister in a field which is totally outside his departmental responsibility. It is some other minister's baby, some other minister's problem . . .

... in a large area of government ... what might be called a mutual blackball system exists. By that I mean that if a minister wishes to do something within his own field which the prime minister profoundly disapproves of, then the prime minister has a blackball which he or she can cast. He or she may choose not to cast it, but that blackball is there. Equally, however, unless the minister concerned is completely spineless – and that is occasionally the case, but not normally – then if the prime minister wants something done in a particular area, and the minister responsible disagrees with it, then it will not happen because he will effectively veto that idea: he has a blackball, too. And that does limit the power of the prime minister.

* * *

The most disastrous single decision which the Thatcher government took [the Poll Tax]. That went rigorously through all the procedures the textbook said it should do and, indeed, more; I mean, there was all manner of public consultation, Green Papers, White Papers, the lot, quite apart from a Cabinet committee which sat for a year; nothing could have been done with greater punctiliousness. Yet at the end of the day, we got this appalling decision. The explanation of why this happened lies, I think, in a number of the things I was talking about earlier: the Prime Minister getting out of touch with her own ministers, and ministers themselves acting as merely departmental heads, and even though they were members of the committee, concentrating on the issues that directly concerned them departmentally, which did not include the Poll Tax, even though it was capable of sinking the government.

After the Falklands, and her second election victory, Margaret Thatcher appeared even less willing to consider the views of colleagues. At a meeting on 13 November 1985 about closer European monetary co-operation, attended by William Whitelaw (Deputy Prime Minister), Nigel Lawson (Chancellor), Leon Brittan (Trade and Industry Secretary), Norman Tebbit (Party Chairman), John Wakeham (Chief Whip), John Biffen (Lord Privy Seal), Robin Leigh-Pemberton (Governor of the Bank of England) and Geoffrey Howe, she vetoed a decision which was reached on a 6–1 majority. Howe described the results.[15]

I think he [Whitelaw] was as surprised as I certainly was by Margaret's instant reaction. She spoke, briefly for her, and made it very plain that she could not and would not accept that view. She brought the meeting quickly to a close, leaving us all wondering where on earth we went next. Nigel invited Willie, Norman and me to join him next door. We were all downcast as well as dumbfounded. What had been the point of the meeting, we asked ourselves, if Margaret was unwilling to heed our collective judgement? The Prime Minister, we knew, was *primus inter pares* but this was the first time that any of us had contemplated her exercising a veto of this kind – and against the very principle of a government policy that we had all been proclaiming for years... The influence of a distant professor[16] had effectively removed the topic from the agenda of collective discussion for the foreseeable future. To change that state of affairs we should, I think, have needed to go almost off the constitutional map.

---

[15] Geoffrey Howe, *Conflict of Loyalty*, Macmillan, London, 1994, p. 450.
[16] Sir Alan Walters, economic adviser to the Prime Minister, whose advice ran counter to the formal advice she was receiving from members of her Cabinet.

Some ministers, more sympathetic to Thatcher's general political outlook, were also more sympathetic to her handling of Cabinet. This is former Environment Secretary and Trade Secretary Nicholas Ridley (1929–93).[17]

It is for each prime minister to decide how to run his or her Cabinet ... Margaret Thatcher was going to be the leader in her Cabinet. She wasn't going to be an impartial chairman ...

All decisions of importance were reported to the Cabinet, except those which were market sensitive, or just plain 'sensitive'. There was thus an opportunity for anyone who wanted to do so to reopen a question if he didn't like a decision. It did sometimes happen, but only rarely. For the most part, Cabinet ministers were so busy that they were only too thankful that other people's complex problems were being sorted out without their having to be involved.

Norman St. John-Stevas (1929–) was one of the first two Cabinet Ministers to be sacked. In 1986 he penned this (ultimately prophetic) article about the Cabinet's enduring influence.[18]

Prime ministers rise and fall; the Cabinet abides. The powers of prime ministers tend to be greatest when they need them least – when things are going well. Conversely, when matters are taking a turn for the worse they begin to fade away. At that point Cabinet once again comes into its own.

---

[17] Nicholas Ridley, *My Style of Government: The Thatcher Years*, Hutchinson, London, 1991, pp. 28, 29–30.
[18] Norman St. John-Stevas, 'Prime Ministers rise and fall, but the Cabinet abides', *Daily Telegraph*, 7 August 1986.

John Hoskyns, head of the Downing Street Policy Unit between 1979 and 1982, is one of the most interesting 'outsiders' to penetrate Whitehall's inner sanctum. An efficiency specialist who was profoundly sceptical of traditional politics and of the civil service in particular, in 2000 he had this to say about the system as he found it.[19]

It seemed to me that Whitehall had no overall strategic capability. In organisational terms, it had turned out to be a headless chicken. The Cabinet Office was an extremely efficient co-ordinating machine. Its briefs to the Prime Minister were of high quality for the despatch of day-to-day and week-to-week business. But Britain was in a state of political and economic discontinuity, and a conventionally efficient government machine was no longer enough. There was no group, team, department, or office, at the apex of government that was set up to determine what actual business had to be despatched, its purpose, sequence, lead times, priorities, enabling steps, internal consistency, politics, constraints, attendant risks; no machinery to mesh together the resulting work of the great Whitehall departments into a coherent whole, and then constantly progress it, revise it and keep it from dissolving into the usual governmental confusion. The lack of such a central 'brain' in the Whitehall organisation (which the CPRS could conceivably have been if Heath had understood strategy and given the CPRS the Whitehall authority it needed) had paralysed successive governments.

---

[19] John Hoskyns, *Just in time: Inside the Thatcher revolution*, Aurum Press, London, 2000, p. 356.

The civil service, of course, had a rather different perspective. In 1987 Lord Bancroft (1922–96), a former Head of the Home Civil Service and Permanent Secretary at the Department of the Environment, described how he saw the role of a department's senior civil servant in relation to a new minister.[20]

How best those [manifesto] policies might be implemented. And here the permanent secretary might have to tread very delicately perhaps suggesting modifications of a relatively minor nature in the priority given to those policies . . . because the permanent secretary must steer a course in which he retains or gains the trust of the new minister but, at the same time, carries out his responsibilities of bringing to the attention of the new minister . . . the difficulties of implementing some of the policies which are in the manifesto . . . It's not that the permanent secretary wants to get in the way of the wishes of the electorate, but he has got, in the words of one of my predecessors, to be 'faithful to the facts'.

John Hoskyns was not, however, an uncritical supporter of Mrs Thatcher's chosen means of dealing with these problems. In 1981 he and his Policy Unit colleagues sent her what they called the 'blockbuster' memorandum on problems with her method of doing things. Because she was actually forced to read it at the time, it is one of the most interesting critiques of her style of government. This is his later summary of its contents.[21]

She was providing political leadership to the country, but not management leadership to the government. She herself broke every

---

[20] Lord Bancroft interviewed by Michael Crick, May 1987, in Peter Hennessy, *Whitehall*, Pimlico, London, 2001, p. 509.
[21] John Hoskyns, *Just in time: Inside the Thatcher revolution*, Aurum Press, London, 2000, pp. 326–27.

rule of good leadership: bullying the weaker colleagues, criticising them in front of each other and in front of their officials. She did not seem to understand that they could not answer back without being disrespectful, in front of others, to a woman and to a prime minister. She was too ready to blame others when things went wrong, and gave too little praise or credit where it was due. None of these things would be forgiven when her position became weaker. The result was demoralisation in government, in the party and in Whitehall. 'No one tells you what is happening, just as no one told Ted.' She would have to rebuild relationships with the colleagues, and lead by encouragement, not by criticism. She should make the members of her team feel 10 feet tall, not add to their own human fears and self-doubt. When speaking of the government's achievements, she should say 'We', not 'I'.

The Prime Minister was becoming isolated and out of touch, as everyone in that lonely position seemed to do. One of her colleagues should have given her that advice. Whitelaw was probably the only one who could have done so, and he may well have tried. According to Lawson, Bernard Ingham was later to have precisely the opposite effect by encouraging her to denigrate her Cabinet colleagues, and then doing further denigrating on her behalf. However it happened, the seeds for her downfall were being sown.

Kenneth Berrill (1920–), a former head of the CPRS, talking to John Hoskyns, then head of the Downing Street Policy Unit, in 1981, had the following to say about the operation of government.[22]

He commented on the small number of political advisers in the present government, compared with its Labour predecessor

---

[22] John Hoskyns, *Just in time: Inside the Thatcher revolution*, Aurum Press, London, 2000, pp. 172–73.

(precisely the point that David, Alfred[23] and I had tried to discuss with Mrs Thatcher before the election). He said that the present Prime Minister was the most 'commanding' in his experience. Prime ministers tended either to act as chairmen, coordinating and steering discussion and then summing up the sense of the meeting or to participate in the discussion right from the start. Berrill warned us not to underestimate Callaghan's skill in leading, so to speak, from behind and then 'coming through to score the goal from time to time'. The danger with leading too much from the front was that it stopped discussion. Why should a peripheral minister, who is not fighting on an issue of crucial importance to his own department, take on the prime minister and possibly have a row, give offence, etc?

And so, he said, we were seeing the pattern of bilateral discussions between the prime minister and those principally involved in each issue, without any wider discussion. 'Busy ministers, facing a big decision as simply one of three items on an agenda, are not really prepared to go beyond one and a half pages of analysis.' He commented on the Cabinet committee on social policy under Shirley Williams in the previous government. On the face of it this was a valid exercise, serviced by the CPRS under a very sympathetic minister. But the thing gradually fizzled out over a few years because there was not enough decision-making involved. Busy ministers needed the pressure of decision. They could not slip into the mould of protracted discussion and self-education.

Bernard Ingham (1932–), Margaret Thatcher's Press Secretary, was an intensely controversial figure. He was frequently accused of briefing against Cabinet ministers, with the Prime Minister's blessing. Here one of those ministers briefed against (he was described as being 'semi-

---

[23] David Wolfson, Chief of Staff in the Number 10 Political Office, and Alfred Sherman, co-founder of the Centre for Policy Studies.

detached'), John Biffen (1930–), describes how he saw that system working.[24]

Margaret Thatcher and Bernard Ingham used the lobby system to promote a prime ministerial view of events which went far beyond anything attempted by Neville Chamberlain or any of his successors...

Margaret Thatcher used the Ingham press lobby to undermine and dispatch ministers who fell out of favour. She preferred this technique to resolving those disputes in the collective privacy of the Cabinet.

The Westland affair was the nadir of Margaret Thatcher's second term in office. It resulted from the attempted sale of a small west-country helicopter manufacturer. The company itself was keen to be sold to an American firm; Defence Secretary Michael Heseltine (1933–) encouraged a European consortium to bid for it and was keen to support their bid. He eventually resigned over the issue, arguing that he had been denied a promised Cabinet hearing at which to put his case. He was followed shortly afterwards by Trade and Industry Secretary Leon Brittan (1939–), whose position became untenable when it emerged that he had authorised the leak of a letter from the Attorney General which appeared to cast doubt on the viability and legality of the Heseltine-backed bid. Mrs Thatcher maintains that proper procedures were, in fact, followed, and that Heseltine had been the one to breach them.[25]

---

[24] John Biffen, 'The revenge of the unburied dead', *Observer*, 9 December 1990.
[25] Margaret Thatcher, *The Downing Street Years*, HarperCollins, London, 1993, pp. 434, 436.

My speech was low-key and strictly factual. It demonstrated that we had reached our decisions on Westland in a proper and responsible way. Indeed, as I listed all the meetings of ministers, including Cabinet committees and Cabinets which had discussed Westland, I half felt that I had been guilty of wasting too much of ministers' time on an issue of relative unimportance. Although it set out all the facts, my speech was not well received. The press were expecting something more fiery.

Michael Heseltine spoke, criticising the way in which collective responsibility had been discharged over Westland and quite ignoring the fact that he had walked out of a Cabinet meeting on Westland because he was the only minister unwilling to abide by a Cabinet decision . . .

. . . to begin with the issues were not as clear-cut as they became. Although, as I was later to stress to the House of Commons, decisions on defence procurement are for the Cabinet as a whole not just for the Defence Secretary, Michael certainly did have a legitimate role to play in deciding Westland's future. The problem was that he did not stick to the limits of that role and not only sought to impose his own views on a private company but did so without respect for collective responsibility in the government.

Geoffrey Howe took a rather different view.[26]

Coming from the past mistress at marginalising Cabinet committees and deciding issues in bilaterals, this was quite a statement. Margaret Thatcher developed over time a clear determination to limit dialogue within government. As Chancellor and, to a lesser extent, as Foreign Secretary, I was lucky enough to be one of those who very

---

[26] Geoffrey Howe, 'The Triumph and Tragedy of the Thatcher Years', *Financial Times*, 24 October 1993.

often had to be present. But one has little doubt – and at the time had few illusions – that she came to see collective discussion as an irritating inconvenience.

Michael Heseltine obviously agreed. He had walked out in the middle of the Cabinet meeting, and later that day offered a 22–page resignation statement. He argued that he had several times been denied a hearing at a Cabinet committee, and claimed that the commitment had been deliberately excluded from the Cabinet minutes, only reinstated at his request. This was the conclusion of his statement.[27]

To serve as a member of a Tory Cabinet within the constitutional understandings and practices of a system under which the Prime Minister is *primus inter pares* is a memory I will always treasure.

But if the basis of trust between the Prime Minister and her Defence Secretary no longer exists, there is no place for me with honour in such a Cabinet.

Margaret Thatcher's premiership had looked vulnerable during the Westland affair. Echoing the views of other Cabinet members about the Prime Minister's closest advisers, Nigel Lawson described how negative were the longer-term effects of this feeling of vulnerability.[28]

The longer-term effects of the Westland affair, however, were wholly adverse. The lesson Margaret took from it was that her colleagues were troublesome and her courtiers were loyal. From then on she began to distance herself even from those Cabinet colleagues who had been closest to her – certainly those who had minds of their own

---

[27] Michael Heseltine, *Life in the Jungle: My Autobiography*, Hodder & Stoughton, London, 2000, p. 542.
[28] Nigel Lawson, *The View from No. 11: Memoirs of a Tory Radical*, Bantam Press, London, 1992, pp. 680–81.

– and to retreat to the Number 10 bunker, where the leading figures were Charles Powell[29] and Bernard Ingham.

I have already written of Ingham, against whom she would not hear a word said. On the occasions when I complained about his activities, she roundly denied that he could possibly have been guilty of what I was alleging, even though it was well known to the Press that that was exactly what he had been doing. Other ministers met precisely the same response. Charles Powell, the Foreign Office man who had become her foreign affairs private secretary, and for most of the time the dominant force in her private office, was as polished as Ingham was blunt. Highly intelligent, he wrote the best and wittiest notes of meetings of anyone in Whitehall. His closeness to her was reinforced by the unlikely friendship Margaret developed with Powell's vivacious and somewhat less polished Italian wife, Carla. He never saw it as his role to question her prejudices, merely to refine the language in which they were expressed. And like Ingham, he stayed at Number 10 far too long – despite Whitehall's efforts to persuade her to make a change and the Foreign Office's repeated attempts to lure him away with the promise of ever more attractive ambassadorial posts.

With things drifting in this undesirable direction, I was both surprised and immensely heartened when, on the flight back from the May 1986 Tokyo summit, Margaret took me aside and said she was considering forming an inner Cabinet: what did I think? It was, of course, what I had for some time felt to be the crucial missing ingredient in the Thatcher government, and I told her I thought it was an excellent idea. Soon afterwards she asked Geoffrey to join us, and we discussed the membership. It seemed to boil down to herself, Willie, Geoffrey, Norman Tebbit, John Wakeham and myself. But

---

[29] Charles Powell (1941–), Foreign Affairs Private Secretary to Margaret Thatcher.

no sooner had she arrived back in London, than the plan changed. Perhaps she changed her mind unaided, perhaps she was persuaded against it by the courtiers, whose role would have diminished. There was no point in asking her, as she would inevitably have replied that it was her unaided decision.

Over time, Nigel Lawson and Margaret Thatcher, as was inevitable for two strong and temperamental personalities, fell out. Lawson adopted the policy of shadowing the German Deutschmark without mentioning it to the Prime Minister; Thatcher had begun to take advice from American economist Sir Alan Walters which undermined Lawson's constitutional position as the manager of economic policy. At the end of 1989, Lawson resigned. This is from his resignation statement.[30]

No one, however long he has held the post, lightly gives up the great office of Chancellor of the Exchequer. Certainly I did not. As the resignation letter that I wrote to my right hon. friend the Prime Minister clearly implies, it was not the outcome I sought. But it is one that I accept without rancour despite what might be described as the hard landing involved. I would only add that the article written by my right hon. friend's former economic adviser was of significance only inasmuch as it represented the tip of a singularly ill-concealed iceberg, with all the destructive potential that icebergs possess . . .

 . . . for our system of Cabinet government to work effectively, the prime minister of the day must appoint ministers whom he or she trusts and then leave them to carry out the policy. When differences of view emerge, as they are bound to do from time to time, they should be resolved privately and, whenever appropriate, collectively.

---

[30] HC Debs, 5 Series, Vol. 159, 31 October 1989, col. 208.

A year later, another resignation statement was to prove even more dramatic. Geoffrey Howe's speech to the House of Commons (on 13 November 1990) was electrifying because it was so critical, because he had been so loyal over so many years, and because it issued a call to arms for anyone who wished to challenge her. While the core of his criticism was directed towards their growing differences on European policy, he also argued that her behaviour was now out of control.[31]

In my letter of resignation, which I tendered with the utmost sadness and dismay, I said: 'Cabinet government is all about trying to persuade one another from within.' That was my commitment to government by persuasion – persuading colleagues and the nation. I have tried to do that as Foreign Secretary and since, but I realise now that the task has become futile: trying to stretch the meaning of words beyond what was credible, and trying to pretend that there was a common policy when every step forward risked being subverted by some casual comment or impulsive answer.

The conflict of loyalty, of loyalty to my right hon. friend the Prime Minister – and, after all, in two decades that instinct of loyalty is still very real – and of loyalty to what I perceive to be the true interests of the nation, has become all too great. I no longer believe it possible to resolve that conflict from within this government. That is why I have resigned. In doing so, I have done what I believe to be right for my party and my country. That time has come for others to consider their own response to the tragic conflict of loyalties with which I have myself wrestled for perhaps too long.

---

[31] Geoffrey Howe, *Conflict of Loyalty*, Macmillan, London, 1994, pp. 702–03.

Howe's statement did indeed produce a leadership challenge. It came from former Defence Secretary Michael Heseltine, who won enough votes in the first round of voting amongst Conservative MPs to force a second. Mrs Thatcher originally announced her intention to fight on in that second round, and decided to consult her Cabinet colleagues about her chances.[32]

The earlier meetings had persuaded me that it was essential to mobilise the Cabinet ministers not just to give formal support, but also to go out and persuade junior ministers and back-benchers to back me. In asking for their support, however, I was also putting myself at their mercy. If a substantial number of Cabinet colleagues refused their backing, there could be no disguising the fact afterwards. I recalled a complaint from Churchill, then Prime Minister, to his Chief Whip that talk of his resignation in the parliamentary party – he would shortly be succeeded by Anthony Eden – was undermining his authority. Without that authority, he could not be an effective prime minister. Similarly, a prime minister who knows that his or her Cabinet has withheld its support is fatally weakened. I knew – and I am sure they knew – that I would not willingly remain an hour in 10 Downing Street without real authority to govern.

Her Cabinet did not provide the looked-for solace. Very few of them were prepared to offer her any comfort about the likely result, although they invariably declared that they would personally support her.[33]

I was sick at heart. I could have resisted the opposition of opponents and potential rivals and even respected them for it; but what grieved

---

[32] Margaret Thatcher, *The Downing Street Years*, HarperCollins, London, 1993, pp. 850–51.
[33] Ibid., p. 855.

me was the desertion of those I had always considered friends and allies and the weasel words whereby they had transmuted their betrayal into frank advice and concern for my fate. I dictated a brief statement of my resignation to be read out at Cabinet the following morning. But I said that I would return to No. 10 to talk to Denis before finally taking my decision.

Margaret Thatcher's period in office was controversial in so many ways, her style not least amongst them. In the last seven excerpts in this chapter, Thatcher-watchers who had worked with her, and those who had studied her from afar, consider the effects of that style on the operation of Cabinet government. Was it a temporary aberration or did it herald something more fundamental in the underlying operation of the system? For some here it did mean exactly that – the end of consensual Cabinet government. However, others disagreed, including George Jones, proponent of an 'elastic theory' of Cabinet government – that it could be 'stretched to accommodate an activist, interventionist prime minister, but also contract to contain a more passive prime minister.'[34] In this piece, he claims that Thatcher's style merely tipped the system away from Cabinet government, and didn't entirely alter it.[35]

The British system of government cannot really be called prime ministerial government, nor can it be called Cabinet government. The right term is ministerial government, because *legally* powers are given in Acts of Parliament to ministers. No powers are given to the prime minister or Cabinet: they do not exist legally; they are conventions.

---

[34] George Jones: 'Cabinet Government and Mrs. Thatcher', *Contemporary Record*, Vol.1 No.3, Autumn 1987, p.11.
[35] G. W. Jones, 'The Prime Minister's Aides', in Anthony King (ed.), *The British Prime Minister* (second ed.), Macmillan, Basingstoke, 1985, pp. 72, 87–88, 94–95.

* * *

[A prime minister's] department might weaken the prime minister because what the prime minister needs are flexible arrangements, which can adapt easily to each prime minister's needs. Prime ministers have different needs, different temperaments, different styles of working, and over the years the basic structure at Number 10 has adapted easily to what the various prime ministers have required . . . a prime minister's department would be a revolution in the constitution, a move from a ministerial Cabinet system to prime ministerial government . . . A prime minister's department is not required.

* * *

She is the most interventionist Prime Minister since Lloyd George, and has sought to mould the staff around her to enable her to find out more of what the departments are doing, to scrutinise their activities and to provide other options to their proposals. While she has been strengthening her own personal staff resources, she has weakened those at the disposal of her Cabinet colleagues for the performance of their collective deliberations by abolishing the CPRS. She has tipped the system a little away from collective to presidential government. But the tipping is only slight. The political and policy aides who serve her are few, junior, inexperienced in government, and fluctuating. They do not stay for long to assist her. They are not as stable a component as the private office nor any real rival to the formidable array of bureaucratic resources available to ministers in their departments.

Some practitioners also disagreed on the need for a prime minister's department. Since Harold Macmillan's comment about the lack of support for a prime minister made Dame Evelyn Sharp consider the need for greater support,[36] academics and politicians have debated the desirability of a prime minister's department – which exists in other countries, for example Australia. In an article making that case, Kenneth Berrill (former head of the CPRS and Chief Economic Adviser to the Treasury) highlighted the additional workload which new international commitments have imposed, and the logical consequences of that workload.[37]

The head of government must know the facts and views on the objectives, the strategy and the tactics across a very wide range of issues in their international context ... No matter what his priorities, in today's world it is just not open to a head of government to devote himself very largely to his country's domestic problems.

* * *

The prime ministerial load is already too heavy to take on yet more detailed responsibilities. What in my view is at issue is whether a prime minister should have a support system with time to work on problems in some depth across the width of government activities.

---

[36] Chapter 7, p. 115.
[37] Kenneth Berrill, 'Strength and the Centre – The Case for a Prime Minister's Department', in Anthony King (ed.), *The British Prime Minister* (second ed.), Macmillan, Basingstoke, 1985, pp. 249, 256.

Academic Anthony King, assessing Thatcher's style of government in a 1985 essay, predicted that, while she dominated her government for the time being, this dominance would eventually result in an eye taken off the political ball, with negative long-term consequences.[38]

Following the Falklands, Thatcher could still on occasion be defeated in Cabinet, but her position of overall dominance was never again in doubt.

* * *

The greater a prime minister's public prestige is thought to be by his Cabinet colleagues – the greater is likely to be his capacity to bend those colleagues to his will.

* * *

She therefore had no choice, given her aims and determination, but to lead in an unusually forthright, assertive manner. Partly this was a matter of her personality; she is a forthright and assertive person. But it was at least as much a matter of the objective situation in which she found herself. She was forced to behave like an outsider for the simple reason that she was one.

* * *

An understandable desire to pull decisions into 10 Downing Street – to be in charge and to seen to be in charge – will result in dilatoriness as well as in weakening the authority of departmental ministers. Her involvement in the taking of all major decisions, and many minor ones, means that many of them do not get taken for a very long time. Delay is likely to have adverse consequences in itself; it could in time

---

[38] Anthony King, 'Margaret Thatcher: The Style of a Prime Minister', in Anthony King (ed.), *The British Prime Minister* (second ed.), Macmillan, Basingstoke, 1985, pp. 107, 109, 116, 135.

come to be portrayed, however inappropriately, as a consequence of indecision. As her tenure of Number 10 lengthens there is also the danger that, although hitherto an assiduous listener, she may stop listening; that, although previously a very careful weigher of other people's power, she may neglect to do her sums or may come up with the wrong answer; that, although in the past a cautious respecter of other people's power, she may in the future fall into the trap of exaggerating her own. Hubris is a danger to Thatcher no more, but no less, than other political leaders.

The Thatcher era also saw the use of all manner of phraseology and constitutional assumptions fall into disuse. Anthony King explained why this was so for one particularly crucial one.[39]

... as an analytical device for exploring the relations between prime ministers and their Cabinet colleagues it [the phrase *primus inter pares*] is so vague as to be completely useless.

Robert Armstrong (1927–), Thatcher's Cabinet Secretary from 1979–88 and one of Whitehall's key figures throughout the era, accepted the new terminology. At a 1994 seminar he argued that the debate had moved so far from Cabinet government that it was now between prime ministerial and presidential government.[40]

After that [the Falklands] experience there was some revival in the more traditionally conventional processes of Cabinet government. There were more meetings of Cabinet committees and fewer *ad hoc* groups; the thing was more formally organised and there was a

---

[39] Anthony King (ed.), *The British Prime Minister* (second ed.), Macmillan, Basingstoke, 1985, p. 4.
[40] Nigel Lawson and Lord Armstrong of Ilminster, 'Cabinet Government in the Thatcher Years', *Contemporary Record*, Vol 8, Winter 1994, Number 3.

repetition of that after the Westland affair of 1986 when the principle of collective responsibility once again came under strain. I think that the importance of Cabinet government did, as it were, revive in those periods. I agree with Nigel very much that, on the old Crossman argument, between prime minister and presidential government, we still have prime ministerial government, even after Thatcher, much as Thatcher might have wished it otherwise.

Historian John Vincent took the view that the Thatcher had inclined towards, but not reached, the presidential.[41]

Mrs Thatcher is an exponent more of presidential than of Cabinet government. These things are relative. She has not sought to build up a White House. Indeed, she rejected plans for a prime minister's department and abolished the Think Tank: hardly the actions of a centraliser. Rather, the conduct of business has turned on personality and on faction. By temperament Mrs Thatcher is not a good listener. Her Cabinet technique, it is said, is a brisk exchange of fire with individual ministers on their special topics, not an Asquithian waiting game as discussion unfolds around the table. Moreover, her assertion that her aim is to get things done has to be taken seriously. The Cabinet stopped things getting done. The long list of her defeats in Cabinet is one reason why meetings of the full Cabinet have been kept to the minimum.

---

[41] John Vincent, 'The Thatcher Governments, 1979–1987', in Peter Hennessy and Anthony Seldon (eds.), *Ruling Performance: British Governments from Attlee to Thatcher*, Basil Blackwell, Oxford, 1987, p. 288.

David Butler was able to offer a balanced view which reflected the new consensus: Cabinet government was, if not dead, then fundamentally altered, and unlikely to revert to the status quo ante.[42]

The style of government has changed. It is arguable how far the full Cabinet was ever the central forum of decision-making. Prime ministers have always fixed many of the key issues in advance with one or more of their senior colleagues, so that to use the phrase 'rubber stamp' about the Cabinet could at times be almost as fair as to use it about Parliament. None the less there have been many critical moments round the table at No. 10 when . . . argument has changed the course of events. And prime ministers, notably Macmillan and Wilson, have testified to the extent that their behaviour was conditioned by considerations of what the Cabinet would stand.

Richard Crossman argued in 1963 that the Cabinet had become a dignified, not an efficient, instrument and that Cabinet government had been superseded by prime-ministerial government. Experience of office in 1964–70 led him to retreat slightly from this view, and Patrick Gordon Walker offered a stoutly revisionist picture of the importance of the Cabinet, which found support in many of the accounts of how affairs were managed in the 1970s. But it does seem that a change has taken place since then. Certainly, after her first few years, Mrs Thatcher took to acting more autocratically in No. 10, allowing fewer papers to come to Cabinet and tolerating less discussion. Cabinet committees and unrecorded *ad hoc* meetings of small groups of ministers have become more important. In 1983–86 the number of hours a week spent by full Cabinet was less than at any time since the war.

[42] David Butler, 'British Politics 1945–1987', in Peter Hennessy and Anthony Seldon (eds.), *Ruling Performance: British Governments from Attlee to Thatcher*, Basil Blackwell, Oxford, 1987, pp. 327–28.

11
Reaction, 1990–1997

Michael Heseltine returned to government under John Major (1943–), first as Employment Secretary, then Trade and Industry Secretary (and President of the Board of Trade, for which title he was much mocked). He eventually combined the latter role with that of Deputy Prime Minister and became a lynchpin of Major's administration. These two sections from his autobiography again testify to the difference in personal style between the two Prime Ministers he served, and how that affected Cabinet.[1]

I learnt quickly that it was all too easy to find one's arguments cut off in midstream by prime ministerial interruption, to have the case one wished to deploy hijacked by premature conclusions and often hectoring interventions. One either gave in to it or one learnt to fight back. Hard experience taught me to wait until Mrs Thatcher paused for breath and then I began again – and again – and again – until I was satisfied that what I had to say had been clearly heard. It was wearying, but those who shrank from it soon found themselves marginalised in the endless power struggle of Cabinet life.

* * *

---

[1] Michael Heseltine, *Life in the Jungle: My Autobiography*, Hodder & Stoughton, London, 2000, pp. 232, 488.

Curiously enough, considering the pressure under which senior politicians live and the pace with which business must be got through, the exchanges between Cabinet colleagues tend to be remarkably good-tempered. Often the differences of view are real and genuine. Every day there are winners and losers. But such is the kaleidoscope of interests involved that a pattern of mutual tolerance gradually emerges. There is, of course, a good reason for this: in the morning you may find yourself at loggerheads with a particular colleague but then arguing passionately on his or her side on a different issue that same afternoon. And it has to be said that John Major was entitled to a great deal of the credit for the improved atmosphere, particularly in Cabinet. In contrast to the Thatcher years, everyone was allowed their say. Arguments were countered by reasons and not interrupted or shouted down. Personal abuse and raised voices were never part of the currency. There may have been occasional and very human lapses even on John's part – but they always took place in circumstances which he had every reason to believe were private.

John Major had sought consciously to achieve this change. In his autobiography, he eloquently described the differences between his style of Cabinet government and the practice of his predecessor.[2]

Margaret [Thatcher] had often introduced subjects in Cabinet by setting out her favoured solution: shameless, but effective. I, by contrast, preferred to let my views be known in private, see potential dissenters ahead of the meeting, encourage discussion, and sum up after it. A different approach, but, I believe, one that is equally effective. Margaret had been at her happiest confronting political dragons; I chose consensus in policy-making, if not always in policy.

[2] John Major, *The Autobiography*, HarperCollins, London, 1999, p. 209.

We were each a product of our times, our characters and our parliamentary positions. She followed a disastrous Labour decade, and was able to boldly attack her inheritance. I had to talk up my inheritance, while moving with the minimum of fuss to correct my own party's mistakes.

Part of Major's new direction was his decision, in 1992, to publish Questions of Procedure for Ministers *(QPM). This meant, for the first time, that the public had some kind of job specification for those who governed them. Yet Cabinet Secretary Robin Butler (1938–) argued that such was the prime minister's power, he could easily scrap the document if he so decided.*[3]

It would be perfectly possible for an incoming prime minister to scrap the whole thing and to devise new rules. The fact that it has been published, would, of course, lead to a debate about that and he would, no doubt, be questioned about the reasons for changes. But it is entirely at the discretion of the new prime minister to scrap this lot of rules and . . . deal with the administration in the way that he chooses.

Gillian Shephard (1940–), who sat in John Major's Cabinet for most of his time as Prime Minister, later wrote a memoir describing several revealing episodes both about Major and the balance of power in Cabinet.[4]

He demonstrated immense self-control at Cabinet, even when he was enraged by the latest series of leaks or briefings against him.

---

[3] Amy Baker, *Prime Ministers and the Rule Book*, Politico's, London, 2000, p. 106.
[4] Gillian Shephard, *Shephard's Watch: Illusions of power in British Politics*, Politicos, London, 2000, pp. 32, 147.

The strongest sign of irritation he showed was to throw down his pencil ...

There was a fair amount of showing-off, too. Someone might say, 'I don't know if anyone heard me on the *Today* programme this morning. I said X.' This went on for years, until one day, John Major said, 'I never listen to the *Today* programme.' There was a sudden silence, and a perceptible reappraisal around the table.

John Major's first Cabinet, which contained no women, was known as the 'Cabinet of chums', containing an above-average number of Cambridge contemporaries even though Major himself had not received a university education. Here John Hoskyns questions how valuable has been the high intellectual calibre of Cabinet ministers since the War.[5]

There can't be many multinational boards with five or more directors who were all contemporaries at Cambridge, as was the case in John Major's Cabinet. In politics the academic experience seems to leave a strong imprint. Denis Healey, in his memoirs, refers to one of Harold Wilson's Cabinets containing eight people with first-class degrees from Oxford. But what did all that brainpower achieve? There is another problem. The closed nature of the system, and the 'musical chairs' resulting from most job changes, mean that professional MPs become, almost by definition, amateur ministers, moving from one half-understood portfolio to another at twelve- to eighteen-month intervals. As a normal rule, the system produces ministers who can preside quite competently over something that works. But they are unlikely to know how to handle large-scale systemic emergencies. For that, they will look to the civil service; and they will look in vain.

[5] John Hoskyns, *Just in time: Inside the Thatcher revolution*, Aurum Press, London, 2000, p. 393.

In a speech at Brunel University on 10 November 1993, Lord Wakeham (1932–), at that time an influential member of the Cabinet and chairman of a number of its committees, became the first such minister to speak on the record about current practice. He confirmed a number of developments perceived by outsiders, and his comments on the committee to oversee public spending were of particular interest.[6]

The increasing use of Cabinet as a reporting and reviewing body, rather than a decision-taker is, I think, an irreversible consequence of the complexity of modern government.

* * *

One new phenomenon which neither Lord Hailsham nor anyone else foresaw six years ago was the setting up of a Ministerial Committee on Public Expenditure to consider collectively and recommend to Cabinet the approach to be adopted to meet the government's public expenditure remits. The so-called 'Star Chamber' chaired by Lord Whitelaw which met occasionally to resolve particularly bitter public expenditure disputes was a precursor of a sort. But the setting up of a Standing Ministerial Committee as a regular part of the government machine marks quite a strong movement towards greater collective involvement in the annual public expenditure survey. The arrangement is only into its second year, but it is already, I believe, beginning to change the quality of the public expenditure discussions, in particular by bringing in a wider range of ministerial experience and a broader perspective at the early stages.

---

[6] Lord Wakeham, 'Cabinet Government', *Contemporary Record*, Vol. 8, Winter 1994, Number 3.

In her book Presidentializing the Premiership, *Sue Pryce argued that there is a clear relationship between the centrality of the public role played by a prime minister, his or her need for better (and independent) advice and the subsequent short-circuiting of the role of departmental ministers as policy initiators and advisers.*[7]

... this often meant advice that would enable them [prime ministers] to challenge the accepted wisdom of departmental civil servants mediated by their Cabinet colleagues ... as a consequence of this, by the 1990s the Cabinet was beginning to look uncomfortably like its American counterpart. It could be seen as just one among many advisory bodies orbiting the prime minister, and its members were becoming frontmen who were expected to sell the prime minister's policies to the political nation and the public. Prime ministers seemed to consider themselves free to exploit tensions between their cabinets, advised by Whitehall, and the various alternative advisers on their personal staff.

Under John Major, a number of 'machinery of government' reforms and much institutionalisation of previous practice took place. Martin Burch and Ian Holliday argue that this was in fact an extremely significant period, and that the scope of 'central executive studies' now needs to be further broadened.[8]

Its approach can partly be seen as a tidying-up operation following the extreme semi-formality and informality of the Thatcher years, although it amounts to far more than these. The Major period has in fact witnessed a substantial consolidation of the changes which have

---

[7] Sue Pryce, *Presidentializing the Premiership*, Macmillan, Basingstoke, 1997, p. 4.
[8] Martin Burch and Ian Holliday, *The British Cabinet System*, Prentice Hall, Hemel Hempstead, 1996, pp. 280–81, 46.

taken place incrementally since 1974, and especially since 1979. The system of ministerial standing committees has been streamlined through consolidation of overarching domestic and overseas committees in EDP and OPD, reduction in the number of standing committees, and redistribution of responsibilities between then. Business has also been concentrated in formal ministerial standing committees of Cabinet, with the result that the use of *ad hoc* and official committees has experienced a precipitate decline. Similar changes have been made to the organisation of Cabinet Office secretariats. On the domestic side, the economic and home and social affairs secretariats have effectively been fused, thus accentuating the distinction between domestic and overseas business. When these developments are analysed together, what emerges is a Cabinet and committee machine which is both leaner and sharper and in which activities are drawn more closely into formal structures. Consolidation is further reflected in the creation of OPS [Office of Public Service] within the Cabinet Office. This has provided a new location for many functions which have been brought within the centre over a period of years. The placing of OPS under a Cabinet minister has served to regularise this accumulation of functions. Under Major and Cabinet Secretary Butler, the Cabinet system has thus become more institutionalised and more firmly embedded in the established framework of government. Theirs has been a period of great significance, akin to the period of expansion and consolidation which took place under Attlee and Cabinet Secretaries Bridges and Brook.

* * *

Conventional accounts of the formal structure of the Cabinet system tend to highlight the position of prime minister, a small number of key ministers, Cabinet acting collectively, and some key officials ... the formal structure of the Cabinet system is far more comprehensive than is suggested by such accounts. The number of functions that are located in the Cabinet system, and the multiplicity of formal Cabinet system arenas within which key personnel interact, mean that a large range of formal organisations and key positions have to be brought within analysis. While the positions identified in conventional accounts are obviously important, they therefore need to be both added to and in some cases subjected to important qualification.

Peter Madgwick agreed that it would be wrong to underestimate the importance of Cabinet committees, and even informal meetings, as part of the core executive. Calling the full Cabinet the Cabinet 'Council', he accepted that its importance had diminished.[9]

The Cabinet Council is by convention at the centre or apex of the Cabinet system since by convention the Cabinet has the final authority to ratify and legitimate decisions. But this authority must be understood as informing, shaping and capping the Cabinet system, rather than as a supreme authority wielded daily over the development of policy and the taking of decisions. The Cabinet is formally but not operationally at the top of a hierarchical structure.

In this 1993 article, Diana Woodhouse charted the decline in resignations under the doctrine of ministerial responsibility. She concluded that the situations in which ministers would now resign had dramatically narrowed over time.[10]

---

[9] Peter Madgwick, *British Government: The Central Executive Territory*, Philip Allan, Hemel Hempstead, 1991, p. 53.

[10] Diana Woodhouse, 'Ministerial responsibility in the 1990s: when do ministers resign?', *Parliamentary Affairs*, Volume 46, Number 3, July 1993.

The answer to the question 'when do ministers resign?' is therefore elusive, at least as it relates to departmental fault. It appears that the following conditions are required before a resignation is likely to occur.

The minister must have made a grievous and foreseeable error in very high policy resulting in evident and grave consequences for a large number of people enjoying public regard and sympathy.

The policy must be easily dissociated from the government as a whole.

There must be no civil servant or law officer in sight to take the blame.

The prime minister should be happy to lose the minister (but not have a reshuffle in mind) and have a replacement at hand.

The parliamentary party and the tabloid press should be out for blood, with the heavy press demanding resignation.

The minister must have a sense of constitutional propriety.

In all other circumstances ministers can hide in the complexities outlined above and expect to survive – at least until the next Cabinet reshuffle, and frequently beyond.

Douglas Hurd had been Political Secretary to Edward Heath and was later a senior Minister himself, serving under both Margaret Thatcher and John Major. From this perspective, he reached the conclusion that a prime minister had less freedom of manoeuvre than was sometimes assumed.[11]

The prime minister can neither govern – as governing occurs through a myriad of institutions – nor actually make decisions without dependence on a whole range of other actors and

---

[11] Quoted in Martin J. Smith, *The Core Executive in Britain*, Macmillan, Basingstoke, 1999, p. 105.

institutions, and without taking account of the structural context. What the prime minister does is play a tactical game that creates the necessary alliances for achieving goals.

In 1993 Michael Foley published his book The Rise of the British Presidency, *in which he argued that the parallels between the British prime minister and American president were now too close to ignore. He accepted that substantial structural differences meant that the context in which they operated was different, but that the means by which presidents and prime ministers confronted challenges, and the nature of many (but not all) of these challenges, were very similar. He argued that, far from nullifying his analysis, the fall of Margaret Thatcher had in fact confirmed it.*[12]

The development and forces underlying the changes in the political position of the British prime minister are not merely similar to those experienced in the White House, but are exemplified and illustrated most fully in their nature by the American presidency. The analytical and interpretative insights afforded by studies of the American presidency can, therefore, be exploited to great effect to increase further the understanding of contemporary developments in the British premiership and to illustrate the many political and social repercussions that flow from the intensification of these trends. This is not to underestimate the importance of the structural differences that exist between the two systems. But it is to draw attention to, and to recognise the significance of, the dramatic extent to which even within two such different contexts certain profound similarities have arisen. In spite of the clear contrast in institutional superstructures, the underlying points of resemblance are so exceptional that there is

---

[12] Michael Foley, *The Rise of the British Presidency*, Manchester University Press, Manchester, 1993, pp. 263–64, 277–78, 282–83.

now evidence to support the contention that the similarities between the two offices are more revealing than their differences. Furthermore, these similarities are increasing in scale and importance all the time.

It is now a plausible contention to claim that the pressures and opportunities, the expectations and motivations, and the restraints and problems associated with the business of being and remaining a prime minister are sufficiently analogous to the equivalent conditions faced by an American president to justify the term 'president' being applied to the occupant of Number 10. In fact, it would be no exaggeration to assert that what this country has witnessed over the last generation has been the growing emergence of a British presidency.

It is important to point out that such an assertion is not implying a convergence of the British premiership with the American presidency. But neither does it carry the implication that the two positions are following diverging courses of development. What is being suggested is that they have come to move along parallel paths. Their separation is still significant, but the changes in the politics of the British premiership have now had the effect of pulling the conditions and properties of British political leadership in the same direction as the contemporary evolution of the American presidency. These forces underlying the presidency's development are now so clearly evident in the British context that they provide compelling grounds for establishing the existence of what is to all intents and purposes a *de facto* British presidency.

* * *

At present what is important is the recognition of a British presidency in formation. It is presidential because of its similarities with recent developments in the American presidency. But it is also very much a British phenomenon. The presence of a *de facto* presidency in the British system has been occasioned by British circumstances and traditions. Furthermore, it has been assisted and supported by some of the most central components of the British system. Parties, for example, have come not only to sponsor the issue of leadership in political competition, but also to project their leaders as individual summations of public hopes, anxieties and ideals. Cabinets – filled as they are with professional politicians who know what is required for governmental and electoral viability in modern conditions – underwrite prime ministerial prominence and leverage as the necessary instruments for remaining in office. Many of the prime minister's colleagues around the Cabinet table will still aspire to his position, but their highest priority will be to remain in government. They will therefore condone and even encourage a prime minister to go out and cultivate a presidential status in the public battle to provide high-profile popular leadership. This amounts to collective peer group pressure to a prime minister to breach the collective ethos of the Cabinet and to assume both a public persona and an individual pre-eminence for the sake of the Cabinet and the party as a whole. As Mrs Thatcher found to her cost, the pressure can work both ways. A prime minister whose stock declines in the public arena not only loses authority in the Cabinet and the party, but risks being removed as party leader.

* * *

In this respect, John Major is probably far more significant than Margaret Thatcher. In seeking to break away from, and to act as an antidote to, the *grande dame*, he has in fact demonstrated the influence of her conditioning precedents. He arguably acted out of character, and contrary to expectations to change the Thatcher government into a wholeheartedly Major government. He was obliged to replace one form of high-profile leadership with another. He personalised policy changes to give emphasis to the idea of a new administration taking its identity from the man at the top. He engaged in publicised interventions in government; he exploited international summitry to build up his personal reputation of leadership and governmental competence; and he came to embody and even to dramatise his own 'big idea' of the Citizen's Charter. In other words, he revealed the underlying evolutionary progression of the office. He showed that behind the surface fluctuations of individual incumbents, the position of the chief executive is developing in accordance with the compulsive inheritance of the past and with the present imperatives of a changing political environment.

12
Command and Control, 1997–

Before the 1997 General Election, Labour Leader Tony Blair (1953–) had refashioned the party's constitution and infrastructure to make it more responsive to leadership. Early decisions in government suggested that he intended to do the same now he was Prime Minister. One such was the overhaul of the Ministerial Code (the old Questions of Procedure for Ministers), which meant a dramatic centralisation. This was the response from journalist Peter Riddell.[1]

Goodbye Cabinet government. Welcome the Blair presidency. The Ministerial Code – the new and expanded version of Questions of Procedure for Ministers – is the most revolutionary publication produced by the government since the election. It sets out in a formal code of conduct, to be obeyed by all ministers, the biggest centralisation of power seen in Whitehall in peacetime.

All the familiar textbooks about the Cabinet system will have to be rewritten. The idea that heads of department have an independent standing has been torn up. The Ministerial Code is a remarkably frank document. The section on 'Ministers and the Presentation of Policy' has been totally rewritten. In the previous version, there is merely a reference to the organisation of a press conference. Now, this has been supplemented by a section on co-ordination of government policy . . .

---

[1] Peter Riddell, 'Tories should focus on what really matters', *The Times*, 1 August 1997.

So much for Cabinet ministers being independent heads of departments with their own responsibilities. Now they have to check in with Downing Street if they want to talk to the press, and they have to put on record even having a quiet drink with a journalist.

Moreover, such centralisation will, in practice, be impossible to sustain. If government is to work, ministers have to be allowed to get on with their allotted responsibilities without all the time having to check in with Downing Street. No Prime Minister's Office can, or should, micro-manage the activities of nearly one hundred ministers. The new code reinforces the centralised practice of the new government, though this is combined with Tony Blair's personal preference for focusing on a few important issues. There is often little collective discussion by the Cabinet, even of major political matters.

This is the offending passage from the Ministerial Code (2001 version) which significantly tightened up the requirement for Ministers to check and report their contacts with journalists.[2]

In order to ensure the effective presentation of government policy, all major interviews and media appearances, both print and broadcast, should be agreed with the No. 10 Press Office before any commitments are entered into. The policy content of all major speeches, press releases and new policy initiatives should be cleared in good time with the No. 10 Private Office. The timing and form of announcements should be cleared with the No. 10 Strategic Communications Unit. Each department should keep a record of media contacts by both ministers and officials.

[2] http://www.cabinet-office.gov.uk/central/2001/mcode/p08.htm

Amy Baker's study of the Ministerial Code was published in 2000. She argued that, particularly since John Major's decision to make it public, it had assumed a place as a 'quasi-constitutional' document.[3]

As a result of the public's use of QPM as a quasi-constitutional document, it is, arguably, *becoming* a quasi-constitutional document. And the cycle of evolution appears to be self-perpetuating – the more frequently it's used as the criteria of constitutional conduct, the greater the pressure will be to develop and reform the document to create a more comprehensive set of rules and principles.

The Ministerial Code still belonged to the Prime Minister. A series of scandals about ministerial propriety raised questions about who was best-placed to enforce it, though.[4]

The tendency of all prime ministers to offer a blanket denial of any impropriety, whether actual or apparent, in the face of allegations against ministers raises the question of whether the prime minister (or his adviser on the rulebook, the Cabinet Secretary) is the best person to enforce the Ministerial Code. However, it is notable that Sir Gordon Downey[5] was unable to enquire into any alleged breaches of the Ministerial Code, which remains a matter for the prime minister. As the leader of a political party, and head of a Cabinet team, one wonders whether the prime minister can always be an entirely impartial judge of the standards of his colleagues'

---

[3] Amy Baker, *Prime Ministers and the Rule Book*, Politico's, London, 2000, p. 108.
[4] Ibid., p. 93.
[5] Sir Gordon was the Parliamentary Commissioner for Standards, 1995–1999.

conduct. Any prime minister is always going to be primarily concerned with sustaining his government in office.

Criticism of Blair's 'command and control' approach was widespread. Fewer substantial matters came before Cabinet, and the meetings were commensurately shorter than ever before. In a film to look back at his first 1000 days, BBC journalist Michael Cockerell asked the Prime Minister about his attitude to Cabinet.[6]

Look I would be pretty shocked if the first time I knew a Cabinet minister felt strongly about something was if they raised it at the Cabinet table – I would expect them to come and knock on my door and say, 'Look Tony, I've got this problem here: I disagree with this,' or 'I disagree with that'. And that happens from time to time, and people do that, and then you, you sit down and you work it out.

As the balance in central government shifted towards the centre, the House of Commons Public Administration Select Committee began a series of inquiries into the new centre. As part of one such inquiry, 'Making Government Work', in 2000, Number 10 gave the committee a basic 'map' of how the different parts of the Prime Minister's Office fitted together. In late 2001, though, Number 10 went much further, providing the Committee with an 'organogram' showing relationships between civil servants and special advisers in Number 10. As further details of reforms to the Cabinet Office were made public, it became clear that Number 10 was increasingly acting as a prime minister's department. The reshuffle which took place later that spring confirmed these suspicions, transferring direct control of the Cabinet Office to Tony Blair and giving full departmental support to the head of government for the first time. The government has steadfastly refused to

---

[6] Michael Cockerell, *Cabinet Confidential*, BBC, 17 November 2001.

acknowledge this development, perhaps for fear of stoking up fears of presidentialism. The relationships in Number 10 and the Cabinet Office have since changed, but this was the original version, published by the Committee in early 2002.[7]

No 10 ORGANOGRAM

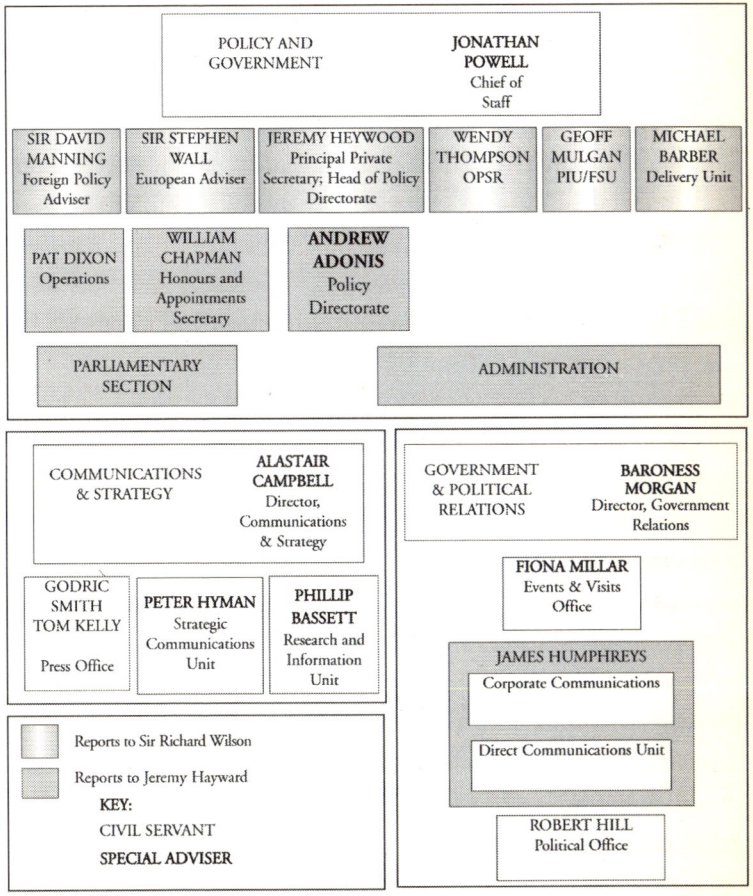

[7] http://www.publications.parliament.uk/pa/cm200102/cmselect/cmpubadm/262/1110101.pdf

Gerald Kaufman (1930–) was Press Secretary to Harold Wilson and later a Labour MP, front bench spokesman and Select Committee Chairman himself. In his witty and incisive book How to be a Minister, *he offered this advice to a junior minister attending Cabinet committee meetings.*[8]

There is no need, of course, for you to pay any attention whatever to these briefs. All you really have to do is to read the Cabinet papers, seek from your department any further information you need, and make up your own mind, assuming of course that your opinion is not contrary to that of your Secretary of State. You can even listen to the discussion at the meeting, and make up your mind on the basis of that. In the Labour government some ministers, such as Edmund Dell and Peter Shore, were notorious for doing this and were consequently branded as simultaneously brilliant and unreliable.

In 2001 David Miliband (1965–), the head of the Number 10 Policy Unit, announced that he would be leaving Number 10 and standing for Parliament at the next election. Duly elected in June, by May 2002 he was already a Minister. In this interview with Nick Robinson for the BBC's One to One *programme, he was able to reflect on the differences between office and adviserdom. In so doing, he also provided a revealing insight into the way in which Cabinet responsibility now operates.*[9]

Robinson: I mean, you're a Minister in an important job, you've only been an MP for a little over a year, is there a bit of you that sometimes thinks, 'my God, is this me?'
Miliband: There's quite a lot of me that's daunted, sometimes

---

[8] Gerald Kaufman, *How to be a Minister*, Faber & Faber, London, 1997, p. 57.
[9] Nick Robinson, *One to One*, interview with David Miliband, BBC, 21 July 2002.

terrified, but I'm also very excited by the huge opportunity that I've got. Being a Minister is a huge honour and a huge challenge as well. They do say, 'Yes Minister', they do say, 'That would be a brave decision, Minister.' You know there's trouble when they say that, but I try and keep my feet on the ground by going out into schools and that's what provides the inspiration for what we're doing in the Education Department.

Robinson: What's fascinating is of course that you were one of Tony Blair's chief policy advisers, and the thinking, the widespread thinking now is that, that's much more important, that if you've got the Prime Minister's ear in Number 10, he basically tells people like you, Ministers, what to do.

Miliband: I think that the jobs are actually quite different, that in the end Advisers advise and Ministers decide and when I sit at my desk now and take decisions I know that they're decisions that are gonna be taken on behalf of the Government. When you're putting up advice to even such a figure as the Prime Minister, he can always, he always does, make up his own mind and I think that there's a responsibility that comes with being a Minister that is quite different from being an Adviser.

But the view sometimes looked very different for a Cabinet minister. Mo Mowlam (1949–), who had been a popular Northern Ireland Secretary and then Secretary of State for the Cabinet Office, had an antagonistic relationship with some in Number 10, alleging on one occasion that 'spin doctors' had been briefing against her. After she retired from Parliament, at the 2001 general election, she explained her views to Michael Cockerell.[10]

---

[10] Michael Cockerell, *Cabinet Confidential*, BBC, 17 November 2001.

Mowlam: I think it's a lot to do with Tony's style. I always likened it in my head to being like a law firm for him. He was one of the partners. He had half a dozen or less partners that he worked with, and ideas filtered down through the business.

Cockerell: Are you saying that a number of people who were not elected had more power than the Cabinet ministers themselves?

Mowlam: Not in terms of their own departments, but they had more power in relation to the Prime Minister in terms of the Cabinet, because the Cabinet seemed to have no power. They seemed to be operating instead of the Cabinet.

Later in the film, Michael Cockerell put to John Prescott (1938–), the Deputy Prime Minister, Mo Mowlam's view that where 'Tony's acting more like a President than a Prime Minister . . . the Cabinet itself is dead.'[11] Having been at the same Cabinet table for the same discussions, he arrived at very different conclusions from Mowlam. And asked about the Cabinet's involvement in a decision over the Millennium Dome, his answers echoed Richard Crossman's lectures of thirty-two years before.[12]

Cockerell: What do you say to someone like Mo Mowlam who says that Cabinet government is now dead?

Prescott: Well, she's daft . . . Just look round that Cabinet table. You think they're going to sit there like sheep and not say what they think? Of course they say what they think, but at the end of the day there's a majority unity and consensus around the policy that's been put forward by the Prime Minister, and there's never been any doubt about that.

* * *

[11] Ibid., p. 37.
[12] Ibid., pp. 37–38, 11–12, 36.

Cockerell: You communicated the discussion that had taken place, but then the Prime Minister took the decision to go ahead with the Dome.

Prescott: He did, yes. And I think about an hour or two later we were at the Dome actually announcing that and looking at it.

Cockerell: But the Cabinet itself hadn't taken that decision to go ahead with the Dome?

Prescott: Well, in the sense that when the Cabinet makes a decision, what we don't have is a vote on it. There's never been a vote. There's this mysterious area of Cabinet, you take soundings and voices. And I gave him the voice, and I gave what I thought the best possible position was, and which would accommodate most of those views of the Cabinet, and he made a decision based on that. I didn't hear of any resignations afterwards, did you?

* * *

Prescott: The Cabinet still plays an essential role, as under any government in Cabinet government in carrying out the policy of the government with the Prime Minister listening to those views and making decisions.

Lord Butler of Brockwell, a former Cabinet Secretary, gave the Attlee Foundation Lecture in 1999. In it he gave some statistics to demonstrate the apparent decline in importance of Cabinet meetings.[13]

During Attlee's Premiership (and excluding the part years of 1945 and 1951) there was an annual average of 87 Cabinet meetings and of 340 circulated papers. The lowest year for circulated papers was 1949 when there were 252.

[13] Lord Butler of Brockwell, 'Cabinet Government', The Attlee Foundation Lecture, Mansion House, London, 18 March 1999, pp. 7–8. I am grateful to Lord Butler for allowing me to have a copy of his speech.

By the early 1970s, when I first sat in the corner of the Cabinet Room as a Junior Private Secretary in Mr Heath's Office, there was an average of 60 meetings a year and of 140 Cabinet memoranda per year.

By the early 1990s, a significantly different pattern had emerged. There were, by then, no more than 40 meetings of the Cabinet per year (and, if statistics were kept of the length of meetings, much shorter ones). More significantly, there was a very marked reduction in the number of memoranda considered. In only one year of the 1990s were more than 20 memoranda circulated.

Freed from the constraints both of office and of collective responsibility after the 2001 election, Labour MP Graham Allen (1953–) produced one of the furthest-reaching analyses of the relationship between prime minister and Cabinet. Dismissing out of hand the idea that Britain had Cabinet government, he argued instead that there was already a presidential system, that this wasn't necessarily a bad thing, and that the powers of this 'authentically British president' should be codified and curtailed.[14]

No one today other than the most self-deluding Cabinet minister or frustrated Permanent Secretary pretends that the Cabinet is an important policy forum ... The increasing marginalisation of formal Cabinet committees, the supervision of Cabinet ministers by what the Deputy Prime Minister has called the 'teenagers' from No. 10's Policy and Political Offices, the increased use of 'Bi-laterals' with individual ministers, No. 10 dealing directly with issues without the relevant minister being present (exemplified by the Ecclestone interview and No. 10 on Formula One and Tobacco advertising): all these acknowledge the end of Cabinet ...

[14] Graham Allen, *The Last Prime Minister: Being Honest About the UK Presidency*, Politico's, London, 2001, pp. 25, 28.

So, while the British Cabinet continues to meet regularly each week it seems to do so as much as a status perk than an executive board meeting. The Cabinet is a relic of pre-presidential government which satisfies a number of political needs, an audience, a chance to touch the cloth, a canvas on which to paint an acceptable gender and racial mix, a bit of networking outside the door but hardly ever now the opportunity to debate a key policy issue on the back of a weighty Cabinet paper.

If, as Graham Allen and Michael Foley had previously claimed, Tony Blair was now a British president, the role and power of the Chancellor, Gordon Brown (1951–), were also unprecedented. Peter Hennessy attempted to put them into some kind of constitutional context.[15]

Power-sharing with his Chancellor of the Exchequer, however, was a matter of daily importance, and the Blair-Brown partnership was as much the bedrock of the government as the Attlee-Bevin axis between 1945 and 1950 . . . Brown is, in effect, overlord of the economic and domestic front. It is a bi-stellar administration with policy constellations revolving round the two stars in Downing Street. It was an old Cabinet Office hand, Jonathan Charkham, who first alerted me to the policy range encompassed by Brown's Budgets – a scope imaginable only for prime ministers before the late 1990s. Mr Charkham saw Brown as comparable to a French prime minister with Blair as a kind of Fifth Republic president.

The core of that power was, for David Lipsey (1948–), an academic and former special adviser, the new Comprehensive Spending Review system, which he describes here.[16]

[15] Peter Hennessy, *The Prime Minister: The office and its holders since 1945*, Penguin, London, 2000, pp. 512–13.
[16] David Lipsey, *The Secret Treasury*, Viking, London, 2000, p. 165.

... the CSR was a triumph for a strong Prime Minister and a strong Chancellor, working together. Nothing illustrates this more clearly than the brutality of its execution. The two just called in ministers and told them how much they were getting. There was no appeal. But Mr Blair and Mr Brown could do that because they were strong. If that strength erodes, so could the CSR system.

The Blair era saw a continued decline in collective decision-taking, a process which had continued more or less unchecked under most governments, of all persuasions, for much of the post-war era. And yet the doctrine of collective responsibility – at least in its public aspects – has survived largely unchanged since Salisbury spelt it out in 1878.[17] Simon James explains why, and describes the three key components of the Cabinet system as it exists today.[18]

The rationale for this seeming absurdity is the need for the government to present a united front. If ministers may contradict each other in public and abide by some decisions but not others, confusion and division will soon set in. The position of a minister who is publicly criticised by his colleagues will become untenable, and a government whose policies are under fire from its own members will lose its authority. It is an illogical, even distasteful doctrine, but there is no practical alternative to it. Collective responsibility is an organised hypocrisy, but a necessary one.

* * *

First, the main component units of the system are individual departments and, particularly, their secretaries of state: the dynamics of the system are dominated by this predominance of

---

[17] See Chapter 2, p. 10.
[18] Simon James, *British Cabinet Government* (second ed.), Routledge, London, 1999, pp. 7, 172.

individual ministerial authority.

Second and simultaneously, the system retains a fundamentally collegiate character and ministers still take the most important decisions and share responsibility collectively.

Third, this collegiality is nonetheless attenuated by the diffusion of power and responsibility from the Cabinet to smaller decision-making fora – committees, *ad hoc* groups and bilateral discussion. The closely-knit pre-war Cabinet machine has become more diffused and, as collegiality has weakened, there is an even greater emphasis on the personal relations between each minister and the prime minister. The system is similar to an exploding galaxy: as the central gravitational force weakens, different elements of the system begin to drift out of synchronisation with each other, disjointing the coordination of the system but still strongly influenced by, and influencing, the central force.

If the value of a collective approach to Cabinet government had already been agreed from the perspective of other Cabinet ministers, good government and good public policy, there remained one further area where it was also worked: the burdens on a prime minister could be reduced, a need which by 1999 had become substantial.[19]

There are several worrying features about excessive prime ministerialism in the conduct of British central government. It cuts against the collective grain, which runs that way for a purpose – as just about the only barrier against undesirable accumulation of power which can all too easily accrue around a single figure under Britain's constitutional arrangements. An excessive focus on the premier can both overburden the Prime Minister (Mr Blair acknowledged publicly that he found the job 'remorseless' just

---

[19] Peter Hennessy, *The Prime Minister: The office and its holders since 1945*, Penguin, London, 2000, p. 507.

before the Balkans War began) and, in the words of an American journalist applied to President Clinton during the conflict, 'threaten to drain the political oxygen available for other projects' if the head of government is faced by too many huge sappers of time and energy simultaneously. Mr Blair had no shortage of these in the spring of 1999. Kosovo and Northern Ireland alone were enough to induce the oxygen starvation effect. The Prime Minister was in danger of wearing himself out, as Roy Jenkins wrote of Mr Gladstone, in 'fighting his endless battle for the victory of activity over time'.

Martin Smith's 1999 book about the core executive placed a heavy emphasis on the notion of inter-dependency between different actors in the 'core': that those actors effectively shared powers. This section is a good summary of his argument.[20]

- All actors within the core executive have resources.
- In order to achieve goals resources have to be exchanged.
- Notions of prime ministerial government, Cabinet government or presidentialism are irrelevant, because power within the core executive is based on dependency, not command.
- In order to understand the operation of the core executive we need to trace the structures of dependency.
- These structures of dependency are often based on overlapping networks. Frequently these networks do not follow formal organisational structures, and this can lead to fragmentation and conflict over responsibility and territory.
- Even resource-rich actors, such as the Prime Minister, are dependent on other actors to achieve their goals. Therefore, government works through building alliances rather than command.

[20] Martin J. Smith, *The Core Executive in Britain*, Macmillan, Basingstoke, 1999, pp. 1–2.

- Actors operate within a structured arena. Traditional approaches to central government have placed too much emphasis on personality. Prime ministers, officials and ministers are bound by external organisation, the rules of the game, the structures of institutions, other actors and the context. Therefore, the nature and form of the core executive do not change with personality.
- The degree of dependency that actors have on each other varies according to the context. As the political and economic situation changes, actors may become more or less dependent. Economic success may provide the Chancellor with more freedom, or electoral success may provide the Prime Minister with greater room for manoeuvre. Economic failure means the Chancellor needs more support from the Prime Minister. Political failure means the Prime Minister needs more support from the Cabinet.
- Because of the distribution of resources, the strength of departments and overlapping networks, the core executive is fragmented and central coordination is extremely difficult.

The relationships between ministers, between ministers and officials and between ministers and the Prime Minister do not primarily depend on personality. They are structured relationships, which are shaped by the rules of the Whitehall game, the institutions of government, past policy choices and the external political and economic context. Asking whether there is prime-ministerial government does not take us far in understanding the operation of central government.

When former Home Secretary Michael Howard (1941–) became the new Conservative Party leader in November 2003, he dramatically altered the shape of the party's opposition team. He halved membership of the Shadow Cabinet and, in a distinct nod to Winston Churchill's 1950s experiment with 'overlords', gave oversight of several major departments at a time to Shadow Cabinet members. Within months, key aspects of the new arrangements had been abandoned. Peter Riddell offered this analysis at the time.[21]

Michael Howard has undermined a good idea with a muddled one. Cutting the size of the Shadow Cabinet from an unwieldy 26 to 12 looks sensible in theory. This creates the type of streamlined inner-core/executive committee which many prime ministers and party leaders have sought over the years. It is a manageable group where it is possible to have a sensible discussion. Then, the trouble starts. Who is in, and who out?

. . . as Mr Howard's team argues, there is no need for the shadow team to match exactly the Whitehall boundaries. There are different jobs in and out of Parliament in developing an alternative programme and scrutinising the government.

But Mr Howard's structure is a recipe for confusion. The new titles would have sounded cumbersome for Pooh-Bah as Lord High Everything Else in *The Mikado*.

Tim Yeo is supposed to be the public face for health and education, replying to statements by John Reid and Charles Clarke. But can he be on top of such a vast area? And where does that leave Tim Collins and Andrew Lansley, described as Shadow Secretaries for Education and Health respectively? And David Curry is going to have to work overtime to master Local Government (including Housing), the Regions, Northern Ireland, Scotland and Wales.

[21] Peter Riddell, 'Slimline team of 12 is recipe for confusion', *The Times*, 11 November 2003.

This set-up is designed for Opposition and is not supposed to imply any view about how a Tory government would work. But first, Mr Howard has to show that his overlords and spokesmen will not trip over themselves.

On 18 April 2004, Tony Blair, previously on record as not having a reverse gear, instead gave the handbrake a sharp tug and executed the sharpest U-turn of his premiership. Newspapers reported that he would now hold a referendum on the proposed European constitution, reports confirmed when he announced the decision in the House of Commons two days later. Plans to discuss it in Cabinet the following Thursday had apparently been abandoned, so this dramatic and hugely controversial decision was greeted with fury by some in his Cabinet. Journalists immediately sought out who had persuaded Blair, and attention soon focused on the Foreign Secretary, Jack Straw (1946–). In the Independent, *political columnist Steve Richards brought the discussion back down to earth.*[22]

Are we witnessing a sudden and astonishing outbreak of Cabinet power? The Foreign Secretary, Jack Straw, prevails in his view that the EU constitution should be the subject of a referendum. The Education Secretary, Charles Clarke, lets the media know he is livid about the rushed announcement. The Home Secretary, David Blunkett, hints he is not thrilled with the handling of this momentous decision either. A rare outbreak of silence from the Leader of the House, Peter Hain, speaks volumes about his unease.

Meanwhile, newspapers report that Mr Blunkett is not pleased with those ministers who oppose him and Mr Blair in their desire to introduce compulsory identity cards. This has not stopped some, including Jack Straw again, from being associated with reports they

[22] Steve Richards, 'Don't be fooled by this chorus of dissent from disgruntled Cabinet ministers', *Independent*, 27 April 2004.

have triumphed in neutering the proposal. Mr Blair's ministers are starting to make the unruly Labour Cabinets of the 1970s seem docile.

Or do they? The stirring of ministerial voices is deceptive. The loud cacophony confirms the weakness of most Cabinet ministers rather than their strength. Indeed some of the noises off are quite openly protesting about their puny influence. 'Why weren't we consulted over the referendum decision?' some ministers ask with an impotent squeal.

In my view the most astonishing element of the decision to hold a referendum was the fact that the announcement preceded a full meeting of the Cabinet. When ministers complain subsequently it is hardly a sign of their new intimidating authority. The excuse for the rushed announcement, that we live with 24-hour media, highlights the prime ministerial disdain for Cabinet government. The 24-hour media could have waited for a few more hours . . .

It was Mr Blair who decided to hold a referendum on the constitution. The reasons did not include overwhelming pressure from the Cabinet. Similarly on ID cards, it is Mr Blair who is keen and so the moves to their introduction continue in spite of significant Cabinet opposition. He still rules over a largely timid Cabinet and worries more about editorials in the *Sun* than the views of most ministers.

The key relationship in the government remains the one between Mr Blair and Mr Brown. Senior Downing Street insiders tell me that the business of government is relatively smooth when they are getting on and bumpy to the point of paralysis when they are not. The main responsibility of other ministers is to navigate between the two centres of power.

One of the more remarkable facts about Tony Blair's premiership is that, at the time of writing, it has sent British troops to five military conflicts[23] – a post-war record. The last of these – Iraq 2003 – was intensely controversial, both for the decision to go to war in the first place and, later, for its conduct. Both questions are intimately related to the issues of collective scrutiny and involvement in decision-taking, addressed in this book. Peter Hennessy had previously enumerated six requirements for the proper conduct of 'limited wars' and in May 2004, as Britain looked ever less likely to emerge early from the Iraqi imbroglio, he updated those original six with some new lessons, painfully learned.[24]

- The War Cabinet should have as close and continuous a relationship with the full Cabinet as possible.
- The War Cabinet should consist of no more than six constant ministerial attenders. For the efficient conduct of affairs, diplomatic or military, it needs to meet regularly and have a bias towards the taking of decisions rather than deferring them. The War Cabinet needs to have adequate military, civil service and diplomatic service back-up, an efficient advice system and a constant flow of high-quality intelligence assessments from the Joint Intelligence Committee.
- The War Cabinet should take pains to avoid the tunnel vision and technical overload that can afflict small groups directed towards a single overriding purpose under conditions of great stress.
- There needs to be a constant awareness of the needs, priorities and attitudes of allies (or potential allies) and the politics of those international organisations in which, to whatever extent, the conflict is being monitored or played out.

---

[23] The five military conflicts were Kosovo, Iraq (December 1998), Sierra Leone, Afghanistan and Iraq again (from March 2003).
[24] Peter Hennessy, 'The procedures of war', *The Tablet*, 28 May 2004.

- Full, accurate and timely disclosure on matters affecting the conflict or near-conflict should be made to Parliament, the media and the public.
- Ministers in the War Cabinet should remember at all times, as a thoughtful airman once put it, that the essential nature of armed conflict is 'to destroy things and kill people', and that the highest duty of politicians in authority is, therefore, to ensure that all steps that can be taken to avoid war – whether through preventative action, diplomacy or intelligence – are taken.

These six requirements reflected a certain kind of limited war – one which effectively came out of the blue in the sense of being precipitated by a crisis which had not been foreseen. Such a war would be Korea in 1950, Suez in 1956, the Falklands in 1982 or the Gulf in 1990. Since then we have moved into a new world with Iraq – of wars of exemplary pre-emption. Tony Blair changed the terms of trade here with his Chicago speech in 1999 at the time of the Kosovo war. The Iraq war was cranked up over a long period. Hence the requirement to supplement those six criteria.

In what way? For a start, number five, the parliamentary one, requires stiffening. The Foreign Secretary, Jack Straw, believes that it already had been. For Straw and the then leader of the House of Commons, Robin Cook, persuaded Blair that there should be a substantive motion – not just a technical one that 'This House do adjourn' – put to the Commons before the UK's armed forces went into action. Straw is convinced that, henceforth, it will be impossible for any future prime minister to take Britain into war without such specific parliamentary sanction. I certainly hope so.

I would add one more criterion . . . I do not believe the UK can engage in a future war of pre-emption – a premeditated war, in other words – without it being accepted that Parliament and the public need and deserve as full a briefing on its legality as that given to the

Cabinet. A summary of the Attorney General's opinion – which is all we have for the Iraq war so far – simply will not do. If the balance of that opinion is a fine one, we really do have a right to know, and *before* the event. This cannot and should not be the exclusive preserve of the prime minister and the Cabinet.

One of the most contested aspects of the war in Iraq was the argument the government made for it – their claim that to hold evidence that Iraq possessed weapons of mass destruction when, as it rapidly became clear after the war, there were none. In July 2004, former Cabinet Secretary Lord Butler published his committee's report on the intelligence failures which led to that claim being made. In it, he concluded that no one in government was guilty of deliberately misrepresenting the available intelligence, and that no individual could be singled out for making mistakes. But he did make some pointed observations about how changes in the Cabinet Office and the informality of the Blair style of government had contributed to the problems, and suggested that 'informed collective political judgement' should be returned centre-stage. Returning centre-stage with it came the Cabinet versus premiership debate, demonstrating once again its enduring relevance to how we are governed.[25]

We received evidence from two former Cabinet members, one of the present and one of a previous administration, who expressed their concern about the informal nature of much of the government's decision-making process, and the relative lack of use of established Cabinet committee machinery.

Two changes which occurred over this period had implications for the application of intelligence to collective ministerial decision-

---

[25] Lord Butler of Brockwell, *Review of Intelligence on Weapons of Mass Destruction, Report of a Committee of Privy Counsellors*, HC 898, HMSO, London, 2004, paragraphs 606–611.

making. One was the splitting of the Cabinet Secretary's responsibilities through the creation of the post of Security and Intelligence Co-ordinator. The latter is able to devote the majority of his time to security and intelligence issues in a way that the Cabinet Secretary, with all the many other calls on his time, could not. It was represented to us that this change was particularly necessary after the terrorist attacks of 11 September 2001. However, the effect is that the Cabinet Secretary is no longer so directly involved in the chain through which intelligence reaches the Prime Minister. It follows that the Cabinet Secretary, who attends the Cabinet and maintains the machinery to support their decision-making, is less directly involved personally in advising the Prime Minister on security and intelligence issues. By the same token, the Security and Intelligence Co-ordinator does not attend Cabinet and is not part of the Cabinet Secretariat supporting Cabinet ministers in discharging their collective responsibilities in defence and overseas policy matters. We understand that the Intelligence and Security Committee will shortly review how this arrangement has worked.

The second change was that two key posts at the top of the Cabinet Secretariat, those of Head of the Defence and Overseas Secretariat and Head of the European Affairs Secretariat, were combined with the posts of the Prime Minister's advisers on Foreign Affairs and on European Affairs respectively. We believe that the effect of the changes has been to weight their responsibility to the Prime Minister more heavily than their responsibility through the Cabinet Secretary to the Cabinet as a whole. It is right to acknowledge that the view of the present post-holders is that the arrangement works well, in particular in connecting the work of the Cabinet Secretariat to that of the Prime Minister's office. We should also record that it was clear from the departmental policy papers we read that there was very close co-operation between officials in the Prime Minister's office and in the FCO in policy-making on Iraq. It is nonetheless a shift which acts to concentrate detailed knowledge and effective decision-making in fewer minds at the top.

In the year before the war, the Cabinet discussed policy towards Iraq as a specific agenda item 24 times. It also arose in the course of discussions on other business. Cabinet members were offered and many received briefings on the intelligence picture on Iraq. There was therefore no lack of discussion on Iraq; and we have been informed that it was substantive. The Ministerial Committee on Defence and Overseas Policy did not meet. By contrast, over the period from April 2002 to the start of military action, some 25 meetings attended by the small number of key Ministers, officials and military officers most closely involved provided the framework of discussion and decision-making within government.

One inescapable consequence of this was to limit wider collective discussion and consideration by the Cabinet to the frequent but unscripted occasions when the Prime Minister, Foreign Secretary and Defence Secretary briefed the Cabinet orally. Excellent quality papers were written by officials, but these were not discussed in Cabinet or in Cabinet committee. Without papers circulated in advance, it remains possible but is obviously much more difficult for members of the Cabinet outside the small circle directly involved to bring their political judgement and experience to bear on the major decisions for which the Cabinet as a whole must carry responsibility. The absence of papers on the Cabinet agenda so that Ministers could obtain briefings in advance from the Cabinet Office, their own departments or from the intelligence agencies plainly reduced their ability to prepare properly for such discussions, while the changes to key posts at the head of the Cabinet Secretariat lessened the support of the machinery of government for the collective responsibility of the Cabinet in the vital matter of war and peace.

We do not suggest that there is or should be an ideal or unchangeable system of collective government, still less that procedures are in aggregate any less effective now than in earlier times. However, we are concerned that the informality and circumscribed character of the government's procedures which we saw in the context of policy-making towards Iraq risks reducing the scope for informed collective political judgement. Such risks are particularly significant in a field like the subject of our Review, where hard facts are inherently difficult to come by and the quality of judgement is accordingly all the more important.

In opposition, Labour and the Liberal Democrats had had detailed discussions about constitutional reform, resulting in the 'Cook/Maclennan' agreement on the shape of that reform. At one stage, private discussions between Tony Blair and Liberal Democrat Leader Paddy Ashdown (1941–) had gone so far as to include coalition. This never materialised, but what did emerge was the Joint Cabinet Committee (JCC), on which Labour Ministers and Liberal Democrat MPs sat to discuss constitutional reform. It operated as a committee of Privy Councillors, and although other issues were later added to its remit, little came of these later discussions. The committee was mothballed in September 2001 after Charles Kennedy (1959–) became leader. This is how Paddy Ashdown recorded the JCC's first meeting, in September 1997, in his diaries.[26]

Wednesday, 17 September, Westminster
At 1.45 I strolled down Whitehall in the sunshine with Alan, Bob, Richard and Ming[27] to Downing Street for the first JCC meeting.

---

[26] Paddy Ashdown, *The Ashdown Diaries, Volume Two, 1997–1999*, Penguin, London, 2002, pp 90–92

[27] Alan Beith (1943), Liberal Democrat Deputy Leader; Robert Maclennan (1936–), Liberal Democrat Party President and co-architect of the Lib–Lab constitutional reform agreement; Lord (Richard) Holme (1936–), Chairman of the Liberal Democrat General Election campaign; and Menzies Campbell (1941–), Liberal Democrat Foreign Affairs Spokesman

Outside the door of No. 10 we stopped for a quick photo op before entering. The meeting started promptly at 2.00. The Labour members[28] of the committee sat on one side of the Cabinet table and we sat on the other. The press came in form some more shots, then Blair shooed them out, took off his jacket and we got straight down to business.

It was an exceptionally warm and friendly meeting, during which Robin Cook, who sat next o Blair, had one or two sharp digs at Straw. Mandelson, a silent brooding presence, sat opposite Richard, chipping in only twice. Ann Taylor, leaning forward and enthusiastically playing weathervane to whatever Blair said. Extraordinary, given that she had apparently been so hostile to all this previously. But she couldn't have been nicer.

The pebble-glassed Jack Straw was owlish and mischievous, as I thought he would be.

At the start, when Alan Beith said something, Blair quickly chipped in with, 'No doubt that accounts for your acerbic comments on the *Today* programme.' I noted that Alan wrote down the word 'acerbic' twice and circled it. Whatever Alan had said on the *Today* programme, it had obviously gone home. But so what? There has to be a hard man in all this and Alan makes a very good one.

Ann Taylor, however, chimed in with a loud 'Yes!' when Blair made this comment and sat nodding her head vigorously like a parcel-shelf dog.

On our side Richard was good, if at times a little Delphic. Though Ming said little, he said it effectively. Bob was slow and measured, as ever. But our star was Alan, who was tremendous: sharp and on the ball. He was very convincing, putting our case across confidently

---

[28] Tony Blair; Robin Cook (1946–), Foreign Secretary and co-architect of the Lib–Lab constitutional reform agreement; Jack Straw (1946), Home Secretary; Peter Mandelson (1953–), Minister without Portfolio; and Ann Taylor (1947–), Government Chief Whip

without any kind of sycophancy. I was glad to have him there.

Fascinating watching Blair. He really is growing into his role. Gone is all that diffidence and his constant deference to Mandelson. He was relaxed and in control of the whole thing. He has adopted an interesting way of pausing in his sentences while he seems to be making up his mind, which makes you believe that he really is thinking about what he says. Whenever there was a difficulty, Blair simply said, 'We'll have a look at that, but there should be a way round it.' He seems serious about genuinely doing business with us and appears determined to make a success of it.

The meeting lasted for ninety minutes and we covered all the ground we wanted to. We left by the front door, stopping to do some press interviews on the way out.

Bibliography and Acknowledgements

The editor and publisher would like to thank the copyright holders for permission to reproduce the excerpts in this book.

Allen, Graham, *The Last Prime Minister: Being Honest About the UK Presidency*, Politico's, London, 2001

Amery, Leo, *Thoughts on the Constitution*, Oxford University Press, London, 1953

Anderson, Rt. Hon. Sir John, *The Machinery of Government: The Romanes Lecture, delivered in the Sheldonian Theatre, 14 May 1946*, Oxford University Press, Oxford, 1946

Ashdown, Paddy, *The Ashdown Diaries, Volume Two, 1997–1999*, Penguin, London, 2002. Reproduced from *The Ashdown Diaries, Volume II* by Paddy Ashdown (Copyright © Paddy Ashdown) by permission of PFD (*www.pfd.co.uk*) on behalf of Paddy Ashdown.

Attlee, Clement, *As it Happened*, William Heinemann Ltd., London, 1954

Attlee, Earl, Letter, *Daily Telegraph*, 9 August 1960

Avon, Earl of, *The Reckoning: The Eden Memoirs*, Cassell & Company Ltd., London, 1965

Bagehot, Walter, *The English Constitution* (ed. Miles Taylor), Oxford University Press, Oxford, 2001

Baker, Amy, *Prime Ministers and the Rule Book*, Politico's, London, 2000

Balfour, Arthur James, *Chapters of Autobiography*, Cassell & Company Ltd., London, 1930

Balfour, Earl of, Introduction to Walter Bagehot's *English Constitution*, Oxford University Press, London, 1926

Barnett, Joel, *Inside the Treasury*, Andre Deutsch, London, 1982

Benewick, Robert and Dowse, Robert E., *Readings on British Politics and Government*, University of London Press, London, 1968

Benn, Tony, *Out of the Wilderness, Diaries 1963–67*, Hutchinson, London, 1987

Benn, Tony, *Office Without Power, Diaries 1968–72*, Hutchinson, London, 1988

Benn, Tony, *Against the Tide: Diaries 1973–76*, Hutchinson, London, 1989

Benn, Tony, *Conflicts of Interest: Diaries 1977–80* (ed. Ruth Winstone), Hutchinson, London, 1990

Biffen, John, 'The revenge of the unburied dead', *Observer*, 9 December 1990

Blackstone, Tessa and Plowden, William, *Inside the Think Tank: Advising the Cabinet 1971–1983*, Heinemann, London, 1988

Blake, Robert, *The Unknown Prime Minister: The Life and Times of Andrew Bonar Law, 1858–1923*, Eyre & Spottiswoode, London, 1955

Bowle, John, *Viscount Samuel: A Biography*, Victor Gollancz Ltd., London, 1957

Brett, Maurice J. (ed.), *Journals and letters of Reginald Viscount Esher*, Vol. 2, Ivor Nicholson & Watson Ltd., London, 1934

Brivati, Brian, and Jones, Harriet (eds.), *From Reconstruction to Integration: Britain and Europe since 1945*, Leicester University Press, Leicester, 1993. Reproduced from *From Reconstruction to Integration* edited by Brian Brivati and Harriet Jones (Copyright © Brian Brivati and Harriet Jones 1993) by permission of Leicester University Press, a Continuum imprint

Brown, George, *In My Way: The Political Memoirs of Lord George-Brown*, London, Victor Gollancz Ltd., 1971

Bruce-Gardyne, Jock and Lawson, Nigel, *The Power Game: An Examination of Decision-Making in Government*, Macmillan, London, 1976

Bryant, Arthur, *The Turn of the Tide, 1939–1943*, Collins, London, 1957

Buckle, George Earle (ed.), *The Letters of Queen Victoria*, third series, Vol. 1, John Murray, London, 1930

Burch, Martin and Holliday, Ian, *The British Cabinet System*, Prentice Hall, Hemel Hempstead, 1996. Reproduced from *The British Cabinet System* by Martin Burch and Ian Holliday (Copyright © Martin Burch and Ian Holliday 1996) by permission of Pearson Education Limited.

Butler, David and Adonis, Andrew, *Failure in British Government: The Politics of the Poll Tax*, Oxford University Press, Oxford, 1994

Butler, David and Stokes, Donald, *Political Change in Britain: The Evolution of Electoral Choice*, second ed., Macmillan, London, 1974

Butler of Brockwell, Lord, *Cabinet Government*, The Attlee Foundation Lecture, Mansion House, London, 18 March 1999

Butler of Brockwell, Lord, *Review of Intelligence of Weapons of Mass Destruction, Report of a Committee of Privy Counsellors*, HC 898, HMSO, London, 2004

Butler, Lord, *The Art of Memory: Friends in Perspective*, Hodder & Stoughton, London, 1982

Callaghan, James, *Time and Chance*, Collins, London, 1987

Campbell, John, *Edward Heath: A biography*, Pimlico, London, 1994

Castle, Barbara, *The Castle Diaries, 1964–1976*, Macmillan, London, 1990

Cecil, Lady Gwendolen, *Life of Robert, Marquis of Salisbury*, Vol. 2, Hodder and Stoughton, London, 1921

Chester, D. N., 'Development of the Cabinet 1914–1949', in Lord

Campion, D. N. Chester, W. J. M. Mackenzie, William Robson, Sir Arthur Street and J. H. Warren, *British Government since 1918*, George Allen & Unwin Ltd., London, 1950

Chessyre, Robert, 'Wilson's new outsiders worry Whitehall', *Observer*, 24 March 1974

Chilston, Viscount Eric Alexander, *Chief Whip: The Political Life and Times of Aretas Akers-Douglas, 1st Viscount Chilston*, Routledge & Kegan Paul, London, 1961

Churchill, Randolph S., *The Rise and Fall of Sir Anthony Eden*, Macgibbon & Kee, London, 1959

Churchill, Winston, *The World Crisis, Volume 2: 1915*, Thorton Butterworth Ltd., London, 1923. Copyright © Winston S. Churchill. Reproduced with permission of Curtis Brown Ltd, London, on behalf of Winston S. Churchill.

Churchill, Winston, *The Second World War, Volume 1: The Gathering Storm*, Cassell & Co. Ltd., London, 1948. Copyright © Winston S. Churchill. Reproduced with permission of Curtis Brown Ltd, London, on behalf of Winston S. Churchill.

Churchill, Winston, *The Second World War, Volume 4: The Hinge of Fate*, Cassell & Co. Ltd., London, 1951. Copyright © Winston S. Churchill. Reproduced with permission of Curtis Brown Ltd, London, on behalf of Winston S. Churchill.

C. 5979, *Preliminary and Further Reports of the Royal Commissioners appointed to enquire into the Civil and Professional Administration of the Naval and Military Departments and the relation of those departments to each other and to the Treasury*, HMSO, London, 1890

Cd. 8490, Dardanelles Commission, *First Report*, HMSO, London, 1917

Cd. 9203, *Report of the Machinery of Government Committee*, Ministry of Reconstruction, London, 1918

Cmnd. 1432, *Control of Public Expenditure*, HMSO, 1961

Cmnd. 4506, *The Reorganisation of Central Government*, HMSO, London, 1970

Cockerell, Michael, *Cabinet Confidential*, BBC Political Documentaries, 17 November 2001

Cole, John, *As it Seemed to Me: Political Memoirs*, Weidenfeld & Nicolson, London, 1995

Cole, Margaret (ed.), *Beatrice Webb's Diaries, 1924–1932*, Longmans, Green & Co., London, 1956

Colville, John, *The Fringes of Power: Downing Street Diaries 1939–55*, Hodder & Stoughton, London, 1955

Colvin, Ian, *The Chamberlain Cabinet*, Victor Gollancz Ltd., London, 1971

Cooper, Duff, *Haig*, Faber and Faber Ltd., London, 1935

Cosgrave, Patrick, *Thatcher: The First Term*, The Bodley Head, London, 1985

Crosland, Susan, *Tony Crosland*, Jonathan Cape, London, 1982

Crossman, Richard, Introduction, to Bagehot, Walter, *The English Constitution*, Fontana, London, 1963

Crossman, Richard, *Inside View*, Jonathan Cape, London, 1972

Crossman, Richard, *The Diaries of a Cabinet Minister, Volume One: Minister of Housing, 1964–66*, Book Club Associates, London, 1977

Crossman, Richard, *The Diaries of a Cabinet Minister, Volume Two: Lord President of the Council and Leader of the House of Commons, 1966–68*, Hamish Hamilton, London, 1976

Crossman, Richard, *The Diaries of a Cabinet Minister, Volume 3: Secretary of State for Social Services, 1968–70*, Hamish Hamilton, London, 1977

Daalder, Hans, *Cabinet Reform in Britain, 1914–1963*, Stanford University Press, Stanford, 1963

Dalyell, Tam, *Dick Crossman: A Portrait*, Weidenfeld & Nicolson, London, 1989

Dell, Edmund and Lord Hunt of Tanworth, 'The Failings of Cabinet

Government in Mid to Late 1970s', *Contemporary Record*, Vol. 8, Winter 1994, Number 3

Donoughue, Bernard, *Prime Minister, The Conduct of Policy under Harold Wilson and James Callaghan*, Jonathan Cape, London, 1987

Eden, Sir Anthony, *Full Circle*, Cassell, London, 1960

Evans, Harold, *Downing Street Diary: The Macmillan Years, 1957–1963*, Hodder & Stoughton, London, 1981

Finer, Herman, *The Theory and Practice of Modern Government*, fourth ed., Methuen & Company Ltd., London, 1961

Fischer, H. A. L., *An Unfinished Autobiography*, Oxford University Press, London, 1940

Foley, Michael, *The Rise of the British Presidency*, Manchester University Press, Manchester, 1993

Foot, Michael, *Aneurin Bevan: A Biography, Volume Two – 1945–1960*, Davis-Poynter, London, 1973

Gardiner, A. G., *The Life of Sir William Harcourt: Volume 1, 1827–1886*, Constable and Company Ltd., London, 1923

Gardiner, A. G., *The Life of Sir William Harcourt: Volume II*, Constable and Company Ltd., London, 1923

Gladstone, W.E., *Gleanings of Past Years, 1875–8*, Vol. 1, John Murray, London, 1879

Gordon Walker, Patrick, *The Cabinet* (revised ed.), Heinemann Educational Books, London, 1973

Grey, Viscount, *Twenty-five years, 1892–1916*, Vol. 1, Hodder & Stoughton, London, 1925

Griffith, John, 'Crichel Down: The Most Famous Farm in British Constitutional History', *Contemporary Record*, Vol. 1, Number 1, Spring 1987, pp. 35–40

Guedella, Philip, *The Queen and Mr Gladstone, 1880–1898*, Hodder & Stoughton Ltd., London, 1933

Hailsham, Lord, 'Elective Dictatorship', *The Listener*, 21 October 1976, pp. 496–500

Hailsham of St. Marylebone, Lord, *A Sparrow's Flight*, Collins, London, 1990

Haines, Joe, *The Politics of Power*, Jonathan Cape, London, 1977

Haldane, Richard, *An Autobiography*, Hodder & Stoughton Ltd., London, 1929

Harris, Kenneth, *Attlee*, Weidenfeld & Nicolson, London, 1995

Harris, Kenneth, 'The Foreign Secretary opens up', *Observer*, 16 September 1962

Harris, Kenneth, 'My kind of Conservatism: Mrs Thatcher talks to the Observer', *Observer*, 25 February 1979

Harrod, R. F., *The Life of John Maynard Keynes*, Macmillan & Co. Ltd., London, 1951

Healey, Denis, *The Time of My Life*, Penguin, London, 1990

Heath, Edward, *The Course of My Life: The Autobiography of Edward Heath*, Hodder & Stoughton, London, 1998

Hennessy, Peter, *Cabinet*, Basil Blackwell, Oxford, 1986

Hennessy, Peter and Seldon, Anthony (eds.), *Ruling Performance: British Governments from Attlee to Thatcher*, Basil Blackwell, Oxford, 1987

Hennessy, Peter, *Muddling Through: Power, Politics and the Quality of Government in Postwar Britain*, Victor Gollancz, London, 1996

Hennessy, Peter, *The Prime Minister: The office and its holders since 1945*, Penguin, London, 2000

Hennessy, Peter, 'The procedures of war', *The Tablet*, 28 May 2004

Hennessy, Peter, *Whitehall*, Pimlico, London, 2001

Herman, Valentine and Alt, James (eds.), *Cabinet Studies: A Reader*, Macmillan, London, 1975

Heseltine, Michael, *Life in the Jungle: My Autobiography*, Hodder & Stoughton, London, 2000

Hill, Christopher, *Cabinet decisions on foreign policy: The British experience October 1938–June 1941*, Cambridge University Press, Cambridge, 1991

Hill of Luton, Lord, *Both sides of the Hill: The Memoirs of Charles Hill*, Heinemann, London, 1964

Home, Lord, *The Way the Wind Blows*, Collins, London, 1976

Hoskyns, John, *Just in time: Inside the Thatcher revolution*, Aurum Press, London, 2000

Howe, Geoffrey, *Conflict of Loyalty*, Macmillan, London, 1994. Reproduced by pemission of Macmillan, London.

Howe, Geoffrey, 'The Triumph and Tragedy of the Thatcher Years', *Financial Times*, 24 October, 1993

Ismay, Lord, *The Memoirs of General The Lord Ismay*, Heinemann, London, 1960

James, Simon, *The Central Policy Review Staff, 1970–1983*, Political Studies, Number 34, 1986

James, Simon, *British Cabinet Government* (second ed.), Routledge, London, 1999

Jay, Anthony (ed.), *The Oxford Dictionary of Political Quotations*, Oxford University Press, Oxford, 1996

Jefferys, Kevin, *Tony Crosland*, Richard Cohew Books, London, 1999

Jenkins, Roy, *A Life at the Centre*, Papermac, London, 1991

Jennings, Sir W. Ivor, *Cabinet Government*, Cambridge University Press, Cambridge, 1936

Jennings, Sir W. Ivor, *Cabinet Government* (third ed.), Cambridge University Press, Cambridge, 1963

Jones, G. W., 'Development of the Cabinet', in W. Thornhill (ed.), *The Modernisation of British Government*, Pitman, London, 1975

Jones, G. W., 'Cabinet Government since Bagehot', in Robert Blackburn (ed.), *Constitutional Studies*, Mansell, London, 1992

Jones, G. W., 'Cabinet Government and Mrs. Thatcher', *Contemporary Record*, Vol. I No. 3, Autumn 1987, p. 11

Jones, Thomas, *A Diary with Letters, 1931–1950*, Oxford University Press, London, 1954

Kaufman, Gerald, *How to be a Minister*, Faber & Faber, London, 1997

Keith, Arthur B., *The British Cabinet System, 1830–1938*, Stevens & Sons Ltd., London, 1939

Kilmuir, Lord, *Political Adventure: The Memoirs of the Earl of Kilmuir*, Weidenfeld & Nicolson, London, 1962

King, Anthony (ed.), *The British Prime Minister: A Reader*, Macmillan, London, 1969

King, Anthony (ed.), *The British Prime Minister* (second ed.), Macmillan, Basingstoke, 1985

Lamb, Richard, *The Macmillan Years, 1957–1963: The Emerging Truth*, John Murray, London, 1995

Laski, Harold, *Reflections on the Constitution*, Manchester University Press, Manchester, 1951

Lawson, Nigel, *The View from No. 11: Memoirs of a Tory Radical*, Bantam Press, London, 1992. Reproduced from *The View From No. 11* by Nigel Lawson (Copyright © Nigel Lawson 1992) by permission of PFD (*www.pfd.co.uk*) on behalf of Lord Lawson of Blaby.

Lawson, Nigel and Armstrong of Ilminster, Lord, 'Cabinet Government in the Thatcher Years', *Contemporary Record*, Vol. 8, Winter 1994, Number 3. Reproduced by permission of Taylor & Francis Ltd (http://tandf.co.uk/journals).

Lipsey, David, *The Secret Treasury*, Viking, London, 2000

Lloyd George, David, *War Memoirs*, Vol. 1 (new edition), Odhams Press Ltd., London, 1938

Lloyd George, David, *War Memoirs*, Vol. 3, Ivor Nicholson & Watson, London, 1934

Low, Sidney, *The Governance of England*, T. Fisher Unwin, London, 1904

Lyman, Richard W., *The First Labour Government 1924*, Russell & Russell, New York, 1975

Lyttelton, Oliver, *The Memoirs of Lord Chandos*, The Bodley Head, London, 1962

Mackenzie, W. J. M. and Grove, J. W., *Central Administration in Britain*, Longman, London, 1957

Mackintosh, J. P., *The British Cabinet*, Stevens & Sons Ltd., London, 1962

Macleod, Iain, 'The Tory Leadership', *Spectator*, 17 January 1964

Macmillan, Harold, *Riding the Storm, 1956–1959*, Macmillan, London, 1971

Macmillan, Harold, *Pointing the Way, 1959–1961*, Macmillan, London, 1972

Macmillan, Harold, *At the End of the Day, 1961–1963*, Macmillan, London, 1973

Madgwick, Peter, *British Government: The Central Executive Territory*, Philip Allan, Hemel Hempstead, 1991

Magnus, Philip, *Gladstone*, John Murray, London, 1954

Major, John, *The Autobiography*, HarperCollins, London, 1999

Marquand, David, *Ramsay MacDonald*, Jonathan Cape, London, 1977

Maurice, Sir Frederick, *Haldane, 1915–1928*, Vol. 2, Faber & Faber Ltd., London, 1939

Montagu, Edwin, 'Mr. Montagu's Reply', *The Times*, 13 March 1922

Moran, Lord, *Winston Churchill: The Struggle for Survival, 1940/1965*, Constable, London, 1966

Morgan, Kenneth O., *Callaghan: A Life*, Oxford University Press, Oxford, 1997

Morley, John, *The Life of William Ewart Gladstone*, Vol. 2, Macmillan, London, 1903

Morley, John, *The Life of William Ewart Gladstone*, Vol. 3, Macmillan, London, 1903

Morley, John, *Walpole*, Macmillan and Co., London, 1890

Morrison, Herbert, *Government and Parliament: A Survey from the Inside* (third ed.), OUP, London, 1964

Mosley, R. K., *The Story of the Cabinet Office*, Routledge, London, 1969

Naylor, John F., *A Man and an Institution: Sir Maurice Hankey, the Cabinet Secretariat and the custody of Cabinet secrecy*, Cambridge University Press, Cambridge, 1984

Nutting, Anthony, *No end of a lesson: The story of Suez*, Constable, London, 1967

Oxford & Asquith, Earl of, *Fifty Years of Parliament*, Vol. 2, Cassell & Co. Ltd., London, 1926

Oxford & Asquith, Earl of, *Memories and Reflections 1852–1927*, Vol. 2, Cassell & Co. Ltd., London, 1928

Pearce, Robert (ed.), *Patrick Gordon Walker: Political Diaries 1932–1971*, The Historians' Press, London, 1991

Percy, Eustace, *Some Memories*, Eyre & Spottiswoode, London, 1958

Phillips, K. M., 'The British Inner Cabinet', *London Review of Public Administration*, Number 10, 1977

Ponting, Clive, *Whitehall: Tragedy and Farce*, Sphere, London, 1987

Prior, James, *A Balance of Power*, Hamish Hamilton, London, 1986

Pryce, Sue, *Presidentializing the Premiership*, Macmillan, Basingstoke, 1997

Rhodes, R. A. W. and Dunleavy, Patrick (eds.), *Prime Minister, Cabinet and Core Executive*, St. Martin's Press, Basingstoke, 1995

Richards, Steve, 'Don't be fooled by this chorus of dissent from disgruntled Cabinet ministers', *Independent*, 27 April 2004

Riddell, Peter, 'Tories should focus on what really matters', *The Times*, 1 August 1997

Riddell, Peter, 'Slimline team of 12 is recipe for confusion', *The Times*, 11 November 2003

Ridley, Nicholas, *My Style of Government: The Thatcher Years*, Hutchinson, London, 1991

Robinson, Nick, *One to One* interview with David Miliband, BBC

Rodgers, Bill, *Fourth Among Equals*, Politico's, London, 2000

Ronaldshay, Earl of, *The Life of Lord Curzon*, Vol. 3, Ernest Benn Ltd., London, 1928

Roth, Andrew, *Heath and the Heathmen*, Routledge & Kegan Paul, London, 1972

Rothschild, Lord, *Meditations of a Broomstick*, Collins, London, 1977

Rush, Michael, *The Cabinet and Policy Formulation*, Longman, London, 1984

Seymour-Ure, Colin, 'British "War Cabinets" in Limited Wars: Korea, Suez and the Falklands', *Public Administration*, Volume 24, summer 1984

Seymour-Ure, Colin, 'The "Disintegration" of the Cabinet and the neglected question of Cabinet reform', *Parliamentary Affairs*, Volume 24, Number 3, 1971

Shephard, Gillian, *Shephard's Watch: Illusions of power in British Politics*, Politico's, London, 2000

Sherwood, Robert E., *Roosevelt and Hopkins: An Intimate History*, Harper & Brothers, New York, 1948

Short, Edward, *Whip to Wilson*, Macdonald, London, 1989

Simon, Sir John, 'Letter to Sir Alfred Mowat, President of the Spen Valley Liberal Association', *The Times*, 18 October 1935

Smith, Martin J., *The Core Executive in Britain*, Macmillan, Basingstoke, 1999

Snowden, Philip, *An autobiography, Volume 2: 1919–1934*, Ivor Nicholson & Watson Ltd., London, 1934

Spender, J.A. and Asquith, Cyril, *Life of Herbert Henry Asquith, Lord Oxford and Asquith*, Vol. 1, Hutchinson & Co., London, 1932

Spender, J.A. and Asquith, Cyril, *Life of Herbert Henry Asquith, Lord of Oxford and Asquith*, Vol. 2, Hutchinson & Co., London, 1932

Steel, David, Diary, *Observer*, 1 April, 1979

St. John-Stevas, Norman, 'Prime Ministers rise and fall, but the Cabinet abides', *Daily Telegraph*, 7 August 1986

Tebbit, Norman, *Upwardly Mobile*, Weidenfeld & Nicolson, London, 1988

Thatcher, Margaret, *The Downing Street Years*, HarperCollins, London, 1993

Thomas, Graham P., *Prime Minister and Cabinet Today*, Manchester University Press, Manchester, 1998

Turner, John, *Lloyd George's Secretariat*, Cambridge University Press, Cambridge, 1980

Wakeham, Lord, 'Cabinet Government', *Contemporary Record*, Vol. 8, Winter 1994, Number 3

Wass, Douglas, *Government and the Governed: BBC Reith Lectures 1983*, Routledge & Kegan Paul, London, 1984

Watt, David, 'The power of the Premiership', *Financial Times*, 5 May 1972

Wheare, Sir Kenneth C., *Government by Committee: An Essay on the British Constitution*, Oxford University Press, London, 1955

Whitelaw, William, *The Whitelaw Memoirs*, Headline, London, 1990

Wigg, Lord George, *George Wigg*, Michael Joseph, London, 1972

Williams, Francis, *The Triple Challenge: The Future of Socialist Britain*, William Heinemann Ltd., London, 1948

Williams, Francis, *A Prime Minister Remembers: The war and post-war memoirs of Earl Attlee*, Heinemann, London, 1961

Williams, Marcia, *Inside Number 10*, Weidenfeld & Nicolson, London, 1972

Williams, Philip M. (ed.), *The Diary of Hugh Gaitskell, 1945–1956*, Jonathan Cape, London, 1983

Willson, F. M. G. and Chester, D. N. (eds.), *The Organization of British Central Government, 1916–1964, A Survey by a Study Group of the Royal Institute of Public Administration* (second ed.), George Allen & Unwin Ltd., London, 1968

Wilson, Harold, *The Labour Government 1964–1970: A Personal Record*, Weidenfeld & Nicolson, London, 1971

Wilson, Sir Harold, *Final Term: The Labour Government 1974–76*, Weidenfeld & Nicolson, London, 1979

Wilson, Sir Harold, *The Governance of Britain*, Weidenfeld & Nicolson, London, 1976

Wolff, Michael, 'The power of the Prime Minister: Should he pick up the ball and run with it?', *The Times*, 24 May 1976

Woodhouse, Diana, 'Ministerial responsibility in the 1990s: when do ministers resign?', *Parliamentary Affairs*, Volume 46, Number 3, July 1993

Woolton, Lord, *The Memoirs of the Rt. Hon. The Earl of Woolton*, Cassell, London, 1959

Young, G. M., *Stanley Baldwin*, Rupert Hart-Davis, London, 1952

Ziegler, Philip, *Wilson: The Authorised Life of Lord Wilson of Rievaulx*, Weidenfeld & Nicolson, London, 1993

Index

admiralty 16–7, 19
agenda papers 30, 32
agreement to differ, the 49–51
Alexander, Lord 97
Allen, Graham 266–7
American
   cabinet 124
   presidency 253–4
Amery, Leo 58–9, 81–2, 95–6
amour-propre 46, 198
Anderson, Sir John 87–8, 90, 95
Ashdown, Paddy 280, 282
Asquith, Herbert 12, 20–29, 41, 60, 82
Attlee, Clement 64–5, 69–70, **72–8**, 83–4, 97, 100, 102, 110–1, 120, 143, 155, 212, 250, 267
Argentina 215
Armstrong, Lord William 163, 169, 196
Armstrong, Robert 177, 241–2
autocratic government 143–4, 194, 243

Badgehot, Walter 1, 6, 123, 160, 167, 208, 215
   the Bagehot template **1–5**
   see also constitution, the English
Baker, Amy 259
Baldwin, Stanley 96, 111, 120
Balfour, Arthur 11, 18–9, 40, 42, 54
Balogh, Tommy 141, 146, 163–4
Banbury, Lord 50
Bancroft, Lord 227
Barnes, John 105–8
BBC 137
Beaconsfield, Lord 7, 11, 40
Beacs, Sir Michael Hicks 11
Beith, Alan 280–1
Benn, Tony 153, 158, 185–188, 192, 199, 202–4
Berchtesgaden 57
Beneš 57

Berrill, Kenneth 228–9, 239
Bevan, Aneurin 79, 139, 145, 167
Bevin, Ernest 70, 72, 79, 111, 267
Biffen, John 224, 229–230
Blackstone, Tessa 220–1
Blair, Tony 220, **257–270**, 273–282
Bligh, Tim 114
blockbuster memorandum 227
Blunkett, David 273
Boyle, Lord 102
Bridges, Sir Edward 59–60, 65, 71–2, 165, 250
Bright, John 9
Brittan, Leon 224, 230
Brook, Sir Norman 79–81, 84–7, 98–9, 114, 117, 250
Brown, George 129–130, 134, 138, 141–2, 150, 153, 170–1
   resignation 156–8
Brown, Gordon 267, 274
Bruce-Gardyne, Jock 161, 213
budget secrecy 215
Burch, Martin 45, 249–251
Butler, David 170, 243
Butler, Lord Robin 246, 250, 265–6, 277–280
Butler, R. A, 98, 108–109, 132–133

cabinet
   appointment 73–4
   collective responsibility 159, 168–9, 187, 191, 197–202, 204, 231, 242, 268–9, 278–280
   collective tolerance 198
   committees 84–7, 92–5, 112, 119, 127, 132, 144, 161–12, 175, 185, 199, 251
   conviction 202
   elastic theory 237
   inner 129, 151, 153–4, 162–3, 170–2, 176–7, 233

leaks 147, 177
minutes 149–150, 169
of chums 247
office 16, 44, 137, 179, 207
overlords 88–97, 150, 165–6, 171, 174, 272
pusillanimity 194
resignations 212, 252
responsibilities of 33–4, 50–6, 74–7, 79–81, 125–6, 262–3
restoration of 34, 37
secretariat 29–34, 41–3, 54, 127–8, 150, 152, 154, 169, 184–5, 278–280
shadow 102–103, 201–2, 272
size of 78
strength of 15, 134
war 28–35, 47–8, 54, 59–60, 62–8, 71, 95, 110, 165, 171, 216–8, 275–6 *see also* war committee
Callaghan, James 130, 134, 136–8, 141–2, 150, 158, 160–2, 182–3, 189–192, **196–206**, 213, 220, 229
Carlton Club, the 13
Carrington, Lord 218
Campbell-Bannerman, Sir Henry 20, 29
Campbell, John 178
Cambell, Menzies 280–1
Castle, Barbara 135–6, 142, 150–2, 158, 188, 191
Central executive studies 249, *see also* core executive studies
Central Policy Review Staff (CPRS) **178–182,** 219–221, 226, 228–9, 238, 242
Centralisation of government 257–8
Charkham, Jonathan 267
Charles II 115–6
Chandos, Lord 66–7 *see also* Lyttelton, Oliver
Chamberlain, Austen 25, 34, 40–3
Chamberlain, Joseph 6–7, 9
Chamberlain, Neville 53, 55–57, 59, 82, 110–111, 120, 193–194, 209, 230
Cherwell, Lord 89, 97
Churchill, Randolph 109–110, 212
Churchill, Winston 25–6, 56–7, 61–8, 84, 87, **91–105**, 109, 111, 113, 116, 120, 133, 143, 236
CID *see* Committee of Imperial Defence
Clarke, Charles 272–3
Clinton, Bill 270
coalition government 23, 25–6
Cockerell, Michael 260, 263–5

collective responsibility *see* cabinet
Collins, Tim 272
colonial office 19
Colville, John 97–9
Colvin, Ian 57
Cook, Robin 276, 281
Cooper, Duff 156, 194
Cooper, Frank 216–7
Committee of Imperial Defence (CID) 16–9, 23–4, 28, 43–4, 46, 100
comprehensive spending review system (CSR) 267–8
concorde project 117
Conservative party 43
government 99, 113
constitution 1–2, 40
the English 1, 42, 123, 160, 208
core executive 270–1
studies 207
creeping bilateralism 221
Crichel Down affair, the 102
Cripps, Stafford 72, 74
Crosland, Susan 136–7
Crosland, Tony 135–7, 192–3, 198–200, 242
Crossman, Richard 123–5, 136, 138–142, 149–150, 155, 160–1, 166, 184, 243, 264
cabinet diaries 138–142, 146–152, 172–3
Harvard lectures 166–170
CRPS *see* Central Policy Review Staff
CSR *see* comprehensive spending review system
Curry, David 272
Curzon, Lord 27, 37–40

Daalder, Hans 17–8, 97, 125–6
Daily Telegraph 110–1
Dalyell, Tam 149
Dardanelles 60
commision 23–4
Davis, Stanley Clinton 189
Dawe, Roger 162
DEA *see* Department of Economic Affairs
defence committee 64, 144, *see also* Committee of Imperial Defence
Dell, Edmund 197–200, 262
Department of Economic Affairs (DEA) 148, 166
Derby, Lord 9
department of health and social security (DHSS) 166

INDEX

Dimbleby, Richard 206
Disraeli, Benjamin 11, *see also* Beaconsfield, Lord
Donoughue, Bernard 183–5, 187–8
Downey, Sir Gordon 259
Downing Street policy unit 183, 221, 226–8, 262
Dugdale, Sir Thomas 102
durante bene placito 11

economic
 policy committee 72
 development committee 139
 strategy committee 163
Economist, The 1
Eden, Sir Anthony 56–7, 64–5, 98, **105–112**, 120, 143, 145, 155, 193–4, 236
Education
 act (1944) 132
 cuts 153
 school leavers age 153
Edward VII 14–5, 18
EEC *see* European Economic Community
Egypt 105–8, 193
Elgin commission 19
elective dictatorship 206–7
Esher, Lord 18–20
European Economic Community (EEC) 175, 184, 186–192, 195
European Union constitution 273
Evans, Harold 115–6

Falklands War 215–9, 224, 276
Fisher, H. A. L. 42–3
Fisher, Sir John 19
Fisher, Sir Warren 43–4
Foley, Michael 253–6, 267
Foot, Michael 188, 192, 198
Ford, Gerald 200
foreign office 38–41, 54
France
 cabinet 56
 Franco-Israeli collusion 106–8
 Suez 109
free trade 49
 fixation of system (1903) 54
Frere, Bartle 10–1

Gaitskell, Hugh 78, 127
garden suburb 34–6, 181
George V 48

Germany, federal 213
Gladstone, William Ewart 6–9, 11–2, 20, 41, 80, 270
gold pool, the 15
Granville, Lord 6, 8
Great War, the *see* World War I
green paper 186, 223
Greenwood, Tony 136
Grey, Earl 46
Griffith, John 102
Grove, J. W. 112
Gulf war 276

Hailsham, Lord 206–7, 248
Hailsham, Viscount 49, 50
Hain, Peter 273
Haines, Joe 134
Haldane, Lord 18, 33
 Haldane committee 33–4, 95
Halifax, Lord 56, 78
Halls, Michael 162, 164
Hankey, Lord Maurice 16–7, 30–3, 43–4, 46–8, 68
Hansardise 14
Harcourt, Sir William 9, 11–3, 52–3
Harris, Kenneth 70, 122–3
Hartington commission (1890) 16
Healy, Denis 197–8, 200–2, 247
Heath, Edward 172–3, **174–9**, 209, 226, 252, 266
Helsby, Sir Lawrence 164–5
Hennessy, Peter 100–1, 165–6, 176–7, 191–2, 197, 216–8, 267, 269–270, 275–7
Herman, Valentine 209–211
Heseltine, Michael 190, 230–2, 236, 244–5
Hill, Christopher 57–8
Hitler, Adolf 55–7, 110
Holliday, Ian 45, 249–251
Holme, Lord Richard 280–1
home affairs committee 60, 139
Home, Sir Alec Douglas (Lord) 117, 122–3, 143, 146, 213
Hoskyns, John 226–9, 247
Houghton, Douglas 165
House of Commons 2–5, 29, 56, 66, 88, 90–1, 194
House of Lords 3, 56, 91
 reform 195
Howard, Micheal 272–3
Howe, Geoffrey 214–5, 224, 231–2, 235–6

299

Howell, Denis 189
Hunt, Norman 127–9, 132–3
Hunt, Lord 199–200
Hurd, Douglas 176–7, 252–3
hydrogen bomb 100–1

IMF *see* International Monetary Fund
Ingham, Bernard 228–230, 233
inner cabinet, *see* cabinet
institutionalisation 249
inteligence departments
 communication between 16–8
inter stellas luna minores 13, 52–3
International Monetary Fund (IMF) 196–7, 200–1
Ismay, Lord 61–2, 216
Israel
 Suez 105–9
Iraq 275–280

Jackson, Margaret 189
James, Simon 180, 268–9
Jay, Douglas 138
JCC *see* joint cabinet committee
Jebb, Gladwyn 108–9
Jenkins, Roy 133, 166, 185–6, 188, 270
Jennings, Sir Arthur 51–6
joint cabinet committee (JCC) 280
Jones, George 142–5, 237–8
Jordan 114
Joseph, Keith 214
journalists, cabinet contact with 258
Judd, Frank 189

Kaufman, Gerald 147, 262
Keith, Arthur Berriedale 26, 34, 51–6, 119
Kennedy, Charles 280
Kennedy, John 116
Kennedy, Ludovic 215–6
Keynes, John Maynard 78
Kilmuir, Lord 121–2
King, Anthony 240–1
Knollys, Lord 15, 18
Kogan, Maurice 193
Korea 216, 218, 276
Kosovo 270, 276

Labour
 government 44–5, 48, 55, 67–9, 72–4, 81, 84, 90
 manifesto 184
Lamb, Richard 113–4

Lansley, Andrew 272
Laski, Harold 81–3
Law, Andrew Bonar 25, 43, 48, 96, 120
Lawson, Nigel 161, 213, 221–4, 228, 232–4, 242
Leathers, Lord 84, 89, 94, 97
Lebanon 114
Lee, Fred 139
Leigh-Pemberton, Robin 224
Liberal Party 48, 122
Lipsey, David 267–8
Llyod, Selwyn 108–9, 121
Lloyd-George, David 16, 26, 28–30, **34–41**, 43–5, 47, 54, 68, 82, 120, 163, 181, 212, 238
Low, Sidney 15–6
Lyttelton, Oliver 64, 66–7 *see also* Chandos, Lord

MacDonald, Ramsey 45, 48–50, 73, 93, 111, 120
Mackenzie, W. J. M. 112
Mackintosh, George 84
Mackintosh, John 110, 119–121, 123, 125, 142, 161
Maclennan, Robert 280–1
Macleod, Iain 123
Macmillan, Harold 100, 109, **113–8**, 120–3, 143, 146, 215–7, 239, 243
 private secretaries 113–4
Madgwick, Peter 212, 218, 251
Major, John 71, **244–252,** 255–6, 259
making government work inquiry, the (2000) 260–1, *see also* organogram
Mandelson, Peter 281, 282
Marconi scandal (1913) 20
Melbourne, Lord 2
Middle-East crisis 114
Miliband, David 262–3
Millennium dome 264–5
Ministerial
 appointments 209
 code 31–2, 257–9, *see also* Questions of Procedure for Ministers
 duration of offices 211
 propriety 20
 special advisors 183
 tenure 209–211
Monckton, Walter 101
monetarist economics 214
Montagu, E. S. 27
Morgan, Kenneth 160–1
Morley, Lord John 12–3, 53

INDEX

Morris, John 190
Morrison, Herbert 70, 72, 83, 88–91
Mowlam, Mo 263–4
Munich crisis (1938) 59, 193

Nasser, Gamal Abdel 105–8
National executive committee, 136, 139, 158–160
National Health Service 79, 152
National Telephone Company 15–6
National Union of Journalists 203
Nazi state 125
night of the long knives, the 121
Northern Ireland 270
nuclear weapons 100–1, 116, 144–5, 153, 155
   British capacity 79
   also see hydrogen bomb
NUJ see National Union of Journalists

OPD see Overseas Policy and Defence Committee
OPS see office of public service
office of public service (OPS) 250
organogram 261
Overseas Policy and Defence Committee (OPD) 151, 250
Owen, David 203–4

Palmerston, Lord
Parkinson's law 135–6
parliament 1–3, 8–9
Parliamentary
   committee 129, 151, 162, see also inner cabinet
   democracy 92
   private secretaries 208
Peart, Fred 190
Peel, Sir Robert 8, 13, 50
Percy, Lord 95–6
PESC see Public Expenditure Survey Committee
picketing 203
Pitblado, David 9
Plowden committee 118
Plowden, William 220–1
poll tax 221, 223
Ponsoby, General 7
Powell, Charles 233
Powell, Enoch 117, 123
Powell, Sir Robert 107
Prentice, Reg 190
Prescott, John 264–5

presidency 253–7
presidential government 242, 266–7
prime ministerial
   government 168, 241, 270
   press service 147
prime ministerialism 110, 142, 153, 160, 170, 269
primus inter pares 12–3, 28, 52–3, 124, 135, 143, 145, 213, 224, 232, 241
Prior, Jim 177, 214
Pryce, Sue 181, 249
Public Expenditure Survey Committee (PESC) 149
Punnett, R. M. 102–3

Questions and Procedure for Ministers (QPM) 131, 246, 257–259
QPM see Questions and Procedure for Ministers

Rees Merlyn 190
Reid, John 272
referendum 273–4
reform act
   (1832) 54
   (1867) 1
reform bills 42
Rhodes, Rod 207
Richards, Steve 273–4
Riddell, Peter 165, 257–8, 272–3
Ridley, Nicholas 225
Roberts, Lord 18
Robinson, Nick 262–3
Rogers, William 189, 192, 201, 205, 220
Rose, Richard 208
Rosebery, Lord 10
Rothschild, Lord 180

Salisbury, Lord 9–10, 13–5, 92, 109, 268
Samuuel, Viscount 48–51
Schmidt, Helmut 200
SEP see Steering Committee on Economic Policy
September 11th (2001) 278
Seymour-Ure, Colin 218–9
Sharp, Dame Evelyn 115, 239
Shepard, Gillian 246–7
Shepard, Lord 190
Shinwell, Manny 139
Shore, Peter 136, 188, 199, 205, 262
Short, Edward 130, 133–4, 189
Simon, Sir John 51
Smith, Martin 270–1

301

Soames, Christopher 98–9
Social Democratic Party 204
Sovereign 6, 8–9
St John-Stevas, Norman 225
star chamber, the 199, 248
Steering Committee on Economic Policy (SEP) 148, 151
Stewart, Michael 170
Strategic Economic Policy Committee 161
Straw, Jack 273, 276, 281
Suez canal crisis 105–3, 144–5, 153, 193, 217–8, 276

Taylor, Ann 281
Tebbit, Norman 224, 233
technocracy **127–173**, 193
terrorist attacks 278
Thatcher, Margaret 71, 176, 182–3, 190, 201–3, **214–243**, 244–6, 249, 252–3, 255
think tank *see* Central Policy Review Staff
Thomas, J. H. 93
Thorpe, Jeremy 122
Tomlinson, George 69
trade unions 159, 204–5
Transition to War Committee 217
treasury 43–4, 52, 112, 134–5, 207, 217
Trend, Burke 114, 131, 146, 150, 152, 168–9, 180
Turner, John 35–6

United States 79, 156, 213
United Nations 108
  security council 106

velut inter ignes Luna minores 28
Victoria I 10–1, 14
Vietnam 116, 135
Vincent, John 242

Wakeham, Lord John 224, 233, 248

Walker, Patrick Gordon 153–6, 243
Walpole, Sir Robert 2, 12–3
Walters, Sir Alan 234
war
  book 46
  committee 23, 47, 59–60
  conduct of 275–7
  council 23–4
  office 16, 19
Watt, David 176
weapons of mass destruction 277
Webb, Beatrice 45
Webb, Sidney 45
Westland helicopter affair 190, 230–2, 242
Wheare, Sir Kenneth 103–4
Whig Party 2
white paper 139, 158, 180, 223
Whitelaw, William 199, 224, 248
Wigg, George 130, 146–7
Wilkinson, Ellen 69
William IV 2
Williams, Francis 69–70, 72
Williams, Marcia 146, 163–4
Williams, Roy 186
Williams, Shirley 188, 205, 229
Wilson, Harold 65, **127–134**, 137–8, 141–3, 146–8, 153, 156, 158–172, **182–196**, 213, 243, 247, 262
Wilson, Sir Horace 59, 194
Wolff, Michael 177, 196
Woodhouse, Diana 251–2
Woolton, Lord 84, 89, 91–2, 94, 97, 101, 112–3
World War I 16, 22–36, 47–8, 60–1
World War II 51, **61–8**, 69, 113
  post war 61–104

Yeo, Tim 272

Zulueta, Philip de 114